JUSTICE REHNQUIST
AND THE CONSTITUTION

JUSTICE REHNQUIST
AND THE CONSTITUTION

SUE DAVIS

Princeton University Press
Princeton, New Jersey

Library of Congress Cataloging-in-Publication Data
Davis, Sue, 1948–
Justice Rehnquist and the Constitution / Sue Davis.
p. cm.   Bibliography: p.   Includes index.
ISBN 0–691–07800–9 (alk. paper)
1. Rehnquist, William, 1924–   .
2. Judges—United States—Biography.
3. Federal government—United States.
4. United States—Constitutional law.   I. Title.
KF8745.R44D38 1989   347.73'2634—dc19   [347.3073534]   88–23413 CIP

This book has been composed in Linotron Trump

Printed in the United States of America
by Princeton University Press,
Princeton, New Jersey

Contents

CONTENTS

Preface

The very large number of studies of justices of the Supreme Court, beginning with Chief Justice John Marshall and including the current members of the Court, attests to a persistent, widespread interest in the individuals who have held positions on the nation's highest tribunal.[1] Indeed, the abundance of judicial biographies strongly suggests a firm belief among legal scholars that knowledge of the individual justices is essential to understanding the Supreme Court as a decision-making body.[2]

Virtually all of the literature that may loosely be termed "Supreme Court biography" falls into one of three categories. First, the conventional biography, usually a book-length study, covers the life of a justice from birth (or before, including a description of the lives of the justice's parents) to death. The emphasis such studies place on an individual's work on the Court ranges from a cursory description to an extensive analysis of a justice's judicial opinions.[3] In contrast, the second variety of biographic study focuses almost entirely on a justice's work on the Court. Prominent in this category are studies that analyze a justice's legal philosophy by utilizing his judicial opinions or papers with the goal of understanding his methods and values and the way they translate into judicial decisions.[4] Studies that attempt to place a jus-

[1] See, for example, Beveridge's classic biography of Chief Justice John Marshall (1916–1919) and Baker 1974. For analyses of current members of the Court, see Heck 1985, 1986; Arledge 1986; Kobylka 1986.

[2] See, for example, Peltason 1964. See also Murphy and Tanenhaus 1972, 13–18. There are many excellent bibliographies and bibliographic essays on judicial biographies, including Abraham 1980, 470–82; Stephenson 1981, 169–263; White 1976, 162–65; Dobie 1957.

[3] In addition to Beveridge 1916–1919 and Baker 1974, see Mason 1956; Swisher 1935; Howe 1957–1963; Simon 1980; White 1982. Excellent biographic sketches of a dozen selected justices from Marshall to Rutledge are contained in Dunham and Kurland 1974. A sketch of the life and career of each of the justices appointed through 1978 is provided by Friedman and Israel 1969 and Friedman 1979.

[4] See, for example, Faulkner 1968; Mendelson 1961; Silverstein 1984; Konefsky 1956. There are relevant law review articles too numerous to list here, but see, for example, Yarbrough 1971; Roche 1957; White 1971. A cursory look at the

tice into proper historical context or demonstrate a particular jurist's impact on the Court are also noteworthy in this category (especially White 1976; Newmyer 1968). Finally, attempts to study decision making scientifically that focus on a justice's votes as a function of values and attitudes and that utilize the tools of empirical analysis, such as scaling and bloc analysis, comprise the third variety of biographic studies (for example, Pritchett 1948; Shubert 1965).

The present work fits squarely into the second category; it is not a full-scale study of the life of Justice William H. Rehnquist, nor is it an empirical analysis of his voting behavior. Instead, this work is a study of the philosophy and the values that shape his judicial decision making. Its purpose is to provide a frame of reference for understanding his work as an associate justice of the Supreme Court.

Index to Legal Periodicals under the heading "Biography" will reveal just how voluminous this work is.

Acknowledgments

I have been fortunate to have the support of many colleagues and friends throughout my work on this project. Walter F. Murphy provided crucial encouragement during the earliest stages of the project by reading a preliminary version of chapter 3. More importantly, however, the example he has set by his work, his confidence in my research, and his friendship have prompted me to endeavor to improve the quality of my scholarship. Melvyn H. Zarr, professor of law at the University of Maine School of Law, provided incisive comments on the early drafts of chapters 8 and 9. John Brigham's insightful reading of chapter 2 was most encouraging during the last stages of the work. Finally, I greatly appreciated the supportive comments of Sheldon Goldman and those of an anonymous reader who motivated me to revise the manuscript one last time.

A grant from the National Endowment for the Humanities for the summer of 1985 and summer research grants from the College of Arts and Sciences at the University of Tulsa in 1982 and 1984 provided much-appreciated financial support for my research. Members of the staff of the Law Library at the University of Maine School of Law—particularly Isa Lang, who was then the reference librarian—were exceptionally enthusiastic and helpful. If they had not so generously allowed me to use Westlaw, the project would certainly have proceeded at a much slower pace. During the two summers that I spent in Portland, Maine, my good friend Yusuf Turner made sure that I took enough time out from my work to maintain a sense of humor.

My colleagues, students, and friends in the Political Science Department at the University of Delaware offered their support in diverse ways. Marian Lief Palley helped me to smooth out some kinks in the analysis, Leslie F. Goldstein commented on an early version of chapter 4, and Bill Boyer allowed me to occupy his study for a fourteen-hour Saturday afternoon so that I might use his printer. Joe Schoell's many trips to the library made the last stages of the work much easier and more pleasant than would otherwise have been the case. Nancy Davis accomplished a task that I would never have believed possible by typing a list of all of Rehnquist's opinions in two days.

PART ONE

The Framework

ONE

1971: Richard Nixon Appoints a New Justice

[I]t may be charged that they are conservatives. This is true. But only in a judicial, not a political sense.—*President Richard M. Nixon, announcing the nomination of William H. Rehnquist and Lewis F. Powell to the Supreme Court* (NEW YORK TIMES, *October 22, 1971*)

My notion would be that [a judicial conservative] attempts to ascertain a constitutional meaning . . . by the use of the language used by the framers, the historical materials available, and the precedents which other Justices of the Supreme Court have decided in cases involving a particular provision.—*William H. Rehnquist, testifying before the Senate Judiciary Committee* (U.S. Congress 1971a)

Richard Nixon made the Supreme Court a major issue in his campaign for the presidency in 1968. In an attempt to appeal to voters by emphasizing law and order, he blamed decisions of the Warren Court for high rates of crime and little punishment. Judicial decisions, he said, "have had the effect of seriously hamstringing the peace forces in our society and strengthening the criminal forces" (quoted in Simon 1973, 8). Nixon adopted the term "strict constructionist"[1] to describe the type of jurists he would place on the Court if he had the opportunity—justices who would "interpret the Constitution strictly and fairly and objectively," unlike some "who have gone too far in assuming unto themselves a mandate which is not there, and that is, to put their social and economic ideas into their decisions" (ibid.).

In October of 1971 President Nixon announced his nomination of William Rehnquist to the Supreme Court, presenting the future justice as a judicial conservative whose judicial philosophy would reflect the view that: "[i]t is the duty of a judge to interpret the Constitution, and not to place himself above the Constitution or outside the Constitution. He should not twist or bend the

[1] Simon (1973, 5) described "strict constructionist" as "a flabby phrase that drew its meaning primarily from the political views of the speaker." Levy (1974, 31) noted that "strict construction in the mouth of President Nixon was like the word love in the mouth of a whore, except that Nixon deceived only the public, not himself. As a lawyer and politician, he knew that inherently vague words cannot be strictly construed." Dworkin (1977, 131–37) provided an excellent explanation of the inherent meaninglessness of the term "strict constructionist."

3

Constitution in order to perpetuate his personal, political, and social views" (*New York Times*, October 22, 1971). Implying that there is some correlation between judicial conservatism and a tough stand against crime, Nixon stated that as a judicial conservative himself, he believed that "some Court decisions have gone too far in the past in weakening the peace forces as against the criminal forces in our society" (ibid.). The president declared that Rehnquist was a conservative only the judicial, not the political, sense, apparently in order to assure the public that the nominee's political preferences would not influence his judicial decisions.

William Rehnquist had the qualifications that Nixon prescribed for a justice since he could be expected to act as a "judicial conservative"—a "strict constructionist" who would give "the peace forces . . . the legal tools they need to protect the innocent from criminal elements" (ibid.). More specifically, in criminal cases Nixon expected Rehnquist to "strictly" construe the Bill of Rights and the due process clause of the Fourteenth Amendment to reverse the Warren Court's expansion of protections for the criminally accused. As a "strict constructionist" he could also be expected to favor "judicial restraint," and thereby to help steer the Court toward a more modest role in the American political system.

The president's confidence in his nominee was based, in part, upon Rehnquist's record in the Justice Department, where he served as assistant attorney general for the Office of Legal Counsel from 1969 until 1971. In that position, he supported inherent executive authority to order wiretapping and surveillance without a prior court order, no-knock entry by the police, preventive detention, the abolition of habeas corpus proceedings after trial, and the abolition of the exclusionary rule (U.S. Congress 1971a, 139–40, 185, 313–15). He also supported the suspension of normal procedures for arrest in order to facilitate the detention of 12,000 antiwar protesters in Washington, D.C., during the May Day demonstrations in 1971 (ibid., 43–48).

Rehnquist's tough position regarding crime was only one of several qualities that made him attractive to the Nixon administration. He also possessed impressive academic credentials, intelligence, and integrity. Only two years had passed since the Senate had rejected the nomination of, first, Clement F. Haynsworth and then G. Harrold Carswell to fill the vacancy left by Justice Abe Fortas's resignation in 1969. When Justices Hugo Black and John Marshall Harlan II retired in 1971, Nixon sent a list of six possible nominees—all of whom possessed marginal qualifications—to the American Bar Association Standing Committee on Federal Judiciary.[2] The president subsequently avoided another embarrasssing failure for the administration by dropping "The Six" and selecting instead Rehnquist and Powell, whose qualifications were strikingly impressive by comparison.

REHNQUIST'S BACKGROUND AND RECORD

Rehnquist was born in 1924, grew up in a suburb of Milwaukee, attended Kenyon College in Ohio for a year, and served for three years in the Army Air Corps during World War II as a weather observer, stationed in North Africa. He used the G.I. Bill to attend Stanford University, from which he received his undergraduate degree (1948) and M.A. (1949) in political science. He received a second M.A. in government from Harvard University (1950). In December of 1951, when he graduated first in his class from Stanford Law School, Justice Robert Jackson selected him as his law clerk. He served in that position from February 1952 until June 1953; during that time he met his future wife, who was then working for the Central Intelligence Agency.

Rehnquist firmly established his reputation as an active and outspoken conservative early in his legal career. During the late 1950s, for example, he publicly criticized the Warren Court, making statements that left him open to charges of extremism and even of McCarthyism. In 1957 he argued that the Court was devoted to a political philosophy that included "extreme solicitude for the claims of Communists and other criminal defendants, expansion of the Federal power at the expense of state power, [and] great sympathy for any Government regulation of business."[3] In an article that appeared in the *American Bar Association Journal* in 1958 he stated that "Communists, former Communists, and others of like political philosophy scored significant victories during the October 1956 term of the Supreme Court of the United States, culminating in the historic decisions of June 17, 1957" (Rehnquist 1958, 229).[4]

---

[2] For a chronicle of President Nixon's nominations, see Abraham 1985, chs. 2, 11.

[3] U.S. Congress 1971a, 28, quoting Rehnquist, "Who Writes Opinions of the Supreme Court?" *U.S. News and World Report*, December 13, 1957, 57.

[4] Rehnquist was referring to Schware v. Board of Examiners, 353 U.S. 232, and Konigsberg v. State Bar of California, 353 U.S. 252. In both cases the Court held

During his sixteen years as an attorney in Phoenix, Rehnquist participated in various political activities and became involved in local controversies, always taking the conservative position. He was actively involved in Barry Goldwater's presidential campaign of 1964. He appeared as a witness before the Phoenix City Council in opposition to a public accommodations ordinance—an action that he later justified by stating: "I am opposed to all civil rights laws," because they infringe on the rights of businesses.[5] He publicly opposed efforts to end de facto segregation in Phoenix high schools and asserted that "many . . . would feel that we are no more dedicated to an 'integrated' society than we are to a 'segregated' society."[6] As a lawyer for the Republican party from 1958 through 1966 he was involved in a program to challenge voters at the polls. Rehnquist later explained the program as an effort to stop tombstone, or absentee, voting; however, there were allegations that the challengers intentionally harassed, intimidated, and interfered with blacks' and Hispanics' ability to vote (U.S. Congress 1971a, 71–72, 296, 490–92).

It was at the urging of another lawyer from Phoenix, Deputy Attorney General Richard Kleindienst, that John Mitchell appointed Rehnquist to the position of assistant attorney general for the Office of Legal Counsel. As the president's lawyer's lawyer, his principal duty was to draft position papers on the legality of the administration's actions. The positions he took in favor of, for example, inherent executive authority to order wiretapping, preventive detention, and abolition of the exclusionary rule exemplified Rehnquist's agreement with the Nixon administration's attitude toward crime. He also shared the administration's abhorrence of student unrest in the late 1960s, once characterizing the dissenters on the campuses as "the new barbarians"

---

that state bar associations' determinations not to admit people to the bar on the basis of their past association with the Communist party were not rationally justified and, therefore, constituted a denial of due process.

[5] An Arizona state senator submitted an affidavit to the Senate Judiciary Committee stating that after the council meeting he had asked Rehnquist why he opposed the ordinance; Rehnquist had replied, "I am opposed to all civil rights laws" (U.S. Congress 1971a, 320). Rehnquist wrote a letter to the editor of the *Arizona Republic* in which he argued that "[t]he ordinance summarily does away with the historic right of the owner by a wave of the legislative wand, hitherto private businesses are made public facilities, which are open to all persons regardless of the owner's wishes" (ibid., 306–7).

[6] As quoted in U.S. Congress 1971a, 309. He made that statement in a letter to the editor of the *Arizona Republic*.

("Reagan's Mr. Right," 1986, 25). Additionally, his views on school desegregation fit comfortably with those of the administration. In 1970 he drafted a proposed constitutional amendment prohibiting busing to achieve desegregation and a memorandum in support of the amendment (Weaver 1974, 99). Of course, Rehnquist's support for the policies of the administration was not extraordinary—after all, it was his job. If he had not shared the views of the administration, he would not have been selected for a position in the Justice Department. Still, he endorsed the policies with enthusiasm and energy. During his two years as assistant attorney general he explained the administration's policies to Congress eighteen times, on topics including obscenity, campaign reform, wiretapping, war powers, executive privilege, and the Equal Rights Amendment (ibid., 98). Once he disagreed with the administration's position, and although he did not make his views explicit, his presentation was, perhaps purposely, quite unpersuasive. The Nixon administration supported the Equal Rights Amendment but when Rehnquist testified before the House Judiciary Committee in April of 1971, he admitted that he did not believe that the amendment was necessary.[7] When asked why he supported it, he responded, "Because the President has committed himself to it and the importance of a general statement in the Constitution establishing the principles of equality of women outweighs the disadvantages that might flow from enactment of the amendment" (quoted in U.S. Congress 1971a, 429).

THE CONFIRMATION

It was clear that Rehnquist had the credentials and the "brilliant and analytical mind" (U.S. Congress 1971a, 10) to qualify him for the Supreme Court.[8] Nevertheless, there were serious questions regarding his fitness to serve as a justice. A chronicle of his activities as an attorney in Phoenix and as assistant attorney general described the career of an extremely conservative political activist. The controversy surrounding his confirmation reflected uncertainty that Nixon's "judicial conservative" would be an im-

[7] Rehnquist drafted a memo in which he summarized his objections to the Equal Rights Amendment, but the existence of that memo was not revealed until after the hearings on his nomination for chief justice in 1986. See ch. 10, n. 5.

[8] That description was in a letter to Sen. James O. Eastland from Robert H. Bork.

partial, fair decision maker rather than a jurist who would use his position on the Court to further his own, as well as the Nixon administration's, political agenda.

The American Bar Association Standing Committee on Federal Judiciary's report to the Senate Judiciary Committee on his nomination was unanimous in the view that the nominee was qualified for the appointment, but three of the nine members gave him a rating of "not opposed." The reservations expressed by judges, lawyers, and law school deans who were interviewed for the report centered on his personal views. One judge expressed concern that Rehnquist had "such deep convictions on social and economic problems that he might be unduly and injudiciously influenced by those views in deciding cases" (ibid., 3).

The questions that several members of the Senate Judiciary Committee addressed to Rehnquist during the hearings on his nomination also manifested a concern for objectivity and fairness. Sen. John McClellen (D., Ark.), who questioned the nominee first, queried, "Would you feel free, as a justice, to take the text of the Constitution particularly in its broad phrases—'due process' . . . 'unreasonable search and seizure'—and to read into it your personal philosophy, be it liberal or conservative?" (ibid., 18–19). Rehnquist answered simply that he would not. When McClellen inquired whether Rehnquist as a jurist might alter the positions he held as a lawyer for the Justice Department, he answered in the affirmative. Sen. Philip Hart (D., Mich.) tried to probe more deeply by asking how one could resolve the meaning of constitutional provisions such as the due process clause without reference to personal philosophy. Rehnquist's response was that he would certainly take to the Court "what I am at the present time. There is no escaping it. I have lived for 47 years, and that goes with me." He went on to avow that "I will try to divorce my personal views as to what I thought [the Constitution] ought to mean from what I conceived the framers to have intended" (ibid., 24).

As Hart questioned the nominee about the impact of his personal views on his judicial decision making, he uncovered a major inconsistency in Nixon's proclaimed intention to appoint a "judicial conservative" to the Court. Nixon's judicial conservative, as Hart pointed out, "would not be too much of an activist, who interpreted the Constitution strictly and did not try to include [sic] his decisions towards a particular political or social view he thought desirable" (ibid., 26). At the same time, however, he would help to swing the pendulum away from the protection of the rights of the accused and toward the power of government. Hart pondered, How could a justice be expected "to follow strictly the mandates of the Constitution, without regard to a personal philosophy of law and order, or desired results in a particular area of the law" (ibid., 26–27)—particularly in light of the fact that he had been put on the Court for the express purpose of shifting the balance toward government? How could Rehnquist resolve such an apparent inconsistency? The nominee responded that the president might not see any inconsistency if he believed that "the pendulum had been swung too far toward the accused not by virtue of a fair reading of the Constitution but by virtue of what was conceived to be some outside influences such as the personal philosophy of one or more of the justices" (ibid., 27). As for his own personal philosophy, Rehnquist maintained that he would disassociate it as much as possible from his role as a justice.

Members of the Judiciary Committee also attempted to elicit information about Rehnquist's judicial views on the role of the courts, the role of precedent, and the interpretation of the Constitution. In response to questions, the nominee stated that he was opposed to lawmaking by the judiciary and affirmed repeatedly his belief that a justice should rely on the intent of the framers rather than his personal views in interpreting the Constitution. For example, when Sen. John Tunney (D., Calif.) inquired how Rehnquist would apply the due process clause in a case that raised the question of whether television should be allowed in the courtroom—a case with no relevant precedent—he responded that he would

> read the amendment, and you suggest that there are no precedents, yet certainly there would be cases that would be not too far off and I would be inclined to go back to the debates, the Bingham explanation of what he meant by the 14th amendment, other explanations on the floor, and I am sure you would come up with something that obviously would not have included a particular discussion of whether a trial could be televised or not. . . . [but] I think it would be wrong for me to simply read in my own subjective notions of fairness. (Ibid., 190)

When he was asked about his view of the role of precedent, he reiterated the tradition that precedent carries greater weight in statutory construction than in constitutional interpretation (ibid., 138–39). In an exchange with Sen. Edward Kennedy (D., Mass.), he stated "to the extent that a precedent is not that authoritative in the sense of having stood for a shorter period of time, or having been handed down by a sharply divided court, then it is of less weight as a precedent" (ibid., 55).

Discussions about the role of precedent led to questions concerning the nominee's views of Brown v. Board of Education (347 U.S. 483 [1954]). At one point, responding to questions asked by Sen. Birch Bayh (D., Ind.), Rehnquist noted that, although he strongly believed that the Court should not reinterpret the Constitution to bring it up to date, he supported the Court's decision in 1954 that segregated schools violated the equal protection clause of the Fourteenth Amendment (U.S. Congress 1971a, 167). Asked how he would justify the Court's departure from the doctrine of "separate but equal," which the Court established in 1896 in its decision in Plessy v. Ferguson (163 U.S. 537), he answered that all the justices in *Brown* examined the specific issues and the historical intent of the framers of the Fourteenth Amendment, and concluded that the Court had been incorrect in *Plessy*. He defended the Court's 1954 decision: "[I]f nine Justices, presumably of the same varying temperaments that one customarily gets on the Supreme Court at the same time, all address themselves to the issue and all unanimously decide that the Constitution requires a particular result, that, to me, is very strong evidence that the Constitution does, in fact, require that result" (ibid., 167). He suggested further that reinterpretation of the intent of the framers might justify departure from precedent: "If you became convinced that the *Plessy* Court had not properly interpreted that intent, that it had simply adopted a view that was too narrow to be consistent with what the framers of the Fourteenth Amendment intended, then I think you would be entitled to disregard *Plessy*" (ibid., 168).

Considered together, Rehnquist's statements regarding the role of precedent implied that, in his view, precedent of recent vintage, particularly if established by a divided Court, may be overturned if a substantial majority of the Court agrees that the interpretation of the Constitution upon which that precedent was based was incorrect. His statements suggested that he would not have trouble voting to overturn the decisions of the Warren Court, particularly in the area of the rights of the accused. Clearly, his view of the role of precedent belied the notion that

Rehnquist would be a justice who fit the description of a "judicial conservative."

The nominee's personable manner created an impression that he was cooperating with the committee, but he actually did not provide the senators with much of the information they were seeking, particularly in regard to his political views. He seemed to answer candidly about his past activities, flatly denying allegations of harassment of voters, for example. But when asked for his views regarding the Justice Department's policies in such areas as wiretapping, preventive detention, or the scope and extent of executive privilege, he demurred, stating that he had acted as an advocate, presenting the positions of the administration, but that if he had found any of them to be personally obnoxious, he would not have acted as he did. He could not state his own views, he said, and invoked the attorney-client privilege as a basis for his refusal.

Moreover, he was reticent about explaining his judicial philosophy, as suggested by the following exchange:

Senator Kennedy: Why do you think the President believes that your appointment there will move the Court closer to the peace forces and away from the accused?

Mr. Rehnquist: I think it would be inappropriate for me to comment on what the President's thought processes were, if I knew them.

Senator Kennedy: Well, I suppose he says he believes your judicial philosophy is that you are a judicial conservative, is what it gets down to. Do you feel so?

Mr. Rehnquist: Well, if by judicial conservative is meant one who will attempt to—

Senator Kennedy: What do you think he meant by that?

The Chairman: Wait a minute. Let him answer the question.

Mr. Rehnquist: I simply cannot speak for him, Senator.

Senator Kennedy: Well, how do you—why do you not speak for yourself then? Do you think you are a judicial conservative?

Mr. Rehnquist: Well, let me tell what I think I am, and then you decide whether I am a judicial conservative or not. (Ibid., 54–55)

Finally, he declined to state his positions on specific constitutional issues, such as the breadth of the equal protection clause, on the grounds that they were either presently before the Court or would be in the near future.[9]

Civil rights groups provided the strongest opposition to Rehnquist's confirmation. Clarence Mitchell, director of the Washington Bureau of the NAACP and the legislative chairman of the Leadership Conference on Civil Rights, and Joseph Rauh, counsel for the Leadership Conference on Civil Rights, made a joint appearance in which they testified that Rehnquist was not committed to the achievement of equal justice under the law for black Americans. Mitchell charged that with the nomination of Rehnquist, "the foot of racism is placed in the door of the temple of justice" (Graham 1971a, 21). Rauh told the committee that Rehnquist's lack of compassion for human rights and his lack of fidelity to the Bill of Rights were grounds for his rejection. Reviewing Rehnquist's activities in Phoenix in opposition to civil rights legislation and school desegregation, Rauh contended that the nominee would be "a judicial activist seeking to put over political conservatism" who would probably be further to the right than any member of the Supreme Court in the twentieth century (U.S. Congress 1971a, 304).[10] Rauh also castigated the nominee for his lack of candor before the Judiciary Committee.

The president of the National Organization for Women, citing the nominee's earlier testimony before the House Judiciary Committee regarding the Equal Rights Amendment, stated that "with friends like this, proponents of . . . women's justice need no additional enemies" and described that testimony as indicative of

[9] For example, Senator Bayh asked Rehnquist how women should be treated under the Fourteenth Amendment. He answered, "Certainly the equal protection of the laws clause in the 14th amendment protects women just as it protects other discrete minorities, if one could call women a minority" (U.S. Congress 1971a, 163). Bayh also asked, "Do you concur in the general concept related in *Griswold v. Connecticut* . . . as the way they describe [the right to privacy], the broad basis of it?" Rehnquist answered, "I think it is not appropriate for me to get any more specific. To say whether I agree with the doctrine of a particular case or not I think would be entirely inappropriate for a nominee" (ibid., 164).

[10] Rauh also called for an FBI investigation of Rehnquist's alleged involvement in voter harassment. The charge was never fully resolved, although the FBI report confirmed that there were incidents of voter harassment, including a "scuffle." The majority of the Judiciary Committee accepted the word of a local judge as evidence that Rehnquist was not involved. The dissenting members of the committee argued that the charges were not completely refuted (U.S. Congress 1971b, 8–10, 41–43).

"lack of scholarship and of insight to the real status of women" (ibid., 429–30). The president of the National Lawyers Guild warned that the reinterpretation of the Constitution promised by the nominee would force the struggles of oppressed groups outside the system (ibid., 456). The American Civil Liberties Union, characterizing Rehnquist as a "dedicated opponent of individual civil liberties," sent a letter to all members of the Senate calling for his defeat (Abraham 1985, 316 n.100).[11]

The Judiciary Committee delayed sending the nomination to the floor of the Senate for a week so that some of the members could review the issues raised during the hearings—particularly Rehnquist's alleged insensitivity to racial minorities. But the majority was unpersuaded by the testimony of scholars and representatives of civil rights groups[12] and found the charges against Rehnquist to be totally unfounded. The majority of the committee reviewed his record and views on civil rights and civil liberties and recommended his confirmation, concluding that he had a balanced approach and "deep and unwavering commitment to the Constitution" (U.S. Congress 1971b, 20). Four committee members—Edward Kennedy, Birch Bayh, Philip Hart, and John Tunney—disagreed. In a thirty-page *Minority Report*, in which they reviewed all the issues, the four dissenting senators concluded:

> Mr. Rehnquist's record reveals a dangerous hostility to the great principles of individual freedom under the Bill of Rights and equal justice for all people. He has persistently opposed the use of law to eliminate racial injustice in America, and he has just as persistently analyzed legal problems in a way which minimizes the importance of civil liberties

[11] Other groups that opposed Rehnquist's appointment were the Americans for Democratic Action, AFL-CIO, UAW, Congressional Black Caucus, National Bar Association, National Legal Aid and Defender Association, Washington Council of Lawyers, and National Catholic Conference for Interracial Justice (U.S. Congress 1971b).

[12] Gary Orfield, then an assistant professor at Princeton University, submitted a statement cautioning that "[h]e seems disposed to view narrowly the responsibility of both courts and legislators in protecting minority rights. In fact there is damaging evidence of his hostility to the rights of black Americans. While Mr. Rehnquist's writings suggest that he would narrowly interpret some sections of the Bill of Rights and the Fourteenth Amendment, he has often read the Constitutional grants of power to the executive branch very broadly indeed" (U.S. Congress 1971a, 445).

values and maximizes the importance of executive power.
(Ibid., 54–55)

The members of the minority asserted that Rehnquist's legal
analysis was not based upon a balanced approach but on a double
standard whereby constitutional provisions that promote the interests of civil liberties are read narrowly while provisions that
limit individual liberties are construed broadly (ibid., 54).

After the Judiciary Committee's favorable report, the discussion on the floor of the Senate initially consisted of long speeches
by Rehnquist's opponents to a vacant chamber (Graham 1971b,
26). But after the "Jackson Memorandum" became public, Rehnquist's confirmation became the subject of considerable controversy.[13] The nominee, *Newsweek* reported, prepared the memorandum for Justice Jackson in 1952, when the Court was
preparing to consider *Brown v. Board of Education*. Entitled "A
Random Thought on the Segregation Cases," the one-and-a-half-
page memorandum read in part:

> One hundred and fifty years of attempts on the part of this
> Court to protect minority rights of any kind—whether those
> of business, slaveholders, or Jehovah's Witnesses—have all
> met the same fate. One by one the cases establishing such
> rights have been sloughed off and crept silently to rest. If the
> present Court is unable to profit by this example, it must be
> prepared to see its work fade in time, too, as embodying only
> the sentiments of a transient majority of nine men.
>
> I realize that it is an unpopular and unhumane proposition
> for which I have been excoriated by "liberal" colleagues but
> I think *Plessy v Ferguson* was right and should be re-af-
> firmed. If the Fourteenth Amendment did not enact Spen-
> cer's *Social Statics*, it just as surely did not enact Myrdal's
> *American Dilemma*. (*Congressional Record*, 1971, 45441)

Thus, the question of whether the memorandum represented
Rehnquist's views or those of Jackson became the focus of the
Senate's debate. Three days after the memorandum became pub-
lic, the nominee sent a letter to Senator Eastland, the chair of the
Judiciary Committee, attesting that the memo "was intended as
a rough draft of a statement of [Justice Jackson's] views at the

---

[13] *Newsweek* (December 13, 1971, 32–33) published excerpts from the memorandum. The issue appeared on December 5. The *New York Times* published the
memorandum on December 9, 1971.

conference of the Justices, rather than as a statement of my views." He also pointed out that during the hearings he mentioned the Supreme Court's decision in *Brown v. Board of Education* in the context of an answer to a question concerning the binding effect of precedent, and "I was not asked my views on the substantive issues in the *Brown* case. In view of some of the recent Senate floor debate, I wish to state unequivocally that I fully support the legal reasoning and the rightness from the standpoint of fundamental fairness of the *Brown* decision" (ibid., 45440).

Several Senators raised questions about the likelihood that the memorandum actually reflected Jackson's views rather than Rehnquist's. Two people, Rehnquist's fellow law clerk and Jackson's secretary, offered information regarding the memorandum; the latter flatly disputed Rehnquist's account.[14] The memorandum did not represent Jackson's views as exemplified by his record in minority rights cases. Moreover, Rehnquist's activities as a Phoenix attorney and statements he was known to have made, such as "we are no more dedicated to an 'integrated' society than to a 'segregated' society," suggested that the memo did, indeed, reflect his own views.[15]

After five days of debate, the Senate confirmed Rehnquist by a vote of 68 to 26 on December 10, 1971, notwithstanding his conservative views, his record of conservative activism, and his probable position in 1952 that *Plessy v. Ferguson* should have been upheld. It is possible that some senators who voted for him did so because they were impressed with his distinguished credentials and intellectual stature, particularly in light of President Nixon's previous attempts to appoint justices with marginal legal skills. In addition, the Senate's perceived role in giving "advice and consent" to the president may have been crucial to Rehnquist's confirmation. A nominee may be "qualified" in the

[14] Donald Cronson, Rehnquist's fellow law clerk, sent a message to Rehnquist that was placed into the *Congressional Record* (1971, 45816). Cronson remembered two memos that he and Rehnquist had prepared for Jackson: one supported the proposition that *Plessy* was wrongly decided and another argued that it was correctly decided. Kluger (1975, 607) noted that Elsie Douglas, Justice Jackson's secretary, told the *Washington Post* that Rehnquist had "smeared the reputation of a great justice" by attributing pro-segregationist views to Jackson. She told *Newsweek* that Rehnquist's explanation of the memo was "incredible on its face."

[15] See, for example, the memorandum placed into the record by Senator Brooke (*Congressional Record*, 1971, 45815–6). See also Kluger 1975, 606–9.

sense that he or she possesses the requisite personal integrity and professional competence to be a Supreme Court justice. Is the Senate then obligated to give its consent to the president's nomination? A narrow construal of the Senate's role in the appointment process would call for an affirmative answer. But the Senate's role may entail more—perhaps its members should look beyond formal qualifications to a nominee's philosophy and probable impact on the Supreme Court. In that view, a Senator would be obligated to vote against the confirmation of a nominee whose presence on the Court he or she believes would be harmful to the country. And fundamental disagreement on major constitutional questions would provide sufficient reason for a Senator to vote "no."[16] But in Rehnquist's case the Senate focused on the nominee's impressive credentials and his character, welcomed his assurance that his personal views would not influence his judicial decision making, and confirmed him. In so doing, the Senate embraced the narrow view of its "advice and consent" role and seemingly took the advice of Tom Wicker, who in November of 1971 wrote in an editorial in the *New York Times*: "It may be argued that Mr. Nixon should not have handed Senators this dilemma by appointing an activist political figure to a nonpolitical court; but the precedents are ample, and the Senate is likely to compound the damage if it denies Mr. Rehnquist his Court seat solely because of his political views" (quoted in *Congressional Record*, 1971, 45814).

REHNQUIST AND THE BURGER COURT: EARLY VIEWS

Rehnquist took his oath of office as an associate justice on January 7, 1972. Scholars, lawyers, and other observers of the Court began almost immediately to predict the impact that a man with such conservative views and keen intellectual ability, who had taken his seat at the early age of forty-seven, would have on the decisions of the Supreme Court. Alexander Bickel predicted that Rehnquist would serve as the Court's resident conservative ideologue, a "man with a first rate independent intellect who would keep the other justices' toes to the fire" (quoted in Simon 1973, 241). In 1972 one commentator characterized the new justice as "an activist. . . . With a majority of Rehnquist's on the Court, it is at least conceivable that the Court could return to the pre-1937

---

[16] See, for example, Black 1970 and Tribe 1985b. Black's article was placed into the record of the hearings (U.S. Congress 1971a, 299–303).

days when its major interest was the protection of private property, not human rights" (ibid., 292).

As soon as Rehnquist had been on the Court a sufficient length of time to establish a voting record, observers began to examine his votes and opinions. At the beginning of Rehnquist's third full term on the Court an article appeared in the *New York Times Magazine* in which the author asserted that

> Rehnquist has established himself firmly as a one-man strong right wing, a constructionist so strict as to make Chief Justice Warren Burger look permissive on occasion, a man seemingly dedicated to cleansing, singlehandedly if necessary, the Augean stable that conservative dogma perceives as the Supreme Court of the nineteen-fifties and nineteen-sixties. . . . [Moreover, a] sizable number [of lawyers] regard Rehnquist as having the best mind on the Court. (Weaver 1974, 36)[17]

In 1975 another commentator argued that "judicial restraint" was the dominant theme of Rehnquist's opinions regarding civil liberties (Rydell 1975). After analyzing his opinions and votes during his first four and a half terms, still another Rehnquist-watcher, who found that the "unyielding character of his ideology" had a detrimental effect on the quality of his opinions, explained his decision making on the basis of three propositions. First, conflicts between an individual and the government should, whenever possible, be resolved against the individual. Second, conflicts between state and federal authority, whether on an executive, legislative, or judicial level, should, whenever possible, be resolved in favor of the states. Finally, questions of the exercise of federal jurisdiction, whether on the district court, appellate court, or Supreme Court level should, whenever possible, be resolved against such exercise (Shapiro 1976, 294).

The early studies were constrained by the fact that they were of necessity "preliminary assessments" and could not resolve disturbing questions of possible inconsistencies in Rehnquist's judicial behavior. For example, he was characterized as both an "activist" and as a justice whose decisions were based on "judicial restraint"; he was described as a "strict constructionist" and

---

[17] Weaver's article was also quite prophetic. He noted that Rehnquist's "arrival in his lifetime post at a relatively early age could easily make him a leading candidate for Chief in some subsequent conservative administration" (1974, 36).

as a justice who interpreted constitutional provisions involving individual rights narrowly, while he construed constitutional grants of power to the Executive broadly.

In 1980 one commentator who was dissatisfied with the justice's performance said that: "Rehnquist surely is not consistent; he is neither libertarian, strict constructionist, nor conservative. Rather, the Court's youngest justice appears to be a complex man beset by the unfocused but pervasive fears of modern America" (Soifer 1980, 28). That indictment articulated the basic elements of what was to become the standard liberal critique of Rehnquist. That critique posited essentially that the justice's reasoning was inconsistent, unprincipled, and result oriented—that he used his position on the Court to achieve the goals of his own conservative political agenda.

Since 1980, some analysts of Rehnquist's judicial work have attempted to explain his decision making with reference to some underlying theme. Among them are those who have asserted that the key to his behavior can be found in a particular devotion to the protection of property rights. Fiss and Krauthammer (1982, 21), for example, asserted that the justice "prefers state autonomy because it is more consonant with classical laissez-faire theory which reduces the function of government to protecting private exchanges and the aim of the Constitution to protecting the rights and expectations of property holders."

Others have argued that Rehnquist's state-centered federalism is the major theme that runs through his votes and opinions (see especially Powell 1982 and also Lind 1980; Riggs and Proffit 1983; Kleven 1982; Luneburg 1982). Still others who have analyzed his opinions have discovered the underlying theme in extraconstitutional principles such as moral relativism (Justice 1980) or in a social vision based on individualism, reward for the successful competitor, and rejection of paternalism (Denvir 1983).

What follows is an examination of Rehnquist's work as an associate justice of the Supreme Court from the beginning of his tenure in 1972 until the end of the Court's 1985–86 term when he was nominated for chief justice. I argue that the justice's decision making is based on a judicial philosophy with legal positivism at its core and a particular ordering of judicial values. He places a preeminent value on federalism; indeed, the theme of state autonomy runs throughout his opinions, while he assigns a subordinate value to private property. He relegates individual rights to the bottom of his hierarchy of values.

The thesis of this work is that Rehnquist's decision making can be understood with reference to the interaction between his judicial philosophy—made up of the democratic model, moral relativism, and his approach to consitutional interpretation—and his ordering of the values of federalism, property rights, and individual rights. I present the thesis by analyzing his opinions in a large number of cases that I have organized into the three categories of individual rights, property rights, and federalism.

———

TWO

Rehnquist's Legal Positivism and His Ordering of Values

In July of 1986 while the Senate Judiciary Committee prepared to convene hearings on Justice Rehnquist's nomination to be the sixteenth chief justice of the Supreme Court, civil rights groups planned, as they had in 1971, to oppose his confirmation. Civil rights leaders alleged that his hostility to civil rights and civil liberties, as well as his consistent stance far to the right of the mainstream, rendered him unfit to head the federal judiciary. Benjamin L. Hooks, chair of the Leadership Conference on Civil Rights, characterized the justice as " 'an extremist . . . an enemy of civil rights' whose rulings in cases involving segregation show a consistent hostility to minorities" (Lardner and Kamen 1986). Eleanor Smeal, president of the National Organization for Women, characterized Rehnquist's record on women's rights as reflective of "a 19th-century view of people" and as a "disaster for women" (ibid.). Moreover, the memorandum that he wrote for Justice Jackson in 1952 threatened to become a major issue, as did the allegations that he harassed and intimidated voters in the early 1960s.

After Rehnquist's fourteen and a half years as an associate justice of the Supreme Court, his record could be summarized as follows: He consistently denied claims of discrimination brought by women, aliens, and illegitimate children, whether such claims were based on civil rights statutes or the equal protection clause of the Fourteenth Amendment. More often than not, he also denied claims of racial discrimination. His votes reflected his opposition both to the busing of schoolchildren to achieve desegregation and to affirmative action programs to remedy the effects of past discrimination in education and employment. He nearly always supported the government—state or federal—against the claims of criminal defendants that their rights to due process of law had been violated. Moreover, he took every opportunity to urge the Court to overrule the decisions of the Warren Court regarding the rights of those accused of crimes. He was a strong supporter of the death penalty against the argument that it violated the Eighth Amendment's prohibition on cruel and unusual punishment. He strongly opposed the Supreme Court's decision in 1973 that the right to privacy encompasses a woman's right to choose to have an abortion during the early stages of a pregnancy. Subsequently, he urged the Court to overrule that decision and to allow the states to prohibit abortion. He only rarely supported a claim that the government had violated the First Amendment's guarantee of freedom of expression. He supported school prayer and state aid to religious schools. He was a strong supporter of presidential power. An advocate of the strict separation of the powers of the federal government, he urged the Court to revive the nondelegation doctrine that it had abandoned in the 1930s. Finally, he staunchly defended judicial deference to legislative decisions except when he believed that federal legislative power infringed on state autonomy.

How can such a voting record be explained? Is Rehnquist simply a right-wing ideologue determined to use the Court to further his own political agenda? Do his votes manifest a desire to protect property rights? Has his judicial record been shaped by a sincere commitment to "judicial restraint"? Is his approach to constitutional interpretation informed by "strict constructionism"? Each of those questions must be answered in the negative. Neither political agenda, property rights, "judicial restraint," nor "strict constructionism" provide adequate explanations of his decision making. The goal of this chapter is to describe the framework that I use throughout the book to analyze Rehnquist's decision making. First, I examine the roots of his judicial philosophy in legal positivism. Second, I divide his judicial philosophy into three components. I then proceed to identify his ordering of values and to examine the relationship between those values and the three components of his judicial philosophy.

Positive Foundations

Legal positivism is a school of jurisprudence that includes two propositions regarding the nature of law: First, the law exists by virtue of an act or decision by the dominant political authority in civil society. Second, the law and morals are separate—the law must be understood as it is, not as it ought to be. John Austin, the nineteenth-century legal philosopher who provided the first systematic statement of legal positivism, identified the law as the commands that emanate from a holder of power (1954). He attempted to analyze law in terms of empirical facts rather than normative concepts, repudiating natural law theory by identifying the crucial characteristic of law as the power to compel obedience.

Although modern legal theorists, most notably H.L.A. Hart (1961), have refined Austinian theory considerably, a sharp separation between law and morality remains central to legal positivism. Modern positivists, furthermore, view law as a set of rules whose validity can be determined by reference to their "pedigree"—the manner in which they were created. Thus, a law is considered valid if it was enacted in a manner consistent with the rules for generating laws. In the American context, if Congress enacted a law following the proper procedures—those which did not violate any express provisions in the Constitution—it is valid.[1]

Oliver Wendell Holmes, Jr., five years before he became an associate justice of the Supreme Court, described the dangers of confusing morality with law. Many laws, he noted, have offended consciences and have been condemned by enlightened opinion. Nevertheless, those laws have been enforced. He contended that "nothing but confusion of thought can result from assuming that the rights of man in a moral sense are equally rights in the sense of the Constitution and the law" (1897, 650). Holmes urged his fellow members of the legal community to wash the law with "cynical acid" and to "expel everything except the object of our study, the operations of the law" (ibid., 652).

---

[1] In H.L.A. Hart's terminology, primary rules are rules that tell individuals how they ought to act in certain circumstances. A society with only primary rules will be uncertain, static, and inefficient, however. Secondary rules, or rules about rules, are therefore needed. The most important type of secondary rule is the "rule of recognition, " which assigns the task of making law to a person or group. Essential to law is the community's acceptance of the "rule of recognition." Legal positivism is much more complex than the brief overview presented here may suggest. For example, in Hart's words: "In a developed legal system the rules of recognition are of course more complex; instead of identifying rules exclusively by reference to a text or list they do so by reference to some general characteristic possessed by the primary rules. This may be the fact of their having been enacted by a specific body, or their long customary practice, or their relation to judicial decisions. Moreover, where more than one of such general characteristics are treated as identifying criteria, provision may be made for their possible conflict by their arrangement in an order of superiority, as by the common subordination of custom or precedent to statute, the latter being a 'superior source' of law" (Hart 1961, 92–93).

Legal positivism, in short, attempts to identify law in a morally neutral way and to strip it of all extraneous notions of morality by limiting it to the body of written law. For an American positivist, the law consists of statutes, the common law, and the Constitution.[2] From such a perspective, it would be meaningless to argue that a law violates principles of morality and, therefore, is not valid, because laws enacted and enforced through the procedures that the community has accepted are, by definition, valid.

A judge who subscribes to legal positivism will be respectful toward legislative decisions. On the grounds that in the American legal system lawmaking is a prerogative of legislators rather than judges, a positivist jurist is likely to endorse judicial review only when a law has been generated by an inappropriate source, when the legislature has failed to follow the proper procedures in enacting a law, or when the lawmaker has clearly violated an explicit constitutional provision. Otherwise, judicial deference to legislative decisions is the proper course of conduct for the legal positivist. In an attempt to adhere to the law as empirical fact, a positivist jurist limits his or her interpretation of the Constitution to the meaning of the words of the text or the intent of its authors. The legal positivist denies the existence of rights that are not expressly provided in statutes or in the Constitution. Thus, property rights have no status for the positivist beyond what is provided in the written law. The due process clause of the Fourteenth Amendment prohibits a state from taking property without due process of law; nevertheless, in the positivist's view, the state can take that property if it follows the proper procedures. Similarly, a legal positivist does not recognize personal rights, such as the right to privacy, that are not expressly guaranteed by the Bill of Rights.

Justice Hugo Black epitomized in several ways the legal positivist's approach to judicial decision making. First, following the tenet that law and morality are separate and distinct, he argued that the due process clause should not be used to invalidate laws that judges see as unwise or unnecessary (see, for example, Griswold v. Connecticut, 381 U.S. 479 [1965]). Second, in interpreting

[2] Ronald Dworkin (1985, 131) noted that in some forms of positivism acceptance of a customary rule qualifies as a law, but in all forms positivism includes the idea that "law exists only in virtue of some human act or decision." He also has noted that the main idea of positivism is that "law is a matter of historical decisions by people in positions of political power" (1986, 34).

the Constitution he followed the plain meaning of the words and the intent of the framers. His absolutist interpretation of the First Amendment and his argument that the framers of the Fourteenth Amendment intended the due process clause to incorporate the Bill of Rights are but two illustrations. In addition, his opinion denying President Truman the authority to take over the steel mills in order to avert a strike not only demonstrated his view that the president's constitutional powers are strictly limited to those listed but that the law should be made by legislators rather than judges (Youngstown Sheet and Tube Co. v. Sawyer, 343 U.S. 579 [1952]).[3]

THREE FACETS

Justice Rehnquist's decision making, though very different from Justice Black's, incorporates a judicial philosophy that has its roots in a jurisprudence of legal positivism.[4] His judicial philosophy includes three components. The first is a democratic model of the American political system. Confident that majority rule is the best principle of governing, he believes that judges should be deferential toward the decisions of elected officials. Moreover, he seems to believe that the political process functions best at the state and local levels, where decisions can most accurately reflect the interests of the people. His democratic model may be contrasted with the model of constitutionalism insofar as it stresses majority rule and the accountability of elected officials through the electoral process while it de-emphasizes the notion that the Constitution protects certain individual rights regardless of the will of the majority (see Murphy 1980, 708).

Rehnquist's commitment to the democratic model has been particularly apparent in his statements urging the Court to apply the presumption of constitutionality to legislative decisions—to uphold a law unless the challenger is able to show that it has no rational basis. For example, he has often urged the Court to up-

---

[3] Yarbrough (1971) presented a clear and convincing analysis of Black as a legal positivist.

[4] The term *positivism* has a broader use in philosophy (i.e., logical positivism), which is associated with empiricism. The reader should note that the use of the term throughout this work is limited to the narrower sense—legal positivism as a theory of law, a way of understanding the law.

hold statutory provisions that distinguish between men and women against challenges under the equal protection clause.[5]

An opinion he wrote in 1972, dissenting from the majority's conclusion that the death penalty, as it was then imposed, was cruel and unusual punishment in violation of the Eighth Amendment, also testifies to his commitment to the democratic model (Furman v. Georgia, 408 U.S. 238). In that opinion he urged judicial deference to legislative enactments, cautioning that, "[w]hile overreaching by the Legislative and Executive Branches may result in the sacrifice of individual protections that the Constitution was designed to secure against the action of the State, judicial overreaching may result in sacrifice of the equally important right of the people to govern themselves" (Furman, 408 U.S. at 470).

In the same opinion he asserted that one of the reasons for judicial deference is the consequence of error. A mistake in favor of an individual's claim against a legislative act, he argued, is more serious than an error in which a court mistakenly upholds a law "while wrongfully depriving the individual of a right secured to him by the Constitution" (ibid., 468). The reason the first type of mistake is more serious than the second, he explained, is that the result of the invalidation of a law is the imposition upon the people of the views of a majority of nine justices who have only a remote connection to the popular will. He subsequently reiterated that argument in his assertion that when the Court mistakenly upholds a law, the result is only to leave in force what has been duly enacted by "the popularly chosen members of the House of Representatives and the Senate and signed into law by the popularly chosen president" (1987b, 318). But when the Court wrongly decides to invalidate a law, it commits an error of "considerably greater consequence; it has struck down a law duly enacted by the popularly elected branches of government not because of any principle in the Constitution, but because of the individual view of desirable policy held by a majority of the nine justices at that time" (ibid.).

His commitment to the democratic model is also manifest in his attempts to revive the nondelegation doctrine, according to which Congress may not delegate its legislative powers to the Executive. Although the Court abandoned that doctrine in the

---

[5] See, for example, Craig v. Boren, 429 U.S. 190 (1976). See the discussion of his opinions in the area of equal protection in chapter 3.

1930s, Rehnquist has argued that the Court has a duty to invalidate unconstitutional delegations of legislative authority and that important choices of social policy must be made by elected representatives rather than nonelected officials in the executive branch.[6] Judges must not usurp the power of the legislators to represent the people; similarly, legislators must not pass the responsibility for making difficult decisions of national policy to nonelected executive officials. His consistent support for extensive presidential power and his devotion to the notion of strictly separated powers of the national government[7] are also explained, at least in part, by his commitment to the democratic model.

Moral relativism, the second component of Rehnquist's judicial philosophy, is apparent in his assertion that no value can be demonstrated to be intrinsically superior to any other—a particular value is authoritative only when it can claim majority support:

> The laws that emerge after a typical political struggle in which various individual value judgments are debated likewise take on a form of moral goodness because they have been enacted into positive law. . . . Beyond the Constitution and the laws in our society, there simply is no basis other than the individual conscience of the citizen that may serve as a platform for the launching of moral judgments. (1976a, 704)

Thus, although individuals may have deeply felt values, they remain merely personal until they are enacted into law either by legislation or by constitutional amendment. Standards or principles of justice are defined by the majority:

> If . . . a [democratic] society adopts a constitution and incorporates in that constitution safeguards for individual liberty, these safeguards indeed do take on a generalized moral rightness or goodness. They assume a general social acceptance neither because of any intrinsic worth nor because of any unique origins in someone's idea of natural justice but in-

---

[6] See Industrial Union Dept., AFL-CIO v. American Petroleum, 448 U.S. 607 (1980); American Textile Manufacturers Institute v. Donovan, 452 U.S. 490 (1981).

[7] Regarding presidential power see, for example, Nixon v. Administrator of General Services, 433 U.S. 425 (1977); Dames & Moore v. Regan, 453 U.S. 654 (1981); Regan v. Wald, 104 S.Ct. 3026 (1984). Regarding separation of powers see, for example, Buckley v. Valeo, 424 U.S. 1 (1976); his vote in Bowsher v. Synar, 106 S.Ct. 3181 (1986).

stead simply because they have been incorporated in a constitution by the people. (Ibid.)[8]

Such statements suggest that Rehnquist subscribes to the principles, associated with the jurisprudence of positivism, that a law derives its validity from the process by which it was enacted and that it is the written law, rather than abstract theories concerning moral principles, that provides the basis for rules of behavior. His statements suggest, moreover, an agreement with Holmes that those who would achieve a true understanding of the law must stop confusing it with morality.

Moral relativism runs through Rehnquist's judicial opinions. He has asserted, for instance, that the states create property rights and may regulate and even take away those rights. Such rights do not exist by virtue of any precepts of natural law but only as a result of their enactment into the positive law. In an opinion he wrote in 1980 he stated, "Nor as a general proposition is the United States, as opposed to the several States, possessed of residual authority that enables it to define 'property' in the first instance" (Pruneyard Shopping Center v. Robins, 447 U.S. 74, 84 [1980]). He has also expressed his disapproval of decisions that have extended judicial protection to personal rights not mentioned in the Constitution. For example, in dissenting from the Court's decision in Roe v. Wade (410 U.S. 113 [1973]), he suggested that he does not find a right to privacy that encompasses a woman's right to decide to have an abortion in the Fourth Amendment or the due process clause of the Fourteenth Amendment.[9] He acknowledged that there may be a right to privacy, but only in the sense that a person is "free from unwanted state regulation of consensual transactions" (Roe, 410 U.S. at 172). Privacy in that conception may be encompassed in the liberty protected by the Fourteenth Amendment, he noted, "[b]ut that liberty is not guaranteed absolutely against deprivation, only against deprivation without due process of law" (ibid., 173). Consequently, the state can take away that privacy so long as it does

---

[8] Rehnquist (1987a, 317) reiterated that view: "Many of us necessarily feel strongly and deeply about the judgments of our own consciences, but these remain only personal moral judgments until in some way they are given the sanction of supreme law."

[9] Rehnquist, at any rate, denied that an abortion involved the right of privacy: "A transaction resulting in an operation such as this is not 'private' in the ordinary usage of that word" (Roe, 410 U.S. at 172).

so through legislation that has a rational relation to a valid state objective.

Rehnquist's moral relativism is illustrated further in his construal of the equal protection clause, which in his view does not symbolize either a goal of social justice or an underlying value of equality. While the clause protects blacks from official discrimination, it does not apply to women, aliens, or illegitimate children; nor does it prohibit private racial discrimination, nor official action that was not intended to discriminate but nevertheless has a discriminatory impact.[10]

The third component of Rehnquist's judicial philosophy is his approach to interpreting the Constitution. I use the term *approach* to refer to an interpreter's basic understanding of the Constitution. Rehnquist's approach includes the belief that the Constitution is limited to the text of the document, the idea that the Constitution has a fixed meaning, and the view that it comprises a set of rules to be strictly followed.[11]

He has asserted that an interpreter should rely on the document itself and confine the meaning to the words of the text. He has allowed that when the words do not suffice, an interpreter may search for the intent of the framers. For example, he has stated that the Fourteenth Amendment was designed to prevent the states from treating black and white citizens differently and that it, therefore, should not be stretched beyond that purpose to embody an affirmative guarantee of equality, nor should it be applied to other disadvantaged groups.

[10] Rehnquist's opinions that illustrate such views are examined in chapter 3.

[11] The literature on constitutional interpretation is too voluminous to list here. For the best comprehensive treatment see Murphy, Fleming, and Harris 1986. Because I have found their terminology to be the most helpful, I have utilized it in this book. See also Carter (1985). Others who have subscribed to an approach akin to Rehnquist's include Berger (1977), Bork (1971), and Monaghan (1981). The approach to constitutional interpretation to which Rehnquist has subscribed has been variously termed interpretivism (Grey 1975; Ely 1980), immanent positivism (Harris 1982, 34–35), preservatism (Carter 1985), originalism and intentionalism (Brest 1980), and the Protestant mode (Levinson 1979). In actuality, more than one approach is represented here. Brest, for example, noted that "[t]he most extreme forms of originalism are 'strict textualism' (or literalism) and 'strict intentionalism.' A strict textualist purports to construe words and phrases very narrowly and precisely. For the strict intentionalist, 'the whole aim of construction, as applied to a provision of the Constitution, is . . . to ascertain and give effect to the intent of its framers and the people who adopted it' " (1980, 204, quoting Home Building and Loan Association v. Blaisdell, 290 U.S. 398, 453 [1934], Southerland dissenting).

The justice has also expressed the belief that the framers did not intend the establishment clause of the First Amendment to require a strict separation between church and state. He dissented when the Court held that an Alabama law providing for a period of silence for meditation or voluntary prayer in the public schools was unconstitutional (Wallace v. Jaffree, 472 U.S. 38 [1985], 105 S.Ct. 2479). In his opinion he reviewed the history of the religion clauses of the First Amendment and suggested that the Court's decisions have been inconsistent with the intent of the framers. A more accurate interpretation, he argued, would permit prayer in the public schools. He characterized Thomas Jefferson's statement that the establishment clause built a "wall of separation between church and state" as a "misleading metaphor" (*Wallace*, 105 S.Ct. at 2509), based on "bad history," that has diverted "judges from the actual intentions of the drafters of the Bill of Rights" (ibid., 2516). He avowed that

> [t]he true meaning of the Establishment Clause can only be seen in its history. As drafters of our Bill of Rights, the Framers inscribed the principles that control today. Any deviation from their intentions frustrates the permanence of that Charter and will only lead to the type of unprincipled decision making that has plagued our Establishment Clause cases. (Ibid., 2520, citations omitted)

Unlike his fellow legal positivist, Justice Black, Rehnquist does not believe that the framers of the Fourteenth Amendment intended the incorporation of the Bill of Rights into the due process clause. He has argued persistently against the Court's selective nationalization of the provisions in the first eight amendments. He has, in fact, referred to incorporation as a "mysterious process of transmogrification" (Carter v. Kentucky, 450 U.S. 288 [1981]).[12]

An alternative approach to consitutional interpretation that stands in stark contrast with Rehnquist's denies that discerning the intent of the framers is either possible or necessary.[13] Rather,

[12] Rehnquist's views on incorporation are also discussed at length in chapter 3.

[13] See, for example, Murphy 1978, 1980, Harris 1982, Barber 1984, Perry 1985, Levinson 1982. Carter has been most explicit: "The case for constitutional interpretation bound strictly to text and history is only slightly stronger than the case for the proposition that we inhabit a flat earth" (1985, 41). See also Justice Brennan's "arrogance cloaked in humility" speech (Taylor 1985a) and Justice Stevens's criticism of Edwin Meese (Taylor 1985b).

when called upon to construe difficult provisions in the Constitution, one should search for underlying values and principles in the overall design of the document. The essence of that approach was captured by Justice William J. Brennan, Jr. (1977, 495):

> For the genius of our Constitution resides not in any static meaning that it had in a world that is dead and gone, but in the adaptability of its great principles to cope with the problems of a developing America. A principle to be vital must be of wider application than the mischief that gave it birth. Constitutions are not ephemeral documents, designed to meet passing occasions. The future is their care, and therefore, in their application, our contemplation cannot be only of what has been but of what may be.

The alternative approach includes the propositions that the Constitution embodies more than the text, that it is evolving to meet the needs of a changing society, and that it is not just a set of rules but represents the nation's goals and aspirations.[14]

Rehnquist has asserted that such an approach is unacceptable because it invariably results in judges' superimposing their own values on the Constitution and, thereby, altering the true meaning of the document. He has expressed his belief that alteration of the Constitution to suit judges' notions of what is good for society controverts democratic principles of governance (1976a, 699). His approach to constitutional interpretation and his democratic model coexist comfortably; it is only by remaining faithful to the text and the intent of the framers that constitutional interpretation can be consistent with the democratic process. His approach to constitutional interpretation is also consistent with his moral relativism insofar as such an understanding of the Constitution precludes judicial substitution of personal values for the rules that have been properly enacted into the law.

A prescription for a minimal role for the judiciary would seem to follow logically from the combination of the three compo-

---

[14] The range of choice in constitutional interpretation represented by the three pairs of alternatives—textualism-transcendence, fixed Constitution–changing Constitution, and the Constitution as rules–the Constitution as vision—was formulated by Murphy, Fleming, and Harris (1986, 290–91). For an enlightening examination of the Constitution as vision, representing the goals of a good society, see Barber (1984). The transcendence-changing-vision approach has been variously termed noninterpretativism (Ely 1980), structuralism (Harris 1982), nonoriginalism (Brest 1980), and the Catholic mode (Levinson 1979).

nents of Rehnquist's judicial philosophy. Indeed, the democratic model seems almost synonymous with "judicial restraint" in its preference for the decisions of elected officials over those of judges. And in fact, the justice has severely criticized the form that modern judicial review has taken. He has expressed agreement with the defense of judicial review that Chief Justice John Marshall articulated in *Marbury v. Madison*, based on the conception of the Constitution as the embodiment of the original will of the people (1976a, 696). For Rehnquist, however, the passage of time has made a crucial difference. In Marshall's time the idea that the Constitution represented the original will of the people rendered judicial review consistent with the democratic process. Not only was judicial review justified, but it was a necessity if the courts were to fulfill their obligation of maintaining the supremacy of the people's will. Given the age in which Marshall lived, Rehnquist has noted, the chief justice may well have had an understanding of the original will of the people. In the twentieth century, however, such an understanding is impossible, and judges no longer function as guardians of the Constitution. Indeed, he has complained, rather than "keepers of the covenant . . . [judges] are a small group of fortunately situated people . . . [who] second guess Congress, state legislatures, and state and federal administrative officers concerning what is best for the country" (1976a, 698). Since judicial review can no longer be linked successfully to the people's original will, it obstructs rather than protects the democratic process.

Thus, the responsibility for preserving the Constitution rests with the popularly elected branches of government rather than the judiciary. Indeed, Rehnquist's criticism of modern judicial review is reminiscent of Justice Gibson's statement in his dissent in Eakin v. Raub (12 S & R 330, Pa. [1825]) that "it is the business of the judiciary to interpret the laws, not scan the authority of the lawgiver." Rehnquist has conceded that the judiciary has the duty to prevent the other branches from transgressing the explicit limits of the authority given to them by the Constitution; but that duty, in his view, does not extend to assessing the substance of policies made by elected officials.

Additional support is provided for a minimal role for the judiciary when moral relativism is joined to the democratic model. The preferences of majorities that have been enacted into the positive law (statutes or the Constitution) provide the basis for defining a society's rules and distinguishing right from wrong.

Following such a line of reasoning, judges have no legitimate basis other than explicit constitutional provisions on which to invalidate legislation.

Rehnquist's approach to constitutional interpretation would also seem to function as a means of minimizing judicial discretion and, thus, the judicial role. An unchanging Constitution, which consists only of its text, would be interpreted with reference to the historical meaning of its provisions, by looking at the words of the text and to the intent of the framers. Judges would therefore presumably be precluded from imposing their own values on the Constitution, and thereby from changing its meaning.

The Ordering of Values

Rehnquist has placed federalism in the highest position in his hierarchy of values, with property rights in second place and individual rights in the lowest position. The three components of his judicial philosophy—the democratic model, moral relativism, and his approach to constitutional interpretation—interact with his ordering of values to form the basis of his decision making.

In cases that involve a conflict between state authority and property rights, he has supported the state's power to regulate such rights so long as the state does not violate any explicit constitutional provision. In his opinion in *Pruneyard*, in 1980, he stated that "[i]t is, of course, well-established that a State in the exercise of its police power may adopt reasonable restrictions on private property so long as the restrictions do not amount to a taking without just compensation or contravene any other federal constitutional provision" (*Pruneyard*, 447 U.S. at 81). When he has found that the state has violated an express constitutional provision, however, Rehnquist, faithful to the written law, has withdrawn his support from the state.[15] He has been even more willing to support a state's authority when it has come into conflict with individual rights. Indeed, he has consistently voted in favor of the state and has given constitutional provisions protecting individual rights the narrowest possible construal.[16]

[15] See the analysis of Rehnquist's votes and opinions in chapter 6.

[16] The reader might object to the implication that property rights and individual rights are separate and distinct. *Individual rights* as used throughout this book refer to the rights—other than property—explicitly provided or implied in the first eight amendments and in the Fourteenth Amendment.

The justice recounted the importance of federalism in a dissenting opinion he wrote in 1977:

> It is too well known to warrant more than brief mention that the framers of the Constitution adopted a system of checks and balances conveniently lumped under the descriptive head of "federalism," whereby all power was originally presumed to reside in the people of the states who adopted the Constitution. The Constitution delegated some authority to the federal executive, some to the federal legislature, some to the federal judiciary, and reserved the remaining authority normally associated with sovereignty to the states and to the people in the states. (*Trimble v. Gordon*, 430 U.S. 762, 778–79)

When he held that the federal law that extended the requirements regarding the minimum wage and maximum hours to state and local government employees was beyond the authority of Congress, he asserted: "[A] state is not merely a factor in the "shifting economic arrangements" in the private sector of the economy, . . . but is itself a coordinate element in the system established by the framers for governing our Federal Union" (National League of Cities v. Usery, 426 U.S. 833 [1976]). Similarly, when a majority of the Court held that the Eleventh Amendment does not afford a state immunity from suit in the courts of another state, Rehnquist dissented. Appealing to the intent of the framers, he contended that

> [a]ny document—particularly a constitution—is built on certain postulates or assumptions; it draws on shared experience and common understanding, . . . when the Constitution is ambiguous or silent on a particular issue, this Court has often relied on notions of a constitutional plan—implicit ordering of relationships within the federal system necessary to make the Constitution a workable governing charter and to give each provision within that document the full effect *intended by the Framers*. (Nevada v. Hall, 440 U.S. 410, 433 [1979], emphasis mine)

The above statements not only testify to the preeminent value that Rehnquist assigns to federalism, but they also begin to suggest the nature of the interaction between that value and his approach to interpreting the Constitution. His conviction that federalism is central to the Constitution as intended by the framers

33

enables him to ground his preference for state autonomy in constitutional theory and, thereby, to avoid the pitfalls of the judge who relies on his own preferences in judicial decision making.

His democratic model also intersects with the high value he places on federalism. He has affirmed his belief that "the people are the ultimate source of authority; they have parceled out the authority that originally resided entirely with them by adopting the original Constitution and by later amending it. They have granted some authority to the federal government and have reserved authority not granted it to the states or to the people individually" (1976a, 696).

Because, in accordance with the democratic model, the laws derive their authority from the fact of their enactment by legislative bodies representing the will of the majority, the laws that are most clearly the product of the majority must be the most legitimate. Rehnquist seems to assume that small units of government, those closest to the people, will most likely reflect the will of the majority. Thus, state laws, which most closely resemble the ideal of the democratic model, are to be highly valued. In short, he finds support for his federalism in his conception of democracy as well as in the Constitution.

Rehnquist's democratic model, his approach to interpreting the Constitution, and his moral relativism go far to explain why he assigns lesser values to property and individual rights than to federalism. In his view, such rights exist only insofar as they are explicitly provided for in provisions of the Constitution and in statutory law. Those rights derive their existence not from moral principles but from their presence in the written law. In a published address Rehnquist (1980) posited that the Bill of Rights—indeed, all of the amendments to the Constitution—draw their authority from the extraordinary majorities required to ratify them. In his view, constitutional provisions are authoritative not because they embody moral principles or values but because they were adopted by the people. It follows that an extraordinary majority might repeal the Bill of Rights, although that might be unwise. To do so would not be illegal or immoral, for in a system based on majority rule "there is no appeal to any higher forum or court than a forum which properly and accurately reflects [the people's] will" (1980, 391).

Rehnquist's subordination of both property and individual rights to federalism is not difficult to explain with reference to the components of his judicial philosophy. But the reason he as-

34

signs individual rights to an even lower position than property rights in his hierarchy of values presents a more complex problem. His democratic model and his moral relativism, which prescribe a minimal role for the judiciary, would seem to leave the protection of both property and individual rights to elected officials. Thus, a preference for one type of right over the other would hardly seem possible. Further, Rehnquist's approach to constitutional interpretation would seem to place the two sets of rights on the same level.

The Constitution explicitly provides for the protection of property in the due process clauses of the Fifth and Fourteenth amendments, in the just compensation clause of the Fifth Amendment, and in the contract clause of Article I, Section 10. There are also express provisions that protect individual rights, primarily the Bill of Rights and the Fourteenth Amendment. Rehnquist construes due process as a procedural protection. Thus, the Fourteenth Amendment's prohibition on states against depriving "any person of life, liberty, or property without due process of law" means that a state may deprive a person of life, liberty, or property *with* due process of law.[17] That interpretation would seem to put property and individual rights (life and liberty) on an equal basis. People could be deprived of either liberty or property so long as the government followed the proper procedures. Moreover, the most explicit protection offered by the Constitution concerns individual rather than property rights. The First Amendment commands that "Congress shall make no law . . . abridging the freedom of speech." Still, Rehnquist minimizes the protection offered by the First Amendment (see ch. 4).

Several explanations, each of which refers to Rehnquist's judicial philosophy, are possible. First, a partial explanation may be found in his view that the First Amendment does not apply to the states, and neither do the other provisions in the Bill of Rights. Second, perhaps he believes that the framers intended the Constitution to protect property more than liberty, although they did not make that explicit in the text of the document. A third possible explanation for his ordering of the values of property and individual rights is that his preference for property rights is grounded in a belief that the protection of property leads to a more stable democratic society. But while the relationship be-

[17] See, for example, Rehnquist's dissenting opinion in *Roe v. Wade*. See chapters 3, 5, and 6 for an extensive treatment of due process.

35

tween his ordering of the values of property rights and individual rights is not fully explained by the components of his judicial philosophy, those components go a long way toward explaining his ordering of values, particularly the preeminent position in which he places federalism.

Taken together, the components of Rehnquist's judicial philosophy prescribe a minimal role for the courts. Still, his opinions in cases in which state and federal laws have come into conflict demonstrate that when he has seen federal action as an encroachment on the states' integrity and their ability to function as governmental units he has been quite willing to exercise the power of judicial review (see, for example, *National League of Cities v. Usery*). In such a situation the implications of the preeminent value that he places on federalism begin to emerge. When state interests are at stake judicial review becomes essential to the preservation of federalism. The necessity of judicial review in the context of federalism is entirely consistent with the democratic model if the states govern in accordance with majority rule, as Rehnquist seems to assume that they do. For Rehnquist, then, the exercise of judicial review in the interest of state autonomy protects not only federalism but the democratic process.

The value that Rehnquist assigns to federalism is so high that it abrogates the prescription for a minimal role for the judiciary. In his view, the courts have a crucial role to play to protect federalism. The maxim of "judicial restraint," in short, applies when property rights or individual rights are involved but not when state autonomy is at risk.

Furthermore, in the interest of protecting federalism Rehnquist's approach to constitutional interpretation has wavered. His opinions suggest that he moves toward the alternative approach to interpreting the Constitution when there is a conflict between a state and the federal government and when explicit constitutional provisions that address individual rights, such as the First Amendment, are invoked. More specifically, while his basic perception of the Constitution has seemed to be one that includes only the text, such phrases as "notions of a constitutional plan—implicit ordering of relationships within the federal system" (*Hall*, 440 U.S. at 443) suggest that when federalism is at issue he is willing to reach beyond that text. He even went so far as to concede that

> it is not the Tenth Amendment by its terms that prohibits congressional action which sets a mandatory ceiling on the

wages of all state employees. Both [the Tenth and the Eleventh] Amendments are simply examples of the understanding of those who drafted and ratified the Constitution that the States were sovereign in many respects, and that although their legislative authority could be superseded by Congress in many areas where Congress was competent to act, Congress was nonetheless not free to deal with a State as if it were just another individual or business enterprise subject to regulation. (Fry v. United States, 421 U.S. 542, 557 [1975])

On the other hand, whereas the First Amendment would seem to provide an absolute protection for expression, Rehnquist, in order to protect federalism, has appeared to find in that provision less than the text supplies.

Throughout this work I refer to the three-tiered model developed by Murphy, Fleming, and Harris to analyze Rehnquist's orientation to constitutional interpretation. The model, which moves from higher to lower levels of abstraction, includes the interpreter's approach to interpretation, or "the most basic ways an interpreter perceives the Constitution," plus modes of interpretation, or "HOW a person utilizes those approaches in the enterprise of constitutional interpretation," and techniques, which "signify specific interpretive tools" that a justice applies to decide particular cases (1986, 289). The variations in Rehnquist's techniques, modes, and even his fundamental approach to interpretation all serve his goal of protecting federalism.[18]

The next two chapters will examine Rehnquist's treatment of individual rights in the contexts of the Fourteenth Amendment and freedom of expression. The analysis of his decision making in those areas will demonstrate the subordinate position that he assigns to individual rights and will begin to delineate the dimensions of his federalism.

[18] Thomas Kleven made essentially the same point, albeit in terms that needed some clarification, when he stated that "what is most striking about Justice Rehnquist's approach is that in cases involving individual rights he interprets the Constitution very *narrowly*, whereas in cases raising issues of federalism he frequently adopts a *broad* construction" (1982, 12, emphasis mine). Kleven concluded that the unifying theme of Rehnquist's decisions is a desire to use his judicial position as a means of fostering states' rights, which is based on an ideological commitment to decentralization and pluralism.

PART TWO

Individual Rights

———

THREE

Justice Rehnquist's Fourteenth Amendment

Justice Rehnquist delivered a lecture in 1980 that subsequently appeared in the *Missouri Law Review* under the title "Government by Cliché." At the outset of that lecture he stated that he intended to dispel two clichés about the Constitution. First, he wanted to refute the idea that the Constitution is a charter that guarantees rights to individuals against the government. Second, he wished to correct the misconception that the Supreme Court " 'upholds' the Constitution only when it decides a constitutional claim in favor of an individual and not when it decides such a claim against the individual and in favor of the federal, state, or local government" (1980, 381). He alluded to his view of the proper role of the judiciary in the context of individual rights in the following statement:

> It is no more accurate to say of our Court that it is the ulti-
> mate guardian of individual rights than it is to say that it is
> the ultimate guardian of national authority or of states'
> rights. Its function is to decide among these conflicting
> claims as truly and accurately as it can in accordance with a
> fundamental charter and later amendments which have been
> adopted by the source of *all governmental authority*—the
> people of this country. (1980, 393, emphasis in original)

That statement suggested that he had rejected the doctrine whereby the Court's duty to protect individual rights requires the suspension of the usual deference to legislative decisions. He subsequently stated in even more explicit terms that he does not believe that the Court has a special duty to protect individual rights:

> [I]ts role is no more to exclusively uphold the claims of the
> individual than it is to exclusively uphold the claims of the
> government: It must hold the constitutional balance true be-
> tween these claims. And if it finds the scales evenly bal-

An earlier version of part of chapter 3 appeared as "Justice Rehnquist's Judicial Philosophy: Democracy v. Equality" in *Polity* (Fall 1984): 88–117.

anced, the longstanding "presumption of constitutionality" to which every law enacted by Congress or a state or local government is entitled means that the person who seeks to have the law held unconstitutional has failed to carry his burden of proof on the question. (1987b, 318)

Rehnquist's decision making in the context of the Fourteenth Amendment demonstrates not only his repudiation of the view of the Court as guardian of civil liberties but also that he has relegated such liberties to the bottom of his hierarchy of values, below both federalism and property rights.

The Fourteenth Amendment, ratified in 1868, provides in relevant part: "No state shall make or enforce any law which shall abridge the privileges or immunities of citizens of the United States; nor shall any State deprive any person of life, liberty, or property, without due process of law; nor deny to any person within its jurisdiction the equal protection of the laws."

The amendment, in order to protect blacks from discriminatory state action, limited the states' authority and expanded the power of Congress;[1] Rehnquist has noted that the provisions of the Fourteenth Amendment "are by express terms directed at the States" (Fitzpatrick v. Bitzer, 427 U.S. 445, 453 [1976]) and has granted that the Civil War amendments "sharply altered the balance of power between the Federal and State Governments" (Trimble v. Gordon 430 U.S. 762, 778 [1977]). Nevertheless, he has made serious and far-reaching efforts to limit the impact of the Fourteeenth Amendment in the interest of federalism.

REHNQUIST'S INTERPRETATION OF THE FOURTEENTH AMENDMENT

In cases involving the Fourteenth Amendment the justice has adopted a historical mode of analysis whereby he searches for its meaning in the past. With his technique of interpretation he has sought to remain faithful to the words and phrases of the document, confining the meaning, as much as possible, to the text. But when the words of the Constitution do not yield adequate information, he has included an analysis of other historical documents in order to discover the intent of the framers. He has utilized such techniques to support his pronouncements regarding both due process and equal protection.

[1] Section 5 provides: "The Congress shall have power to enforce, by appropriate legislation, the provisions of this article."

Literalism and "intent of the framers" are techniques of constitutional interpretation that coincide with Rehnquist's basic understanding of the Constitution. His perception includes the conviction that the Constitution consists only of the text of the document plus the belief that the Constitution has a fixed rather than a changing meaning and that the document constitutes a set of rules rather than a vision of the good society.[2] That understanding is reflected clearly in his opinions regarding the equal protection clause. He has argued that the clause was designed to protect blacks from discriminatory state laws, not "to solve problems that society might confront a century later" (1976a, 700).[3] Moreover, in his view, equal protection should not be expanded to cover other groups nor should it be used as a guarantee of complete racial equality. His interpretation of the due process clause also reflects a perception of an unchanging Constitution, composed of a set of rules, that is limited to its text. He has argued that the due process clause does not incorporate the Bill of Rights and that it creates no substantive rights; rather, it merely guarantees that government must follow fair procedures before it takes life, liberty, or property.[4]

Rehnquist's opinions that have involved, first, questions of the application of the Bill of Rights to the states through the due process clause and, second, the equal protection clause are the subjects of the remainder of this chapter.

DUE PROCESS: THE BILL OF RIGHTS AND THE STATES

The Supreme Court initially held that the Bill of Rights placed restrictions only on the federal government, not the states (Bar-

[2] See the discussion of constitutional interpretation in chapter 2. For an extensive overview of approaches to constitutional interpretation, see Murphy, Fleming, and Harris 1986, ch. 8. See Barber 1984 for the view that the Constitution represents a vision of the good society.

[3] But see Rehnquist's statement: "Merely because a particular activity may not have existed when the Constitution was adopted, or because the framers could not have conceived of a particular method of transacting affairs, cannot mean that general language in the Constitution may not be applied to such a course of conduct. Where the framers of the Constitution have used general language, they have given latitude to those who would later interpret the instrument to make that language applicable to cases that the framers might not have foreseen" (1976a, 694). He also stated that "[t]he evil at which Congress was aiming gives some idea of what the words 'equal protection' meant, but certainly the language is broad enough to include other beneficiaries than the freedmen" (1987a, 13–14).

[4] See, for example, Rehnquist's discussion of due process in Roe v. Wade (410 U.S. 113, 172–77 [1973]). See also the cases discussed in chapter 6.

ron v. Baltimore, 7 Pet. 243 [1833]). Thus, the states were free to handle matters involving individual rights as they saw fit. Subsequently, the Court declined to hold that the due process clause of the Fourteenth Amendment incorporated the Bill of Rights (Hurtado v. California, 110 U.S. 516 [1884]; Twining v. New Jersey, 211 U.S. 78 [1908]). Gradually, however, through a process of selective incorporation, the Court has held that nearly all of the provisions in the first eight amendments apply to the states because they are essential to due process (for example, Mapp v. Ohio, 367 U.S. 643 [1961]; Gideon v. Wainwright, 372 U.S. 335 [1963]).

Rehnquist would prefer a different approach—one that would allow the states to depart from the requirements set forth in the Bill of Rights. He has expressed his disagreement with the doctrine of incorporation in cases that have involved the rights of the accused, nontraditional property, and free speech. He has meticulously placed quotation marks around the word "incorporation" as if to deny its legitimacy and has characterized the incorporation of the Bill of Rights as a "mysterious process of transmogrification" (Carter v. Kentucky, 450 U.S. 288 [1981]). Due process, in his view, is not simply a shorthand term for the provisions in the first eight amendments. Indeed, he has asserted that the liberty that a state may not take without due process of law "embraces more than the rights found in the Bill of Rights" (Roe v. Wade, 410 U.S. 113, 173 [1973]). From his perspective, although some provisions in the Bill of Rights may apply to the states, they do so only coincidentally, not by virtue of their automatic applicability through the due process clause. According to Rehnquist, rather than require the states to comply with the provisions in the Bill of Rights the Court should only oblige them to treat individuals with fundamental fairness. It would not only be more consistent with the meaning of the due process clause as the justice understands it for the Court to repudiate the incorporation doctrine and return to the standard of fundamental fairness, but it would demonstrate more respect for the principles of federalism; in such a system a "healthy pluralism" could thrive (Richmond Newspapers v. Virginia, 448 U.S. 555, 606 [1980]).

Rehnquist's opinions in cases involving the rights of those accused and convicted of a crime are notable for their consistent support for law enforcement. He has clearly fulfilled Richard Nixon's dream of a justice who would strengthen the "peace forces" against the "criminal forces," who would help to swing

the pendulum away from the protection of the rights of the accused and toward the power of government. For instance, he
wrote opinions for the majority narrowing the "expectation of
privacy" and restricting defendants' ability to achieve standing to
challenge searches and seizures (Rakas v. Illinois, 439 U.S. 128
[1978]; see also United States v. Salvucci, 448 U.S. 83 [1980], and
Rawlings v. Kentucky, 448 U.S. 98 [1980]). He urged the Court to
abolish the exclusionary rule (California v. Minjares, 443 U.S.
916 [1979]) and joined the majority when the Court approved the
"good faith" exception to the exclusionary rule (United States v.
Leon, 104 S.Ct. 3405 [1984]). He wrote an opinion formulating a
"totality of circumstances" standard that made it easier for police to obtain a warrant on the basis of an informant's tip (Illinois
v. Gates, 462 U.S. 213 [1983]). He wrote for the majority endors-
ing a "public safety" exception to the *Miranda* rules (New York
v. Quarles, 467 U.S. 649 [1984]). He has consistently urged the
Court to retain the death penalty against the charge that it violates the Eighth Amendment (for example, Furman v. Georgia,
408 U.S. 238 [1972]). Finally, he wrote the opinion for the majority when the Court upheld a mandatory sentence of life in prison
pursuant to a Texas recidivist statute (Rummel v. Estelle, 445
U.S. 263 [1980]). Clearly, for Rehnquist, "conflicting claims" between a criminal defendant and the state should be resolved in
favor of the state.

He has taken numerous opportunities to articulate his objections to the application of the provisions in the Bill of Rights to
the states when the rights of the accused are involved. When the
Court held that the First and Fourteenth amendments require
that state criminal trials must be open to the public except under
extraordinary circumstances, he objected that the public trial
guarantee of the Sixth Amendment should not be applicable to
the states. Further, he suggested that a state's reasons for denying
public access to a trial should not be subject to Supreme Court
review and objected that the Court was "smother[ing] a healthy
pluralism which would ordinarily exist in a national government
embracing fifty states" (*Richmond Newspapers*, 448 U.S. at 606).
In another case he contended that Congress, under Section 5 of
the Fourteenth Amendment, does not have the same power to
enforce a constitutional provision that has been incorporated,
such as the cruel and unusual punishments prohibition of the
Eighth Amendment, as it does "with respect to a provision which
was placed in the Amendment by the drafters" (Hutto v. Finney,

437 U.S. 678, 717–18 [1978]). In another case, dissenting from the Court's denial of certiorari, Rehnquist characterized the incorporation of the Sixth Amendment right to counsel as a "judicial building block" (Snead v. Stringer, 454 U.S. 988, 989 [1981]).

Rehnquist has also expressed his objections to the incorporation doctrine when due process outside of the criminal context has been involved. For example, he dissented when the Court held that the due process clause requires a state to provide at least clear and convincing evidence before it may sever the rights of parents in their natural child. He stated that "[b]eyond an examination for the constitutional minimum of 'fundamental fairness' . . . this Court simply has no role in establishing the standards of proof that states must follow in the various judicial proceedings they afford to their citizens" (Santosky v. Kramer, 455 U.S. 745, 771, n. 2 [1982]).

Questions regarding the relationship of the Bill of Rights to the states have most often been raised in the context of state criminal processes. It was freedom of speech, however, that was incorporated into the due process clause in 1925, years before any of the provisions that pertain to the rights of the accused. Rehnquist has opposed the application of the First Amendment to the states and has affirmed a belief, based upon his federalism, that the states are limited only by the "general principle" of free speech (Buckley v. Valeo, 424 U.S. 1, 191 [1976]).[5]

Equal Protection

"One of the majestic generalities of the Constitution," the equal protection clause was intended to prohibit states from treating blacks and whites differently; the equal protection clause made race "an invalid sorting tool" (*Trimble*, 430 U.S. at 777, 779 [1977]). In Rehnquist's view, the protections offered by the clause should go that far and no further.

The *Carolene Products* Footnote, on which much of the modern doctrine of equal protection is based, suggested that the normal presumption of constitutionality would not apply to legislative acts that interfered with the political process or that disadvantaged "discrete and insular minorities" (United States v.

---

[5] See the discussion of the incorporation of the free speech provision of the First Amendment in chapter 4.

Carolene Products Co., 304 U.S. 144 [1938]). Instead, such legislation would be subject to heightened scrutiny. The Supreme Court subsequently developed a two-tier approach to equal protection whereby it used the rational basis test, which required only that a classification be rationally related to achieving a legitimate end, when economic regulations were challenged. When racial classifications were involved, however, the Court used strict scrutiny and required that a classification be shown to be the only means of achieving a compelling state interest. The two tiers developed by the Warren Court subsequently became three when the Burger Court introduced an intermediate standard of review according to which classifications based on characteristics such as sex and illegitimacy were required to be substantially related to an important governmental interest.[6] The Court has used the intermediate standard to examine classifications based on sex and illegitimacy and often to invalidate them without actually declaring these categories to be suspect.

Rehnquist's responses to the developments described above have been as follows: First, he has questioned the legitimacy of the *Carolene Products* Footnote as an authority for judicial doctrine. He has noted, for example, that only four members of the Court joined the opinion in which the Footnote appeared and has quoted with approval Justice Frankfurter's assertion that "[a] footnote hardly seems to be an appropriate way of announcing a new constitutional doctrine, and the *Carolene* footnote did not purport to announce any new doctrine" (Kovacs v. Cooper, 336 U.S. 77, 90–91 [1949], quoted in Sugarman v. Dougall, 413 U.S. 634, 656 [1973]).

Second, he strongly opposed the Court's adoption of the intermediate standard of review. Castigating the Court for using that standard, he once characterized its equal protection decisions as "an endless tinkering with legislative judgments, a series of conclusions unsupported by any central guiding principle" (*Trimble*, 430 U.S. at 779). Moreover, he criticized the majority for adding alienage to the list of suspect classifications. In short, he has suggested that he finds the basis for heightened scrutiny unconvincing; if there must be heightened scrutiny, his preference would be for the two-tier analysis, which would require only a rational

[6] In Craig v. Boren (429 U.S. 190, 197 [1976]), for example, Justice Brennan stated that "to withstand constitutional challenge, previous cases establish that classifications by gender must serve important governmental objectives and must be substantially related to achievement of those objectives."

basis for all classifications except those based on race. Finally, he has attempted to avoid strict scrutiny even when racial classifications have been involved.

Sex Classifications

The Supreme Court has determined that classifications based on sex "must serve important governmental objectives and must be substantially related to achievement of those objectives" (Craig v. Boren, 429 U.S. 190 [1976]). Administrative ease and convenience are not sufficiently important governmental objectives when classifications are based on "archaic and overbroad generalizations" and "gross, stereotyped distinctions between the sexes" (Frontiero v. Richardson, 411 U.S. 177 [1973]).[7]

Rehnquist, with rare exceptions,[8] has disagreed with the majority when the Court has invalidated classifications based on sex. Voicing his objections to the Court's decisions, he has often expressed his preference for a technique of constitutional interpretation based upon the intent of the framers, which, in his view, was to prohibit the states from treating blacks differently from whites. The Court should preserve the original intent of the framers and thus should not extend heightened scrutiny of legislative classifications beyond the area of racial discrimination. While racial classifications must be presumptively invalid,[9] in all

[7] Some examples of classifications based on sex that the Court has invalidated are an Oklahoma law that set the age for purchase of 3.2 beer at eighteen for females and twenty-one for males (Craig v. Boren), a Social Security Act provision that allowed a widower to receive survivors' benefits only if he was receiving one-half of his support from his wife (Weinberger v. Weisenfeld, 420 U.S. 636 [1975]), an Alabama statute that required husbands but not wives to pay alimony (Orr v. Orr, 440 U.S. 268 [1979]), a New York law that permitted an unwed mother but not an unwed father to block the adoption of his or her child by withholding consent (Caban v. Mohammed, 441 U.S. 380 [1979]), and a provision of the Missouri worker's compensation laws that denied a widower benefits from the wife's work-related death unless he proved dependence on her earnings but granted a widow such benefits regardless of such dependence (Wengler v. Druggists Mutual Insurance Co., 446 U.S. 142 [1980]).

[8] See Weinberger v. Weisenfeld, a unanimous decision; and Kirchberg v. Feenstra (450 U.S. 455 [1981]), a unanimous decision to invalidate a Louisiana statute that gave a husband as "head and master" of property jointly owned with his wife the right to dispose of such property without the wife's consent.

[9] In Korematsu v. United States (232 U.S. 214 [1944]) Justice Douglas made explicit the notion, which can be traced back to at least 1880 (Strauder v. West Virginia, 100 U.S. 303), that race is a suspect classification and, therefore, requires

other areas the principle of equal protection requires only "that persons similarly situated should be treated similarly."[10] For Rehnquist, the appropriate standard of review outside the area of race is that of rationality.

He has objected to the Court's development of an intermediate standard of review, arguing that it is simply too subjective. How is a judge to know what objectives are important? How is a judge to determine whether a law is substantially related to the achievement of such an objective? These phrases, he has said, are "so diaphanous and elastic as to invite subjective judicial preferences or prejudices relating to particular types of legislation, masquerading as judgments whether such legislation is directed at 'important' objectives or whether the relationship to those objectives is 'substantial' enough" (Craig, 429 U.S. at 221). Questions concerning governmental objectives are, in his view, appropriately left to elected officials, as judges are not equipped with the data or the expertise to handle them.

In short, the Court should use the rational basis test when reviewing classifications based on sex, and Rehnquist has submitted that such classifications do not, per se, fail that test.[11] Using the language of opinions in which the Court has upheld economic regulations against equal protection challenges, he has paid maximum deference to legislative decisions. Any conceivable relationship between a classification and its stated purpose, no matter how tenuous, has served to vindicate the law.

In 1976 the Court invoked the intermediate standard of review to invalidate an Oklahoma law that set the age for purchase of 3.2 beer at eighteen for females and twenty-one for males (Craig v. Boren). Rehnquist dissented, expressing his disapproval of the intermediate standard, particularly as the majority applied it to a

---

the most stringent review. In Loving v. Virginia Chief Justice Warren articulated the strict scrutiny standard of review: "[I]f [racial classifications] are ever to be upheld, they must be shown to be necessary to the accomplishment of some permissible state objective, independent of the racial discrimination which it was the object of the Fourteenth Amendment to eliminate" (388 U.S. 1 [1967]).

[10] The "similarly situated" language comes from Royster Guano Co., F.S. v. Virginia, 243 U.S. 412, 415 (1920): "The classification must be reasonable, not arbitrary, and must rest upon some ground of difference having a fair and substantial relation to the object of the legislation so that all persons similarly circumstanced shall be treated alike."

[11] David Shapiro (1976) argued that Rehnquist's rational basis test requires only that a challenged classification not be entirely counterproductive with respect to the purposes of the legislation in which it is contained.

law that discriminated against men. The ostensible purpose of the beer law was to promote traffic safety. The majority, presented with statistics on drunk-driving arrests, did not find the fit between driving under the influence and maleness to be sufficient so as to be substantially related to the achievement of the law's objective. Rehnquist countered that the proper standard of review was the rational basis test and avowed that the law could pass that test. In his view, the statistical evidence indicating that males in the relevant age group had an arrest rate for driving under the influence that was ten times greater than the rate for females gave the law the necessary rationality. The Court, he said, was no better qualified than the state legislature to analyze the statistics. The only relevant question was whether the incidence of drunk-driving among men was sufficiently greater than among young women to justify differential treatment, and the statistics gave the legislature a rational basis for believing that it was.

Rehnquist elaborated and clarified his approach to classifications based on sex in an opinion he wrote for the majority in 1981 (Michael M. v. Superior Court of Sonoma County, 450 U.S. 464). The California statutory rape law made men criminally liable for sexual intercourse with females under the age of eighteen. The state supreme court subjected the law to strict scrutiny and found that the classification was justified by a compelling state interest in preventing teenage pregnancies. Rehnquist, speaking for four justices, used the rational basis test to uphold the law. He made only a slight concession to the Court's customary use of an intermediate standard of review for classifications based on sex: "[T]he traditional minimum rationality test takes on a *somewhat* 'sharper focus' when gender-based classifications are challenged" (*Michael M.*, 450 U.S. at 468, emphasis mine). One of the purposes of the statute was to prevent illegitimate pregnancies. The state has a strong interest in such a purpose, Rehnquist noted, because illegitimate pregnancies often result in abortions or additions to the welfare rolls. Because only women can become pregnant, it was clear to Rehnquist that men and women are not similarly situated with respect to the problems and the risks of sexual intercourse.

Rehnquist's use of the phrase "similarly situated" shifted the focus of analysis away from the question of whether a classification bears a substantial relationship to an important governmental objective toward that of whether a classification is reasonable. Under the intermediate standard of review, the state must show that a sex-neutral statute would be a less effective means of achieving its goal. Thus, the state would have had the burden of showing that fewer teenage pregnancies occur under the sex-based statutory rape law than if the law was sex-neutral. Rehnquist, however, simply assumed that a sex-neutral law would be less effective because it would present enforcement problems (if women were subject to criminal prosecution, they would not be likely to report violations of the law). Therefore, he shifted the standard of review from moderate to minimum scrutiny; in fact, he implied that challengers of sex classifications must meet the burden of showing that sex-neutral statutes would be equally effective in achieving their goals.[12]

Rehnquist's position regarding classifications based on sex may be simply stated: the rational basis test is the proper standard of review. The intermediate standard only introduces confusion and excessive reliance on the personal preferences of the justices. Moreover, his version of the rational basis test virtually presupposes the result; it renders the equal protection clause virtually inapplicable to women.

Illegitimacy

Urging the majority to use a standard of rationality when classifications based on the marital status of a person's parents at the time of his or her birth are challenged, Rehnquist has argued that equal protection does not require a state law to be logical or just but only "that there be some conceivable set of facts that may justify the classification involved" (Weber v. Aetna, 406 U.S. 164 [1972]).[13] In 1972, when the Court held that a Louisiana worker's compensation law that subordinated claims of unacknowledged illegitimate children to claims of legitimate children for death benefits failed even the test of rationality, Rehnquist objected that the law in question was clearly rational. He argued that the legislature could have believed that a man would want his com-

---

[12] Rehnquist also used the "similarly situated" approach in Rostker v. Goldberg (453 U.S. 57 [1981]) when he held that the male-only draft registration did not violate the equal protection component of the due process clause of the Fifth Amendment.

[13] The Court has not consistently subjected classifications based on illegitimacy to the intermediate standard of review. The Court has invalidated illegitimacy classifications in the following cases: Trimble v. Gordon; New Jersey Welfare Rights Organization v. Cahill, 411 U.S. 619 (1973); Weber v. Aetna; Gomez v. Perez, 409 U.S. 535 (1973); Jimenez v. Weinberger, 417 U.S. 628 (1974).

pensation to go to his legitimate children, and it was reasonable for the legislature to believe that the law would encourage legally recognized, responsible family relationships (ibid.).

He took the opportunity to reiterate his deferential approach to classifications based on illegitimacy when, in a per curiam opinion in 1973, the Court invalidated a New Jersey welfare law that limited benefits to families consisting of adults who were married to each other and whose children were either natural to both parents or adopted by one or both (New Jersey Welfare Rights Organization v. Cahill, 411 U.S. 619). The majority concluded that the statute operated to deprive illegitimate children of benefits and constituted a denial of equal protection, but Rehnquist argued that it was clearly rational: "[M]arriage can reasonably be found to be an essential ingredient of the family unit that the New Jersey Legislature is trying to protect from dissolution due to the economic vicissitudes of family life" (Cahill, 411 U.S. at 622).

His dissent in Trimble v. Gordon further illustrates his view of the proper way to treat classifications based on illegitimacy while it also exemplifies his approach to equal protection in general. In that case the Court, in a 5-to-4 decision, invalidated an Illinois law that allowed illegitimate children to inherit by intestate succession only from their mother while legitimate children were allowed to inherit by intestate succession from both their father and mother. Rehnquist complained that the majority failed to specify the level of scrutiny it had used. He objected that the Court looked too closely at the purpose of the law and that, in fact, it went so far as to judge the motives of the legislature. He contended that because there will always be some imperfection in the fit between legislative goals and the means of accomplishing them, once the Court begins to examine motives, it puts itself in the untenable position of deciding how much imperfection to allow and what alternatives are available. Judges are no more qualified to make such assessments than legislators; indeed, they are less so, in Rehnquist's view, for the reason that they are not accountable to the people. The Court was, thus, simply "meddling," with the result that "we have created on the premises of the equal protection clause a school for legislators whereby opinions of this Court are written to instruct them in a better understanding of how to accomplish their ordinary legislative tasks" (Trimble, 430 U.S. at 784). In short, for Rehnquist, the only acceptable standard is that of rationality. From his perspective, the

Court's adoption of a more stringent standard of review has led the justices to substitute their own values for those properly enacted into law by the elected representatives of the people.

Alienage

In 1971, the Supreme Court declared that classifications based on alienage "are inherently suspect and subject to close judicial scrutiny" (Graham v. Richardson, 403 U.S. 365, 372). Since then, however, the Court has fashioned the "political function exception," according to which laws that exclude aliens from positions that are related to the process of democratic self-government are not subject to strict scrutiny.[14]

Rehnquist has conveyed his position on alienage classifications in three dissenting opinions. First, he wrote an opinion that

---

[14] In 1973 the Court invalidated New York's law that excluded noncitizens from holding positions in the competitive class of the state civil service (Sugarman v. Dougall). Justice Blackmun, who wrote for the majority of the Court, held that a flat ban on the employment of aliens in the civil service did not withstand "close judicial scrutiny." He noted, however, that states may exclude aliens from public employment where citizenship bears a relationship to legitimate state interests. States have the power and the responsibility "to preserve the basic conception of a political community" (Sugarman, 413 U.S. at 647, quoting Dunn v. Blumstein, 405 U.S. 330, 344 [1972]) and, therefore, to determine qualifications of voters and of people who hold positions in which they "perform functions that go to the heart of representative government" (ibid.). Blackmun stated that "scrutiny would not be so demanding where we deal with matters resting firmly within a state's constitutional prerogatives" (ibid., 648). The state's power to define its political community, Blackmun's opinion implied, includes the power to exclude aliens from participation in its democratic political institutions. Blackmun's suggestion that the exclusion of aliens from political participation would be subject to less than strict scrutiny subsequently became the focus of the Court's analysis of classifications based on alienage. In 1978, for example, when the Court upheld a state law that barred aliens from employment as state troopers, Chief Justice Burger elevated Blackmun's suggestion to the status of a rule when he asserted that "[t]he State need only justify its classification by a showing of some rational relationship between the interest sought to be protected and the limiting classification" (Foley v. Connelie, 435 U.S. 291, 296 [1978]). Thus, classifications based upon alienage are not suspect and are, therefore, subject only to a test of rationality when they distinguish between citizens and aliens in ways that are related to the functions of state government. Justice White clarified the standards of review for alienage classifications when he explained that where sovereign functions of government are involved, citizenship is a relevant ground for determining membership in the political community. Citizenship is not relevant, however, when the state is distributing economic benefits (Cabell v. Chavez-Salido, 454 U.S. 432 [1982]).

applied to the two cases decided in 1973 in which the Court invalidated Connecticut's exclusion of resident aliens from law practice (*In re Griffiths*, 413 U.S. 717) and New York's law that excluded noncitizens from holding permanent positions in the competitive classified civil service (*Sugarman*, 413 U.S. at 634). In that opinion he asserted that classifications based on alienage should be subject only to a test of rationality. Important differences between classifications based on alienage and those based on race, he argued, make strict scrutiny of alienage classifications inappropriate. Central to his opinion was the notion that citizenship is a legitimate classification because it means "something, a status in and relationship with a society which is continuing and more basic than mere presence or residence" (ibid., 652). He pointed out that the Constitution distinguishes between citizens and aliens eleven times. The Fourteenth Amendment, he asserted, does not render alienage a suspect classification; indeed, the first sentence defines citizenship, signifying that the framers intended citizens to be a "rationally distinct subclass of all 'persons' " (ibid.). The amendment, in Rehnquist's view, actually authorizes the states to treat aliens and citizens differently. Consequently, heightened scrutiny of alienage classifications is even less appropriate than it is for laws that classify on the basis of sex or legitimacy.

Rehnquist also objected that the Court had expanded the category of suspect classifications to include alienage on the basis of questionable doctrine—namely, that of the *Carolene Products* Footnote. He noted that even if he considered the Footnote to be authoritative, he would still deny that the label "discrete and insular minorities" applies to aliens. He castigated the majority for its failure to explain why aliens should be placed in that category. The Court, he admonished, seemed to be selecting groups arbitrarily for special protection.

That alienage is not a status or condition that cannot be altered was also an important aspect of Rehnquist's analysis. Because aliens have the opportunity to become American citizens they cannot be "discrete and insular minorities"; they are fundamentally different from racial minorites and cannot claim the same protections.

Advocating the use of the standard of rationality, Rehnquist asserted that laws excluding aliens from certain types of employment were constitutionally sound. He reasoned that because citizenship confers membership in the political community, and since the naturalization process gives aliens the opportunity to show that they understand and accept American values, the laws were rational. While the majority found the civil service law to be too broad insofar as it precluded aliens from holding even low-level non-policy-making positions, such as those of typist and garbage worker, Rehnquist argued that a great deal of de facto policy making took place at low-levels. He also justified the limiting of government jobs to citizens in the interest of efficiency; aliens may not be familiar with our institutions and with our social and political values. For example, he contended that it is not irrational to assume that a person who grew up in a country where bribery was an accepted practice would not perform his duties as well as an American citizen.

In the cases involving the exclusion of aliens from legal practice in Connecticut, the majority rejected the argument that lawyers were government officials and must, therefore, be citizens. Rehnquist, however, stressed the responsibility and trust that are given to lawyers. Connecticut's law, he argued, reflected a rational judgment that a lawyer needs to have an understanding of the American experience in addition to technical skills.[15] In short, the law established reasonable requirements that aliens understand and accept American institutions and values before they hold public positions of responsibility.

Rehnquist further developed the theme of the changeability of alien status in a second opinion in which he dissented from the majority's decision to invalidate a New York statutory arrangement providing that only citizens and resident aliens who had expressed their intention to become citizens were eligible for higher education assistance programs (Nyquist v. Mauclet, 432 U.S. [1977]). He argued that aliens are, in fact, a "discrete and insular minority," but only when they are powerless to change

---

[15] In Supreme Court of New Hampshire v. Piper (470 U.S. 274, 105 S.Ct. 1272 [1985]) the Court held that New Hampshire's rule limiting bar admission to state residents violated the privileges and immunities of Article IV, Section 2. Rehnquist was the lone dissenter. The majority reasoned that under *Griffiths* a lawyer is not an officer of the state; thus, there is no reason for the state to exclude nonresidents from the practice of law. Rehnquist objected that "[w]hatever the merits of that conclusion, my point here is different; whether or not lawyers actually wield state powers, the State nevertheless has a substantial interest in having resident lawyers. In *Griffiths* the alien lawyers were state residents. The harms that a State can identify from allowing *nonresident* lawyers to practice is very different from the harms posited in *Griffiths* as arising from allowing *resident alien* lawyers to practice" (*Piper*, 105 S.Ct. at 1283 n.4, emphasis in original). Throughout his opinion Rehnquist emphasized the important interest the state has in determining who may practice law within its boundaries.

their status. Consequently, the only alienage classifications that should be subject to strict scrutiny are those that categorize aliens for a period of time during which they cannot remove themselves from that status. He saw no reason for strict scrutiny of a classification that allowed an alien to remove himself from the disabled class by either becoming a citizen or declaring his intention to become one. Under such an arrangement, in the justice's view, alien status did not place one in the position of a discrete and insular minority.

In a third opinion, Rehnquist dissented when the majority invalidated, on supremacy clause grounds, Maryland's policy of denying nonimmigrant aliens with G-4 visas in-state status for the purpose of university tuition (Toll v. Moreno, 458 U.S. 1 [1982]).[16] While he disagreed with the majority's decision that the state's policy conflicted with federal law, he also addressed the equal protection issue.[17] He offered an additional rationale for using minimum scrutiny of alienage classifications. The Court, he explained, initially based its decision to treat alienage as a suspect classification on the fact that aliens are excluded from participating in the political process by virtue of their being unable to vote. Aliens were powerless and thus, in the tradition of the *Carolene Products* Footnote, were "discrete and insular minorites." In subsequent decisions, however, the Court concluded that distinctions that exclude aliens from the political process are constitutionally permissible. Thus, there could no longer be any reason for treating alienage as a suspect classification; by the Court's own pronouncements, lack of ability to participate in the political process no longer places one in a protected category. Classifications based on alienage should therefore be upheld unless they are irrational. His reasoning may be confusing and less than persuasive; still, it is significant insofar as it represents a denial of the legitimacy of the doctrine of heightened judicial scrutiny to protect "discrete and insular minorities."

Racial Equality

Because the immediate purpose of the Fourteenth Amendment was to prohibit states from enacting legislation that treated

[16] Students with G-4 visas generally are children of officers or employees of international organizations such as the World Bank.

[17] The lower courts based their decisions to invalidate Maryland's tuition policy on the equal protection clause rather than the supremacy clause.

blacks differently from whites, classifications based on race are suspect and, in fact, are presumptively invalid. Decisions involving such classifications should be relatively simple. According to Rehnquist, the determining factor in such decisions is the presence of purposeful discrimination through legislation or other public policy. For example, in 1985 he wrote an opinion for a unanimous Court invalidating an Alabama constitutional provision that disenfranchised people convicted of misdemeanors involving moral turpitude. He pointed to statements made by the drafters of the Alabama Constitution regarding the purpose of the provision that suggested discriminatory intent, such as, "What is it we want to do? . . . it is within the limits imposed by the Federal Constitution to establish white supremacy" (quoted in Hunter v. Underwood, 471 U.S. 222, 106 S.Ct. 1916, 1921 [1985]). In more typical cases the official, purposeful factors in racial discrimination are not often so blatant, and Rehnquist has taken the position that unless there is official involvement that entails an intent to discriminate, there is no constitutional violation. Moreover, in cases in which the outcome has turned largely on the question of whether the official or purposeful elements were present, he has applied his tools of analysis to resolve that question in the negative.

While the jurisprudence of the Fourteenth Amendment has continued to include the principle that governmental involvement in racial discrimination is a prerequisite for invoking the Fourteenth Amendment, members of the Court have disagreed on just how much involvement is required. When the Court held that the required state action was absent in the liquor licensing scheme of a private club that refused to admit blacks to its restaurant and cocktail lounge, Rehnquist expressed his view in the majority opinion (Moose Lodge v. Irvis, 407 U.S. 163 [1972]). The state liquor license, he held, did not sufficiently implicate the state in the racial discrimination practiced by the club. He argued that the mere presence of a benefit or service from the state or a state regulation did not amount to significant state involvement. In an earlier case the Court had indicated that it would use a flexible case-by-case approach rather than a precise formula to determine when government involvement became sufficient (Burton v. Wilmington Parking Authority, 365 U.S. 715 [1961]). Rehnquist appeared to reject such an approach in favor of the more stringent requirement that the state must be shown to be directly and specifically supporting or encouraging racial discrimination.

In 1986 Rehnquist dissented when seven justices[18] concluded that the use of peremptory challenges by the prosecutor constitutes purposeful discrimination in a trial of a black defendant if they are used to exclude all blacks from the jury solely on the basis of race or on the assumption that black jurors will be unable to consider the case impartially (Batson v. Kentucky, 106 S.Ct., 1712 [1986]).[19] He objected that the use of peremptory challenges does not violate the equal protection clause "so long as such challenges are also used to exclude whites in cases involving white defendants, Hispanics in cases involving Hispanic defendants, Asians in cases involving Asian defendants" (Batson, 106 S. Ct. at 1744). He not only maintained that the use of peremptory challenges to exclude blacks from a jury did not amount to purposeful discrimination, but he went further, hinting that even if such exclusion did amount to purposeful discrimination, it would not amount to a constitutional violation.

Rehnquist's conviction that discrimination must be shown to have been purposeful before a constitutional violation can be found is most apparent in several of his opinions in the context of northern school desegregation. In 1968, convinced that "all deliberate speed" (Brown v. Board of Education, 349 U.S. 294 [1955]) meant continuing segregation, the Supreme Court charged public school boards that had operated dual school systems pursuant to state law in 1954 with an affirmative duty to eliminate their dual systems. The legal status of schools in northern cities, where the law had never required segregation, was unclear. Were these

---

[18] Joining Rehnquist in dissent was Chief Justice Burger.

[19] Peremptory challenges, in contrast with challenges for cause, are limited in number by the presiding judge. No reason for excusing a prospective juror is required with a peremptory challenge. According to long-standing Court doctrine, a black defendant would be denied equal protection if tried by a jury from which blacks had been purposefully excluded (Strauder v. West Virginia, 100 U.S. 303 [1880]). Nevertheless, the Court rejected a black defendant's objection to the prosecutor's use of peremptory challenges to exclude black jurors from his trial (Swain v. Alabama, 380 U.S. 202 [1965]). In that case the Court held that a black defendant could make out a prima facie case of purposeful discrimination on proof that peremptory challenges were being used to exclude black jurors. But in order to make such a case, the defendant would be required to show systematic exclusion of blacks in case after case. Exclusion in only the defendant's case would not be sufficient. In Batson v. Kentucky the Court found such an evidentiary burden to be unacceptable.

school systems obligated to desegregate? Or was the de facto segregation of the North a problem that lay beyond the reach of the
equal protection clause? In its initial pronouncements condemn-
ing de jure segregation the Court suggested that such might be
the case. Subsequently, however, the Court blurred the de jure–
de facto distinction according to which court-ordered desegregation is warranted when there has been purposeful segregation in
violation of the Constitution, but when there has been no official
segregation and, thus, no constitutional violation, no remedy is
warranted.

The issue of northern school desegregation reached the Supreme Court about a year after Rehnquist became an associate
justice, and he has persistently objected to the majority's obscur-
ing of the de jure–de facto distinction. In 1973, when the Court
upheld a districtwide desegregation plan in Denver even though
intentional discrimination had been found in only one part of the
district, Rehnquist was the sole dissenter (Keyes v. School District No. 1, Denver, Colorado, 413 U.S. 189). He emphasized the
factual differences between the segregation existing in the Denver schools and that which has dominated southern school systems. He went further, to object to the Court's imposition in
1968 of the "affirmative duty" to desegregate, characterizing it as
an unexplained extension of *Brown*. While he conceded that such
a duty existed, he maintained that it should only apply to southern school systems where segregation had once been mandated
by law.

In two cases decided in 1979, a majority held that school
boards that intentionally maintained dual systems in 1954 and
subsequently sustained these systems must show why they had
not taken necessary steps to desegregate (Columbus v. Penick,
443 U.S. 449, and Dayton v. Brinkman, 443 U.S. 526). In one of
the cases, the Court stated that "actions having foreseeable and
anticipated disparate impact are relevant evidence to prove the
ultimate fact, forbidden purpose" (*Penick*, 443 U.S. at 464). Thus,
while the Court indicated that it would still require a finding of
de jure segregation as shown by school boards' or administrators'
purposeful segregative action in order to justify a legally imposed
remedy for racially imbalanced schools, the decision facilitated
findings of purposeful segregation.

In his dissent, Rehnquist suggested that schools that were not
legally segregated in 1954 should not bear the responsibility for
achieving a unitary system. He also argued that the burden of

showing a discriminatory purpose should lie with the plaintiffs, and if there was no evidence to prove or disprove the justification offered by a school board for its actions, there should be no finding of a constitutional violation.

Disgruntled with the majority's "radical" departure from the de jure–de facto distinction and disavowing the Court's "new methodology," Rehnquist outlined the following approach: First, in order to impose a remedy for racially imbalanced schools, the lower courts must find action by a school board that was intended to and did, in fact, discriminate against minority students. Second, the court must determine how much segregative effect such action has had on the racial distribution of the schools by comparing the existing distribution with that which would have prevailed in the absence of the objectionable school board action. The remedy must go no further than what is required to redress the difference. If there were violations on the part of the school board in the past, the proper remedy would be "to restore those integrated educational opportunities that would now exist but for purposefully discriminatory school board conduct" (ibid., 524). Rehnquist would therefore have made it considerably more difficult to challenge racially segregated schools by requiring proof that school authorities had engaged in purposeful discrimination. Moreover, his approach would have limited the remedy to removing the effects of the actual violation.

Although the justice would not go so far as to repudiate *Brown*,[20] he would interpret its holding narrowly, to the effect that only legally authorized or mandated segregated schools constitute equal protection violations. He would, in addition, welcome the opportunity to overrule subsequent holdings that, in his view, have virtually obliterated the de jure–de facto distinction.

Rehnquist's conviction that there must be a showing of purposeful discrimination in order to justify a legal remedy is demonstrated further in his opinions concerning affirmative action. His pronouncements also illustrate the technique he has used to constrain the application of not only the equal protection clause but also the antidiscrimination provisions in the federal statutes. In 1978, the Supreme Court held that the admissions program at the medical school of the University of California, Davis, which

[20] See the discussion of the memorandum that Rehnquist prepared for Justice Jackson in 1952 in chapter 1.

reserved sixteen places for minority group members, was illegal (Regents of the University of California v. Bakke, 438 U.S. 265). Rehnquist joined Justice Stevens's opinion asserting that the policy violated Title VI of the Civil Rights Act of 1964, which prohibits racial discrimination in activities or programs receiving federal assistance.

A year later, the Court held that Kaiser Aluminum's policy of reserving 50 percent of the openings in craft training programs for black employees, until the percentage of black craft workers reached a level approximating that of the percentage of blacks in the local labor force, did not violate Title VII of the Civil Rights Act United Steelworkers v. Weber, 443 U.S. 193 [1979].[21] Justice Brennan, who wrote for the majority, reasoned that Title VII should not be construed literally to prohibit all affirmative action plans. Instead, the prohibition against racial discrimination in employment practices must be interpreted within the context of its legislative history. The purpose of the provisions, he found, was to ameliorate economic inequality by opening employment opportunities for blacks in areas traditionally closed to them. He also noted that if Congress had intended to prohibit voluntary affirmative action programs, it would have stated that such programs were neither required nor permitted; instead, the law said only that they were not required. Race-conscious affirmative action programs, instituted voluntarily by private employers, were, therefore, not inconsistent with the purpose of Title VII.

In an extensive and acrimonious dissent Rehnquist accused the majority of reaching its conclusion in an intellectually dishonest way, reminding him of the governmental official in George Orwell's *1984* who was handed a note in the middle of his speech and switched positions without a pause, without even a break in syntax. The majority, he argued, had disregarded previous interpretations as well as the language and legislative history of Title VII. In his view, Kaiser's affirmative action policy was clearly prohibited by the plain language of the provisions. Further, the relevant legislative history revealed that Congress had intended to outlaw all discrimination and preferential treatment. The majority, Rehnquist protested, had called upon the "spirit" of the

---

[21] Title VII, Sections 703(a) and 703(d), prohibits discrimination in employment practices and training programs. Section 703(j) provides that nothing in Title VII shall be interpreted to require an employer to institute an affirmative action program.

act to reach the desired result. If the provision had a "spirit," he said, it was one that was consistent with its language and intent.

In the Court's subsequent decisions regarding affirmative action, Rehnquist has invariably found that race-conscious programs violate antidiscrimination provisions in the law; he has found it unnecessary to address the constitutional question of whether such programs are consistent with the equal protection clause.[22] In his view, the law condemns racial discrimination in employment and education. It matters not whether that discrimination incidentally disadvantages whites for the purpose of increasing economic opportunities for blacks or whether it takes the more traditional form of depriving blacks of opportunities. Like the technique he has adopted in constitutional decision making, his statutory construction, based on literalism and the authors' intent, precludes the recognition of purposes or principles of legislation other than those explicitly stated either in the language of the statute or in the statements of members of Congress.

CONCLUSION: DEMOCRACY, FEDERALISM, AND EQUALITY

The opinions discussed in this chapter may be construed simply as incontrovertible evidence of Rehnquist's insensitivity to the problems encountered by members of disadvantaged groups in American society. His record in the area of racial discrimination

---

[22] Rehnquist joined the majority when the Court invalidated a district court's order, which was a modification of a consent decree, that changed the Memphis Fire Department's layoff plan with the result that white employees with more seniority than black employees were laid off. The otherwise applicable seniority system would have called for the layoff of black employees with less seniority. Justice White wrote the opinion for the Court, reasoning that under Title VII of the Civil Rights Act of 1964 it is inappropriate to deny an innocent employee the benefits of seniority in order to provide a remedy, at least when the modification of the consent decree was not based on any agreement between the parties (Firefighters Local Union No. 1784 v. Stotts, 467 U.S. 516 [1984]). Rehnquist dissented in two affirmative action cases decided in 1986. In those cases Justice Brennan wrote for the majority, upholding a consent decree that provided for affirmative action in the promotion of fire fighters (Local No. 93, International Association of Firefighters v. City of Cleveland, 106 S.Ct. 3023) and a court-ordered affirmative action program that was intended to remedy discrimination by a labor union (Local 28, Sheet Metal Workers v. EEOC, 106 S.Ct. 3019). Title VII, according to the majority, is not limited to relief for actual victims of discrimination. Rehnquist objected that Title VII forbids relief except to actual victims of employment discrimination.

has led observers to conclude that he is " 'an extremist . . . an enemy of civil rights' " (Benjamin L. Hooks, quoted in Lardner and Kamen 1986); his decisions regarding discrimination based on gender have elicited the response, "He's a disaster for women" (Eleanor Smeal, quoted in ibid.). Additionally, his consistency in voting to limit the rights of criminal defendants evidences his preference for the power of the states at the expense of individual rights.

There is no doubt that Rehnquist is not particularly concerned with individual rights. His apparent insensitivity might be attributed to mean-spiritedness, the lack of awareness of an upper-middle class white male, or simply as a testament to a political agenda that includes a commitment to preserving the status quo. I do not attempt to disprove such allegations here, yet I offer a more elaborate explanation of his record on individual rights.

The three components of Rehnquist's judicial philosophy—his democratic model, his moral relativism, and his approach to constitutional interpretation—are all manifest in his decision making in the context of the Fourteenth Amendment. His persistent advocacy of a deferential standard of review for classifications based on gender, illegitimacy, and alienage presents a very clear example of his commitment to the democractic model. From such a perspective, policy should be made by elected officials without interference from the judiciary. Although women could correctly point out that gender-based classifications frequently put them at a disadvantage economically, politically, and socially, Rehnquist would most likely advise them to participate in the traditional channels of the democratic process—to vote, to communicate with elected officials, to campaign for supportive candidates, to organize, and to lobby their elected officials in order to bring about the changes they think necessary. In short, women could attempt to convince a majority that legal distinctions based on gender are unacceptable. If they succeeded, their legislators would abolish such distinctions, but if they failed, those distinctions would legitimately remain part of the law enacted by representatives of the people. He would be likely to offer the same advice to people born out of wedlock, while he would suggest to aliens that they obtain United States citizenship. Likewise, his record concerning racial equality suggests a belief that constitutional provisions guarantee to blacks the right to participate in the political process; no further protection of substantive rights is warranted so long as blacks are able to seek their goals through the channels of the democratic system.

His moral relativism, the second component of his judicial philosophy, is also apparent in his decision making in the context of equal protection. Legislators could abolish all statutory distinctions based on gender if a majority commanded; or if an extraordinarily large number of people agreed, gender equality could become part of the Constitution via an amendment. But equality, for Rehnquist, remains merely a subjective value until enacted into the law. In the same vein, his indictment of affirmative action implies his support for what he views as a neutral stance toward racial minorities rather than what he most likely construes as a personal preference, held by a minority, for helping members of groups that have been victims of discrimination in the past.

He has urged the Court to keep faith with the intent of the framers with regard to both the relationship of the due process clause to the Bill of Rights and the limitation of the application of the equal protection clause to official discrimination against blacks. Rehnquist's approach to constitutional interpretation, the third component of his judicial philosophy, has informed his perception of the guarantee of "equal protection of the laws" as one that is limited to the text. The clause is merely a prohibition on state action that denies equal protection. The meaning of the clause is also, in his view, unchanging. Therefore, its prohibition applies only to classifications based on race, not gender, illegitimacy, or alienage. The clause, for Rehnquist, constitutes simply a rule that "[n]o state shall . . ." It does not represent any societal goal of fairness, equality, or any other abstract moral principle. For him, an unchanging Fourteenth Amendment provides rules constraining state action. The notion of an evolving constitutional guarantee of equality is, in his view, anathema. His fundamental understanding of the Constitution has seemingly led him to employ a historical mode of analysis, whereby he seeks to discern the meaning of constitutional provisions in the past and to utilize the techniques of literalism and a search for support in the intent of the framers.

Rehnquist's decisions in the area of the Fourteenth Amendment also reflect his ordering of values. Federalism prevails over individual rights whether in the context of criminal justice or equality. Moreover, the value he places on federalism is reinforced by the three components of his judicial philosophy. His democratic model and his moral relativism coincide with the view that state elected officials should make policy without "meddling" from the federal judiciary. His approach to constitutional interpretation supports the notion that the breadth of the Fourteenth Amendment is so limited that it puts minimal constraints on the states.

The analysis in part 3 of this work will describe how Rehnquist has usually—but not invariably—supported federalism over property rights. He has written some opinions and cast some votes that may be construed as protective of property against state power. But his opinions in the context of individual rights, specifically in relation to the Fourteenth Amendment, reveal no such inconsistencies or uncertainties regarding the priority that he places on federalism. Clearly, in Rehnquist's scheme of values, "conflicting claims" between individual rights and the state should be resolved in favor of the state.

FOUR

The First Amendment
Speaks with a Different Voice:
Rehnquist and Freedom of Expression

The analysis of Rehnquist's decision making in the context of the due process and equal protection clauses of the Fourteenth Amendment, presented in the preceding chapter, indicated how clearly he supports judicial deference to legislative decisions when individual rights are involved. That deferential posture is in accord with his judicial philosophy, composed of the democratic model, moral relativism, and his approach to constitutional interpretation. His views concerning the Fourteenth Amendment, moreover, reflect his ordering of values whereby a conflict between a state and an individual is resolved in favor of the state; federalism takes precedence over individual rights. Additionally, the three components of his judicial philosophy reinforce the preeminent value he places on federalism.

The present chapter examines Rehnquist's decision making in the area of freedom of expression in order to further explore the relationship between the three components of his judicial philosophy and his ordering of the values of federalism and individual rights.

In 1927 Justice Louis D. Brandeis wrote that

[t]hose who won our independence believed that the final end of the State was to make men free to develop their faculties; and that in its government the deliberative forces should prevail over the arbitrary. They valued liberty both as an end and as a means. They believed liberty to be the secret of happiness and courage to be the secret of liberty. They believed that freedom to think as you will and to speak as you think are means indispensable to the discovery and spread of political truth; that without free speech and assembly discussion would be futile; that with them, discussion affords ordinarily adequate protection against the dissemination of noxious doctrine; that the greatest menace to freedom is an

inert people; that public discussion is a political duty; and that this should be a fundamental principle of the American government. (Whitney v. California, 274 U.S. 357, 375 [1927])

Brandeis's statement contains three rationales for protecting freedom of expression. First, freedom to communicate is essential to self-government. Second, freedom of expression is indispensable in the search for truth.[1] Third, freedom of expression is necessary to individual self-fulfillment, personal liberty, and autonomy. The scope of the protection for freedom of expression depends to a great extent on which rationale is emphasized. If the necessity of free speech to self-government is stressed, for example, expression that is protected by the First Amendment may be limited to that which has political content.[2] In contrast, emphasis on freedom of expression as a means to self-fulfillment would be likely to lead to high regard and protection for all types of speech.

The three components of Rehnquist's judicial philosophy might be expected to lead to particular views regarding freedom of expression. First, the democratic model might well lead him to place a high value on freedom of expression in the belief that in its absence the democratic process would be doomed to fail. The expression that he would find to be protected, however, would most likely be limited to that which contributes to the political discourse. Additionally, the judicial deference to legislative decisions prescribed by the democratic model would leave

[1] The theme of the search for truth was also reflected in John Milton's statement that, "though all the winds of doctrine were let loose to play upon the earth, so Truth be in the field, we do injuriously, by licensing and prohibiting, to misdoubt her strength. Let her and Falsehood grapple; who ever knew Truth put to the worst, in a free and open encounter?" (Areopagitica—A Speech for the Liberty of Unlicensed Printing (1644), quoted in Gunther 1985, 978). Justice Oliver Wendell Holmes, Jr., also referred to the value of free speech in the search for truth in his dissent in Abrams v. United States (250 U.S. 616 [1919]): "[T]he best test of truth is the power of the thought to get itself accepted in the competition of the market."

[2] For example, Alexander Meiklejohn (1965) argued that there were two kinds of speech. The freedom of speech—political speech—was absolutely protected by the First Amendment. On the other hand, private speech could be limited. For a contemporary expression of the view that political speech is the subject of the First Amendment provisions regarding freedom of expression, see Bork 1971.

legislatures a large amount of discretion to limit freedom of speech deemed to be harmful or dangerous to the community.

Second, it is likely that Rehnquist's moral relativism would support a belief that freedom of speech derives its legitimacy solely by virtue of its enactment into the positive law in the First Amendment; it would not find the source of its value in the search for truth, or as a means to self-fulfillment. Still, if he perceives that freedom of expression plays an essential role in the processes of democratic government, he might find that it has some legitimacy beyond its presence in the positive law. Thus, freedom of speech could be a central value for Rehnquist because it is part of the Constitution or because it helps to make the democratic processes work.

Finally, his approach to constitutional interpretation, according to which the Constitution is limited to the text and the intent of the framers and comprises a fixed set of rules rather than a changing representation of the goals of American society, could logically be expected to coincide with the view that the First Amendment provides maximum, perhaps even absolute, protection for freedom of speech. The language of the First Amendment could hardly be more explicit: "Congress shall make no law . . . abridging the freedom of speech, or of the press; or the right of the people peaceably to assemble to petition the Government for a redress of grievances." Rehnquist's approach to constitutional interpretation, however, has not led him to support freedom of expression. On the contrary, he was the justice who gave less support for free speech claims than any member of the Burger Court (see Heck and Ringelstein 1985, table 1).

The following analysis of Rehnquist's decision making in the context of freedom of expression attempts to reconcile the apparent contradictions between his moral relativism, his approach to constitutional interpretation, and his actual pronouncements regarding the First Amendment. The analysis also explores several other themes in his opinions that may shed additional light on his decision making.

THE BURGER COURT AND FREEDOM OF EXPRESSION

One of the grounds on which scholars have criticized the Burger Court has been its failure to develop a coherent approach to the First Amendment. Thomas I. Emerson, for example, examined the Burger Court's treatment of freedom of expression and concluded that as a result of its "predilection for ad hoc balancing, its failure to take proper account of the dynamics of suppression, and its unwillingness to develop innovative doctrines in response to changing needs, the system [of freedom of expression] has become less effective at serving its underlying values" (1980, 423).

In a similar vein, Archibald Cox (1980, 31) commented that "[i]nconsistency marks the pronouncements of the Burger Court." He faulted the Court for failing to "nurture a coherent body of constitutional law" and for paying "little attention to building a systematic body of law, but instead engage[ing] in particularistic and pragmatic balancing" (1980, 26–27).[3] In contrast, other commentators have found the Court's approach to freedom of expression to be quite coherent. Norman Dorsen and Joel Gora (1982), for example, postulated that the Burger Court's free speech doctrine can be summarized by the word "property." The Court, according to their analysis, tended to protect free speech values when those values coincided with or were augmented by property interests. William Van Alstyne (1980, 67–68)[4] also argued that the Court's free speech analysis may be understood in terms of property interests.

Edward Heck and Albert C. Ringelstein, who have analyzed the votes of the Burger Court in freedom of expression cases, com-

[3] In his review of the Court's 1979 term, Cox faulted the justices for writing so many separate opinions when joining in a single opinion would have made a more constructive contribution to the relevant body of law. He also castigated the Court for not giving proper attention to fitting new decisions into the body of precedent. Cox was referring specifically to *Richmond Newspapers v. Virginia*, a case in which there were six opinions supporting the judgment plus Rehnquist's dissent.

[4] Van Alstyne (1980, 77) stated that "[i]n respect to freedom of speech and of the press, there has been at the least an arrest of the expansionary protections characteristic of the preceding decade and, in certain respects, a net diminution in the boundary of the free speech clause for those without money to pay as against the enlarged prerogatives of those with the means to advertise." Further, he noted: "It seems quite clear, . . . that the security of private property as an extension of oneself and the corresponding liberty of free speech with respect to ownership dominion of that private property, is a clear and powerful development of the seventies" (ibid.). He also pointed out that the Burger Court has limited the scope of publicly owned property available for the exercise of free speech. Neither property "owned" by others nor property "owned" by the state is as widely available as decisions in the preceding decade appeared to imply. The free speech claims of private property, commercial property, and entrepreneurial property are more important than before (ibid., 79). See also Nowak (1980), who described the Burger Court as a historical Court dedicated to the promotion of a libertarian political philosophy.

69

mented that "while the Burger Court has not elevated the First Amendment to a preferred position in a hierarchy of constitutional values, neither is the Court as a collectivity actively hostile to the assertion of First Amendment rights" (1985, 4). Their analysis of the 192 plenary docket cases decided during the terms 1969–70 through 1983–84 showed that the Court voted to support the litigant raising a First Amendment claim in 45.3 percent of the cases (87 cases) and rejected First Amendment claims in 54.7 percent of the cases (105 cases).

Rehnquist stands out against such a background as the justice who was least supportive of First Amendment claims. He voted in favor of freedom of speech claims in 23.1 percent of the cases in which he participated.[5] Even in those cases in which he voted in support of a free speech claim, he often did so on narrower grounds than several of the other justices.[6] Moreover, as demon-

[5] The figure of 23.1 percent comes from Edward Heck's (1986) data, which includes the 1984–85 term of the Court.

[6] My purpose in using the statistical analysis at this point is simply to suggest how weak Rehnquist's support for freedom of expression has been. Still, the use of the statistic raises questions regarding the type of exceptional situation in which Rehnquist supports a claim of freedom of expression—Does any pattern emerge? In the hope that I might answer such a question I obtained a list from Edward Heck of the cases in which he considered Rehnquist's vote to support a claim of freedom of expression. Upon examining the cases on that list I found, first, many decisions that I would describe as not really upholding a claim of freedom of expression. For example, in Pinkus v. United States (436 U.S. 293 [1978]), Rehnquist joined the majority in holding that children may not be included as part of the "community" in defining obscenity. But the Court also held that sensitive persons can be included, and members of deviant groups can be considered, in determining whether material appeals to prurient interest in sex. In Miami Herald v. Tornillo (418 U.S. 241 [1974]) the Court invalidated Florida's right to reply law. Rehnquist joined Brennan's concurring opinion, which asserted that the decision did not apply to retraction statutes affording plaintiffs able to prove defamatory falsehoods a statutory action to require publication of a retraction. It is questionable whether the *Miami Herald* decision, which shields newspapers from a requirement that they provide space for disgruntled objects of news stories, actually protects freedom of expression. Second, in a large number of cases on Heck's list, although Rehnquist did, in fact, support a claim of freedom of expression, he did so on narrower grounds than those expressed in the majority opinion (see, for example, Healy v. James, 408 U.S. 169 [1972], and Steffel v. Thompson, 415 U.S. 452 [1974], concurring opinions; Communist Party of Indiana v. Whitcomb, 414 U.S. 441 [1974], in which he joined the concurring opinion); or he either joined the majority or wrote the majority opinion while several members of the Court would have gone further (see, for example, Jenkins v. Georgia, 418 U.S. 153 [1974], holding that the film *Carnal Knowledge* was not obscene and that juries do not have unbridled discretion in determining what is patently of-

strated by the abundance of his dissenting opinions, he has objected to most of the Court's innovations in First Amendment doctrine.

FEDERALISM AND FREEDOM OF EXPRESSION

Rehnquist's opinions regarding freedom of expression manifest most clearly the preeminent value he assigns to federalism. The positions he has taken seem to contradict his approach to constitutional interpretation. Indeed, he seems to pay little heed to the fact that the First Amendment contains an express prohibition on the abridgment of speech. That prohibition, however, is addressed not to the states but to Congress.[7] Rehnquist has made plain his disagreement with the Court's incorporation doctrine[8] and has on numerous occasions expressed the view that the provisions of the First Amendment do not apply to the states.

He has, for example, affirmed his belief in the "limited application of the First Amendment to the States" (First National Bank of Boston v. Bellotti, 435 U.S. 765, 823 [1978]). He has asserted that "not all the strictures which the First Amendment imposes upon Congress are carried over against the States by the Fourteenth Amendment, but rather that it is only the 'general

---

fensive but affirmed that community standards are local; Nebraska Press Association v. Stuart, 427 U.S. 539 [1976], in which Rehnquist joined the majority opinion that struck down a gag order on news media reporting on a murder case. Concurring opinions authored by White, Powell, Brennan, and Stevens would have gone further than the majority to protect freedom of the press).

[7] The Court announced the principle that the First Amendment applies to the states through the due process clause of the Fourteenth Amendment in 1925 when it stated that "freedom of speech and of the press—which are protected by the First Amendment from abridgment by Congress—are among the fundamental personal rights and 'liberties' protected by the due process clause of the Fourteenth Amendment from impairment by the States" (Gitlow v. New York, 268 U.S. 652, 666). It has reaffirmed that principle in subsequent cases and only occasionally has a justice challenged it. The only justices (other than Rehnquist) to question the incorporation of the First Amendment were Jackson, who stated, "As a limitation upon power to punish written or spoken words, Fourteenth Amendment 'liberty' in its context of state powers and functions has meant and should mean something quite different from 'freedom' in its context of federal powers and functions" (Beauharnais v. Illinois, 343 U.S. 250, 288 [1952]), and Harlan: "The states' power to make printed words criminal is, of course, confined by the Fourteenth Amendment, but only insofar as such power is inconsistent with our concepts of 'ordered liberty' " (Roth v. United States, 354 U.S. 476, 501 [1957], citation omitted).

[8] See the discussion of his views on incorporation in chapter 3.

principle' of free speech, that the latter incorporates" (Buckley v. Valeo, 424 U.S. 1, 191 [1976], citations omitted). Further, he has stated that "cases which deal with state restrictions on First Amendment freedoms are not fungible with those which deal with restrictions imposed by the Federal Government" (ibid., 291). When the Court held that the First and Fourteenth amendments require that "[a]bsent an overriding interest articulated in the findings," state criminal trials be open to the public, Rehnquist objected that the public trial guarantee of the Sixth Amendment should not be applicable to the states. He went even further, to suggest that a state's reasons for denying public access to a trial should not be subject to Supreme Court review and objected that the Court was "smother[ing] a healthy pluralism which would ordinarily exist in a national government embracing fifty states" (Richmond Newspapers v. Virginia, 448 U.S. 555, 606 [1980]).[9]

In short, in Rehnquist's view, state action that is challenged as an abridgment of free speech should be examined by the Court to determine only whether it is consistent with the "general principle" of free speech. This suggests that, rather than apply the stringent standard of review requiring a state to show that it has a compelling interest when restrictions on expression are challenged, he will find a challenged state policy to be constitutionally acceptable if it bears a rational relation to a valid state objective. Thus, the apparent contradiction between his approach to constitutional interpretation and the low regard in which he holds freedom of expression may be resolved, at least in part, by his conviction that the First Amendment applies only to Congress.

Broad construal of state power is a theme that prevails throughout his opinions regarding freedom of expression. For example, he wrote for a majority upholding California's prohibition on sexually explicit live entertainment in establishments licensed to dispense liquor by the drink. He found the regulation not unreasonable or irrational and emphasized the states' authority under the Twenty-first Amendment to control the manner and circumstances under which liquor may be dispensed. He also noted that the state regulations that were challenged did not forbid the entertainment; rather, the state merely proscribed such

[9] The Supreme Court of Virginia had denied relief to the local press's request to open the trial to the public and the press.

72

performances in establishments licensed to sell liquor (California v. La Rue, 409 U.S. 109 [1972]).

Rehnquist wrote for the majority when the Court held that California could require owners of private shopping centers to provide access to people exercising their state constitutional rights of freedom of speech (Pruneyard Shopping Center v. Robins, 447 U.S. 74 [1980]). The Supreme Court has ruled that such rights are not protected by the United States Constitution (Lloyd Corporation v. Tanner, 407 U.S. 551 [1972]; Hudgens v. NLRB, 424 U.S. 507 [1976]). Rehnquist held that, nonetheless, the state has the authority to exercise its police powers and a sovereign right to adopt in its own constitution individual liberties more expansive than those conferred by the United States Constitution.

In numerous other opinions he has postulated that the issue at hand was one that was properly a concern of the states. For instance, he has maintained that states have the power to regulate and prohibit commercial advertising (Bigelow v. Virginia, 421 U.S. 809 [1975]), to restrict the activities of members of the bar (*In re* Primus, 436 U.S. 412 [1978]), and to restrict the political activities of corporations (*First National Bank of Boston v. Bellotti*). All such restrictions, in his view, should be treated as economic regulations subject only to rationality review.

PROPERTY RIGHTS AND FREEDOM OF EXPRESSION

In 1982, Owen Fiss and Charles Krauthammer argued that Rehnquist's preference for state autonomy was grounded in his desire to protect property. State autonomy, they contended, "is more consonant with classical laissez-faire theory which reduces the function of government to protecting private exchanges and the aim of the Constitution to protecting the rights and expectations of property holders" (1982, 21).[10]

Rehnquist's opinions in the area of freedom of expression, however, suggest that he is not primarily concerned with protecting rights of private property, at least not in the same way that Fiss and Krauthammer suggested. His dissenting opinions in cases in which the majority indicated a serious concern with pro-

[10] See also "Rediscovering the Contract Clause" (1984), which presented the thesis that Rehnquist assigns more constitutional protection to "just compensation property" than to "due process property." The article attributed that double standard to a social vision of an efficient system of property rights in which people without capital must labor for those people with capital.

tecting property rights indicate that property interests do not provide the focus of his attention. He dissented, for example, when the Court invalidated a conviction for improper use of the American flag of a man who had taped a peace symbol on a flag in order to protest the invasion of Cambodia and the deaths at Kent State (Spence v. Washington, 418 U.S. 405 [1974]).[11] The Court's per curiam opinion noted that the flag was private property—not the property of the government—and that the flag was displayed on private property. Moreover, as the state acknowledged, a form of communication was involved. The majority suggested that the state might have two interests in prohibiting the display of a flag to which another design has been affixed: the interest in preventing misunderstanding concerning governmental endorsement and the interest in preserving the uniquely universal character of the flag as a symbol. Nevertheless, the Court found the statute, as applied, to be unconstitutional because the act of taping the peace symbol to the flag was not only protected expression but it impaired neither state interest.

Rehnquist, in contrast, contended that the statute constituted only an incidental limitation on free speech that was justified by the state's important interest in protecting the flag's integrity. Discounting the consideration of private property in the Court's decision, he analogized: "[N]o one would argue, I presume, that a State could not prevent the painting of public buildings simply because a particular class of protesters believed their message would best be conveyed through that medium" (*Spence*, 418 U.S. at 417). The flag, in Rehnquist's view, is less like private property than it is like a public building—"a national property, and the Nation may regulate those who would make, imitate, sell, possess or use it" (ibid., 422, citations omitted). Thus the state had a valid interest in protecting the flag's integrity by limiting the uses to which it could be put. The state, according to Rehnquist, had not infringed on speech because it had not tried to dictate or to limit the content of communication; rather, it had simply

[11] Three months earlier the Court held that the language of a Massachusetts statute that prohibited treating the flag contemptously was void for vagueness (Smith v. Goguen, 415 U.S. 566 [1974]). Rehnquist dissented, objecting that the statute was designed to preserve the physical integrity of the flag against those who would infringe that integrity for any reason—whether it be for commercial purposes or to disparage the flag as a national symbol. In his view, the government's interest in protecting the flag was unrelated to the suppression of freedom of expression and, thus, easily withstood the First Amendment challenge.

withdrawn a "unique national symbol from the roster of materials that may be used as a background for communications" (ibid., 423).[12]

He also disagreed with the majority when the Court held that New Hampshire could not compel individuals to display "Live Free or Die" on their automobile license plates (Wooley v. Maynard, 430 U.S. 705 [1977]). The presence of the property element in the majority's analysis was evidenced by the assertion that the state may not "constitutionally require an individual to participate in the dissemination of an ideological message by displaying it on his private property in a manner and for the express purpose that it be observed and read by the public" (*Wooley*, 430 U.S. at 713). Rehnquist objected that the state had not forced people to say anything; it had merely required automobiles to bear license plates with the motto. No one was required to affirm the motto, and anyone at any time could express disagreement with it. The private property factor was of less import to his analysis than the fact that the state had used its authority to require the motto on license plates and that its authority had been upheld by the New Hampshire Supreme Court.[13]

Rehnquist's majority opinion in the California shopping center case (*Pruneyard*) also strongly suggests that the protection of property rights is not a central concern for him. He accepted the California Supreme Court's decision in favor of the right to engage in expressive activities in private shopping centers and rejected the owners' contention that they had a First Amendment right to prohibit non-business-related petitioning on the premises of the center.

Rehnquist's opinions, nonetheless, manifest a concern for property rights, albeit of a different nature from those of owners of flags, automobile license plates, or shopping centers. First, they reflect an apparent concern with the property interests of the government as opposed to those of the ordinary citizen. In the flag case, for example, his analysis of the state's interest suggested that he viewed the government as the proprietor of the national symbol. In terms of his ordering of values, he placed the property rights of government above individual rights of free

[12] *Spence* "pitted the tangible property interest in private ownership of a flag against the less tangible interest in public control of the symbol, and the traditional property interest prevailed" (Dorsen and Gora 1982, 206).

[13] Rehnquist noted that the New Hampshire Supreme Court and the United States Supreme Court had reached opposite conclusions.

speech. Federalism would still prevail, however; indeed, state power and property rights would coincide. Second, Rehnquist's opinions evidence his agreement with the Court's recognition of a right, protected by the First Amendment, to spend unlimited sums of money in political campaigns. He joined the majority when the Court invalidated federal restrictions on campaign expenditures (*Buckley v. Valeo*) and restrictions on spending by political action committees (Federal Election Commission v. NCPAC, 470 U.S. 480 [1985]).[14] He seems therefore to have accorded property rights some protection—at least the property rights of government and the right to spend one's money to attempt to influence elections. Still, the priority he gives to federalism helps to explain his position in those cases: the challenged federal laws were subject to a more exacting scrutiny under the First Amendment than comparable state restrictions, which would have been judged only by the general principles of freedom of speech.

Exclusion: Lewd, Commercial, and Corporate Speech

The exclusion of certain types of expression from the protection of the First Amendment finds its basis in the statement that

> [t]here are certain well-defined and narrowly limited classes of speech, the prevention and punishment of which have never been thought to raise any Constitutional problem. These include the lewd and obscene, the profane, the libelous, and the insulting or "fighting" words—those which by their very utterance inflict injury or tend to incite an immediate breach of the peace. It has been well observed that such utterances are no essential part of any exposition of ideas, and are of such slight social value as a step to truth that any benefit that may be derived from them is clearly outweighed by the social interest in order and morality. (Chaplinsky v. New Hampshire, 315 U.S. 568, 571–72 [1942])

The Burger Court modified the "fighting words" doctrine by extending protection to expression that is crude, shocking, and

---

[14] This appears to be entirely congruent with Dorsen and Gora's assertion that "[t]he Burger Court has consistently held that speech may not be restricted in order to redress inequalities in the competitive 'marketplace of ideas' resulting from disparities in wealth" (1982, 196–97).

even personally insulting (see, for example, Cohen v. California, 403 U.S. 15 [1971]; Gooding v. Wilson, 405 U.S. 518 [1972]; Rosenfeld v. New Jersey, 408 U.S. 901 [1972]). The Court, however, was not willing to extend full protection to such expression. It stressed that some types of communication are less valuable than others; while they are not excluded from the First Amendment, they may, nevertheless, be restrained.[15] Rehnquist was opposed to the Court's extension of protection to expression that he considered to be "fighting words" and "lewd and obscene" and "profane."[16] But he grudgingly gave his approval to the assignment of a lower value, and consequent modicum of protection, to certain expression.[17]

Commerical speech was also traditionally excluded from the protection of the First Amendment (Valentine v. Chrestensen, 316 U.S. 52 [1942]), but in 1975 the Burger Court began to extend the zone of protected speech to include commercial communication.[18] The Court suggested that some commercial speech could be protected by the First Amendment when a majority invalidated a Virginia statute prohibiting the sale or circulation of any publication that encouraged procuring an abortion. The statute had been used to convict the editor of a newspaper for publishing an advertisement of a New York organization that offered to arrange low-cost abortions in hospitals and clinics (Bigelow v. Virginia, 421 U.S. 809 [1975]). In dissent, Rehnquist stated that the advertisement was "a purely commercial proposal . . . entitled to little constitutional protection" (*Bigelow*, 421 U.S. at 832). The regulation was a reasonable means of achieving the

[15] For example, in a decision upholding a zoning ordinance that regulated the placement of theaters displaying sexually explicit films, Justice Stevens, in a plurality opinion, stated: "[F]ew of us would march our sons and daughters off to war to preserve the citizen's right to see 'Specified Sexual Activities' exhibited in the theaters of our choice. Even though the First Amendment protects communication in this area from total suppression, we hold that the State may legitimately use the content of these materials as the basis for placing them in a different classification from other motion pictures" (Young v. American Mini Theatres, 427 U.S. 50, 70–71 [1976]). See also FCC v. Pacifica, 438 U.S. 726 [1978]), upholding regulation of offensive words dealing with sex and excretion.

[16] See Rehnquist's opinion in Rosenfeld v. New Jersey, 408 U.S. 901 (1972), dissenting from the decision to vacate and remand, and Papish v. Board of Curators of the University of Missouri, 410 U.S. 667 (1973).

[17] Rehnquist joined the plurality opinions in both *FCC v. Pacifica* and *Young v. American Mini Theatres*.

[18] For useful discussions of the Burger Court's treatment of commercial speech see Dorsen and Gora 1982; Van Alstyne 1980; Cox 1980; Emerson 1980.

state's purpose of preventing commercial exploitation of its citizens. Further, even if the publication of the advertisement in this case involved more than a commercial proposal, he argued, the states have a strong interest in the prevention of commercial advertising in the health field. The justice viewed the Court's holding that a state may not bar a citizen of another state from disseminating information that is legal in that state as a "rigid territorial limitation on the power of the states in our federal system" (ibid., 834). A state, he contended, should be able to prohibit commercial advertising within its boundaries regardless of where the services are provided.

Newspaper advertisements about the availability of out-of-state abortions clearly imposed controls on noncommercial expression and could have been invalidated without extending protection to commercial speech. In 1976 the justices spoke more explicitly about the protection of commercial speech when the Court invalidated a statute that prohibited pharmacists from advertising the prices of prescription drugs. The majority declared that the First Amendment does not deny all protection to "speech which does 'no more than propose a commercial transaction' " (Virginia State Board of Pharmacy v. Virginia Citizens Consumer Council, 425 U.S. 748, 762, citation omitted). In dissent again, Rehnquist reiterated his belief that commercial speech should not be included under the rubric of the First Amendment.

When the Court subsequently invalidated New York's restrictions on advertising of nonprescription contraceptives, in a brief dissent, he rebuked the majority:

> If those responsible for [the Bill of Rights and the Civil War amendments] could have lived to know that their efforts had enshrined in the Constitution the right of commercial vendors of contraceptives to peddle them to unmarried minors through such means as window displays and vending machines located in the men's room of truck stops, . . . it is not difficult to imagine their reaction. (Carey v. Population Services International, 431 U.S. 678, 717 [1977])[19]

The Court further extended First Amendment protection to commercial speech when it invalidated a state supreme court's

---

[19] In *Carey*, the Court also invalidated prohibitions on the distribution of contraceptives to people over sixteen by anyone other than a licensed pharmacist and the sale or distribution of contraceptives to minors under sixteen.

disciplinary rule that prohibited attorneys from advertising (Bates v. State Bar of Arizona, 433 U.S. 350 [1977]). Rehnquist again expressed his view that commercial advertising is not protected by the First Amendment. The protection of freedom of expression, he contended, "long regarded by this Court as a sanctuary for expressions of public importance or intellectual interest, is demeaned by invocation to protect advertisements of goods and services" (*Bates*, 433 U.S. at 404). The Court, it seemed to him, had taken too many steps down the slippery slope toward the abandonment of the distinction between protected and unprotected speech.

Rehnquist reaffirmed his views in his opinions in two cases decided by the Court in 1978 that involved solicitation by lawyers. In one case the majority sustained disciplinary action against an attorney who had engaged in the solicitation of potential personal injury plaintiffs (Ohralik v. Ohio State Bar Association, 436 U.S. 447 [1978]). In the other, the Court held that solicitation of a client on behalf of an association seeking to promote political and ideological goals is entitled to full protection of the First Amendment, at least when the attorney will receive no direct monetary benefit from the particular case (*In re* Primus, 436 U.S. 412 [1978]). Rehnquist objected that the Court had failed to provide a principled distinction between civil liberties lawyers and ambulance chasers. He argued that the rules and their application were reasonable in both cases and that the state should be able to restrict the activities of the members of its bar.

In 1980 Justice Powell articulated a four-part test that a state must satisfy in order to justify a restriction on advertising when the Court invalidated an order of the New York Public Service Commission that prohibited electrical utilities from advertising to promote the purchase of utility services (Central Hudson Gas and Electric Corporation v. Public Service Commission of New York, 447 U.S. 557). According to the test, a court must determine, first, if the speech is deceptive or related to illegal activity. If it is neither, it is protected by the First Amendment. The inquiry does not end there, however. Protected speech may be regulated under certain conditions. The remaining three parts of the test require that if the restriction is to be upheld, the state must have a substantial governmental interest in it; the restriction must directly advance that interest; and the restriction must be no broader than is necessary to advance the state's interest. The Court held that the order was invalid on the basis of the last two parts of the test. The regulation was not carefully designed to achieve the state's goals of energy conservation and distributional fairness in electricity rates. Additionally, a narrower order might have been written that would have achieved those goals. Justices Blackmun and Brennan, in a concurring opinion, objected to the four-part test on the grounds that it did not provide adequate protection for truthful commercial speech regarding activities that the state has not or can not prohibit directly.

In contrast, Rehnquist, the sole dissenter, objected that the test "elevates the protection accorded commerical speech that falls within the scope of the First Amendment to a level that is virtually indistinguishable from that of noncommercial speech" (*Central Hudson*, 447 U.S. at 591). He argued that the order should have been treated as an economic regulation that would be given "virtually complete deference" (ibid.).[20]

In 1986 Rehnquist wrote the majority opinion for the Court when, by a vote of 5 to 4, it upheld Puerto Rico's ban on local advertising of legalized casino gambling against a challenge that the statute and regulations violated the First Amendment (Posadas de Puerto Rico Assoc. v. Tourism Co., 106 S.Ct. 2698).[21] He applied the four-part test that he had objected to in *Central Hudson*, but in his hands it was so deferential that it verged on requiring only that the legislative determination be reasonable.[22]

[20] Rehnquist concurred when the Court held that a federal law that prohibited mailing of unsolicited advertisements for contraceptives violated the First Amendment as applied to manufacturers who advertised products available at drugstores and informational pamphlets discussing the desirability of prophylactics in general (Bolger v. Young's Drug Products Corp., 463 U.S. 60 [1983]). He has rarely supported an overbreadth analysis, but here he found that the provision advanced governmental interests by permitting parents to provide their children with information on contraception in their own way but that it also inhibited that interest by denying parents access to that information. The statute was broader than necessary because it completely banned from the mail unsolicited material suitable for adults.

[21] The Games of Chance Act of 1948, which legalized casino gambling, authorized the Economic Development Administration of Puerto Rico to issue and enforce regulations to implement the act. Tourism Company assumed the regulatory powers of the Economic Development Administration. The regulations at issue prohibited advertising "the gambling parlors to the public in Puerto Rico" (quoted in *Posadas*, 106 S.Ct. at 2972). After being fined for violating the restrictions, Posadas de Puerto Rico filed an action in the Superior Court of Puerto Rico. The court found that the application of the act had been arbitrary and issued a narrowing construction, which made clear that the restrictions applied only to advertising that was directed at residents.

[22] In dissent, Brennan objected that Rehnquist's opinion, "[w]hile tipping its hat

First, he noted that the advertising concerned a lawful activity and was not misleading or fraudulent; he then proceeded to the three remaining parts of the test. He found that the Puerto Rican government's interest in reducing the demand for casino gambling by the local residents in order to avoid harmful effects on the health, safety, and welfare of Puerto Rican citizens was substantial.[23] Applying the third part of the test, Rehnquist held that the regulation directly advanced the government's interest since the legislature had made a reasonable determination that advertising of casino gambling would serve to increase the demand for it. Suggesting that the legal action itself could serve as evidence of the state's interest, he asserted that the appellant would not have litigated the case to the Supreme Court if he did not believe that the ban on advertising decreased the demand for casino gambling. Finally, he found that the restrictions were no more extensive than necessary to achieve the government's interest in light of the fact that the Superior Court had issued a narrowing construction of the statute to make clear that only advertising directed at residents was prohibited.[24]

Rehnquist rejected Posadas de Puerto Rico's contention that the advertising restrictions conflicted with the First Amendment according to the Court's decisions in *Carey* and *Bigelow*. In so doing, he emphasized the difference between the advertising of

---

to these standards, . . . does little more than defer to what it perceives to be the determination by Puerto Rico's legislature that a ban on casino advertising aimed at residents is reasonable. The Court totally ignores the fact that commerical speech is entitled to substantial First Amendment protection, giving the government unprecedented authority to eviscerate constitutionally protected expression" (*Posadas*, 106 S.Ct. at 2983).

[23] Rehnquist accepted the argument presented in the brief for Tourism Company that "excessive casino gambling among local residents . . . would produce serious harmful effects on the health safety and welfare of the Puerto Rican citizens, such as the disruption of moral and cultural patterns, the increase in local crime, the fostering of prostitution, the development of corruption, and the infiltration of organized crime" (Brief for Appellee, 37, quoted in *Posadas*, 106 S.Ct. at 2977). In contrast, Brennan asserted that by legalizing gambling casinos, permitting Puerto Rican residents to patronize them, and permitting various other gambling activities, the legislature had determined that it was not harmful for residents to engage in such activities. He speculated that the legislature may have chosen to restrict advertising because it preferred that Puerto Ricans spend their gambling dollars on the Puerto Rican lottery (ibid., 2983).

[24] Brennan suggested several more limited approaches that Puerto Rico could use to achieve its interest, such as carefully monitoring casino operations and vigorously enforcing criminal statutes (*Posadas*, 106 S.Ct. at 2985).

activities that are constitutionally protected, such as the sale of contraceptives and abortion, and the advertising of activities that the government could prohibit, such as gambling. The government's power to completely ban an activity, Rehnquist asserted, "necessarily includes the lesser power to ban advertising of casino gambling" (*Posadas*, 106 S.Ct. at 2979). Thus, if the legislature has the power to ban an activity but instead chooses to allow it, it can attempt to limit the demand for the activity through restrictions on advertising. By relying so explicitly on the distinction between constitutionally protected and unprotected activities, Rehnquist provided the basis for excluding from the protection of the First Amendment the advertising of products or activities that legislatures can constitutionally condemn, such as cigarettes, alcoholic beverages, and prostitution.[25] His opinion, in short, represented a serious, if not altogether straightforward, attempt to constrain the doctrine that has extended constitutional protection to commercial speech.

The Burger Court's decisions extending First Amendment rights to corporations was closely related to its bestowal of constitutional status on commerical speech. On several occasions Rehnquist took the opportunity to express his view that when the source of expression is a corporation, it should not be accorded First Amendment protection. Statutes that limit corporate expression, in his view, should be subject only to a test of reasonableness. Laws that limit both corporate and other organizations' expression, however, should be more carefully scrutinized because they infringe on values protected by the First Amendment.

In 1978 the Court extended to corporations the right to spend money in political campaigns (First National Bank of Boston v. Bellotti, 435 U.S. 765). The majority invalidated a Massachusetts criminal statute that prohibited businesses engaged in banking from using corporate funds to publish views about referenda issues having no material effect on the business, property, or assets of the corporation. Rehnquist dissented. He alluded to the democratic model when he noted that Congress and thirty states

[25] Justice Stevens, in his dissenting opinion, pointed out a major problem with Rehnquist's use of the distinction. He characterized it as "an inappropriate major premise" because although Puerto Rico could have prohibited all casino gambling, it could not have prohibited residents from patronizing casinos that are open to tourists; thus, by Rehnquist's own reasoning, the restriction could not be justified (ibid., 2988).

have decided that restrictions upon political activity of business corporations are both politically desirable and constitutionally permissible. He then developed a justification for treating corporations differently from persons. He posited that corporations have some liberties that are "necessarily incidental" to their existence. For example, although a corporation cannot be deprived of property without due process of law, the right of political expression is not necessary to its existence and is thus "necessarily incidental." The state grants "properties" of perpetual life and limited liability to corporations and might conclude that those properties pose special dangers in the political sphere. Rehnquist contended that the liberties of political expression are not at all necessary to effectuate the purposes for which states permit commercial corporations to exist. The property interests of corporations are adequately protected.

> So long as the Judicial Branches of the State and Federal Governments remain open to protect the corporation's interest in its property, it has no need, though it may have the desire, to petition the political branches for similar protection. Indeed, the States might reasonably fear that the corporation would use its economic power to obtain further benefits beyond those already bestowed. (*First National Bank*, 435 U.S. at 826)

The justice also discussed corporate free speech rights in his dissent in the 1980 electrical utilities case (*Central Hudson*), which was discussed briefly above in the context of commercial speech. He asserted that the source of the speech may be relevant in determining whether a given message is protected under the First Amendment, and "when the source of the speech is a state-created monopoly such as this, traditional First Amendment concerns, if they come into play at all, certainly do not justify the broad interventionist role adopted by the Court today" (*Central Hudson*, 447 U.S. at 585).

In 1986 the Court held that an order of the California Public Utilities Commission requiring a privately owned utility to include messages in its billing envelopes from a group that disagreed with the utility's views infringed on the utility's rights under the First Amendment (Pacific Gas and Electric Co. v. Public Utilities Commission of California, 475 U.S. 1). Affirming the extension of the First Amendment to corporations, Justice Powell wrote for a four-person plurality that "[t]he identity of the

83

speaker is not decisive in determining whether speech is protected. Corporations and other associations, like individuals, contribute to the 'discussion, debate, and the dissemination of information and ideas' that the First Amendment seeks to foster" (*Pacific Gas and Electric*, 106 S.Ct. at 907, citations omitted). Rehnquist dissented, reiterating his belief that protection of free speech should not be extended to corporations: "To ascribe to such artificial entities an 'intellect' or 'mind' for freedom of conscience purposes is to confuse metaphor with reality" (ibid., 921). He argued that the Court's earlier decision (*Pruneyard*) upholding a right, created by the state, of access to private shopping centers should be controlling.

When the Court has invalidated restrictions on corporate participation in the political process, as it did in *First Bank of Boston*, Rehnquist has objected that corporations do not have the same interest in freedom of expression as natural persons. He has been much more willing to find a violation of the First Amendment when federal and state regulations on campaign spending that apply not only to corporations but to individuals or to other associations have been challenged. In 1976 he joined the majority when it held unconstitutional the Federal Election Campaign Act's limits on expenditures on behalf of candidates for federal office (Buckley v. Valeo). He concurred when the Court invalidated a city ordinance that limited to $250 the contribution that could be made to committees formed to support or oppose ballot measures (Citizens Against Rent Control v. Berkeley, 454 U.S. 290 [1981]), noting that the ordinance was not aimed at corporations but at individuals.

Finally, Rehnquist held that a section of the Presidential Election Campaign Fund Act making it a crime for an independent political action committee to spend more than $1,000 to further the election of a candidate receiving public financing violated the First Amendment (Federal Election Commission v. NCPAC). He noted that the law did not apply to corporations but to any committee or association that accepts contributions or makes expenditures in connection with electoral campaigns. Thus, he held, a PAC's expenditures are entitled to full protection under the First Amendment.

If Rehnquist were primarily concerned with protecting property rights, it seems that he would be much more amenable to extending the protection of the First Amendment to commercial and corporate speech. Instead, he prefers to allow the states to regulate such speech—an indication that he places a higher value on federalism than on property rights. His opinions in the area of commercial and corporate speech also suggest two important distinctions. First, and more readily apparent, is the distinction between business corporations (granted special status by the state, likely to be communicating for commercial purposes, and not entitled to protection under the First Amendment) and other individuals or associations (engaged in political communication and fully protected by the First Amendment).

POLITICAL SPEECH AS "HIGH VALUE" EXPRESSION

The second distinction suggested by Rehnquist's opinions is between political and nonpolitical speech. Rehnquist's opinions in the area of sexually explicit expression, obscenity,[26] and commercial and corporate speech considered together indicate that he considers communication regarding public issues to be more valuable than other forms of speech. For example, arguing that the advertisement of drug prices should not be accorded protection, he stated: "I had understood [the] view [of the First Amendment as an instrument to enlighten decision making in a democracy] to relate to public decision making as to political, social, and other public issues, rather than the decision of a particular individual as to whether to purchase one or another kind of shampoo" (*Virginia State Board of Pharmacy*, 425 U.S. at 787). Disputing the application of the First Amendment to state-created monopolies he acknowledged that the "clear and present danger" test is appropriate in the political context "in light of the central importance of such speech to our system of self-government" (*Central Hudson*, 447 U.S. at 595). In that opinion he asserted:

> Discussion of public issues and debate on the qualifications of candidates are integral to the operation of the system of

[26] Rehnquist has adhered to the Court's doctrine holding that obscenity is not protected. He has written several opinions in this area. See Hamling v. U.S., 418 U.S. 87 (1974) (majority opinion holding that contemporary community standards are not national); Jenkins v. Georgia, 418 U.S. 153 (1974) (majority opinion holding that the film *Carnal Knowledge* is not obscene and that juries do not have unbridled discretion in determining what is patently offensive); Mckinney v. Alabama, 424 U.S. 669 (1976) (majority opinion regarding procedural requirements of notification); Splawn v. California, 431 U.S. 595 (1977) (majority opinion regarding jury instructions in an obscenity trial).

government established by our Constitution. The First Amendment affords the broadest protection to such political expression in order "to assure [the] unfettered interchange of ideas for the bringing about of political and social changes desired by the people." (*Buckley*, 424 U.S. at 14, quoted in *Central Hudson*, 447 U.S. at 595–96)

When his opinions in the flag "desecration" cases and the New Hampshire license plate motto case are also considered, the high value he places on political speech must be qualified. The type of speech that is most deserving of protection under the First Amendment, in his view, appears to be that which is not only concerned with public issues but is also exercised in conventional ways, such as campaigning for candidates for office or spending money for that purpose, rather than expressing disapproval of government policy by means of symbolic communication.

An examination of several opinions in cases that involved restrictions on canvasing, which clearly fell into the category of political expression, suggests that, in spite of his proclaimed commitment to political speech as a highly valued category of expression, Rehnquist has demonstrated very little support for it. In 1976 the Court invalidated an ordinance prohibiting house-to-house canvasing for "a recognized charitable cause, or . . . political campaign or cause" without written notice to the police department "for identification only" (Hynes v. Mayor of Oradell 425 U.S. 610). Chief Justice Burger, in an opinion for the majority, aknowledged "a municipality's power to protect its citizens from crime and undue annoyance by regulating soliciting and canvassing" (ibid., 616–17). The majority, nevertheless, found the ordinance to be unconstitutionally vague because its coverage was unclear and because it did not sufficiently specify what was necessary for compliance. Rehnquist dissented, arguing that the political canvasers had no standing to challenge the ordinance, but even if they did, its language was clear enough to withstand a vagueness challenge.

He dissented when the Court invalidated an ordinance barring door-to-door and street solicitation by charitable organizations that used less than 75 percent of their receipts for charitable purposes (Village of Schaumberg v. Citizens for a Better Environment, 444 U.S. 620 [1980]). The majority held that canvasing for contributions for a charitable or political cause is an activity entitled to some degree of protection under the First Amendment. Clearly, the speech protected here was political in nature; Rehnquist, however, suggested that he considered door-to-door solicitation for financial contributions to be commercial speech: "I believe that a simple request for money lies far from the core protections of the First Amendment as heretofore interpreted" (*Village of Schaumberg*, 444 U.S. at 644).

In a subsequent case he dissented when the Court invalidated a state law that prohibited organizations from paying fund-raisers more than 25 percent of the amount they raised (Secretary of State of Maryland v. Joseph H. Munson Co., 467 U.S. 947 [1984]). While the majority concluded that the restriction infringed on activity protected by the First Amendment, Rehnquist countered that the law functioned merely as an economic regulation setting a limit on fees charged by professional fund-raisers and, thus, regulated only the external relations between charities and professional fund-raisers. In his view, although it was possible that the law had some indirect and incidental impact on expression, it was insufficient to warrant strict scrutiny.

Two cases, both of which involved challenges to federal provisions that limited free speech, further suggest that Rehnquist lacks a strong commitment to political speech. In one case he denied that regulations affecting the financial status of associations that engage in lobbying abridge any rights under the First Amendment. He wrote an opinion for a unanimous Court upholding a provision of the Internal Revenue Code that limits tax exempt status to nonprofit organizations that do not engage in lobbying (Regan v. Taxation with Representation of Washington, 461 U.S. 540 [1983]).[27] The group that challenged the provision, TRW, argued that the provision violated the First Amendment by conditioning tax exempt status on refraining from lobbying—a constitutionally protected activity. Rehnquist characterized tax exemptions as a form of subsidy. The code, consequently, did not

[27] Three justices took a position that was much more supportive of associations' rights to engage in lobbying. Justice Blackmun wrote a concurring opinion, which Brennan and Marshall joined, emphasizing that the challenged provision, viewed in isolation, violated the First Amendment; however, another provision allowed an organization to create an affiliate to pursue its goals through lobbying. Thus, under the IRS code, the organization could retain its tax exempt status and establish an affiliate for lobbying; the right to engage in lobbying activities would not be abridged. But an attempt by the IRS to interfere with the organization's relationship to its affiliate would violate the First Amendment.

infringe on any First Amendment rights nor did it regulate any activity protected by the First Amendment. Congress had simply chosen not to subsidize TRW's lobbying.

In a second case the majority found that a section of the Public Broadcasting Act of 1967, forbidding noncommercial educational broadcasting stations receiving federal funds from engaging in editorializing, violated the First Amendment (FCC v. League of Women Voters of California, 468 U.S. 364 [1984]). Dissenting, Rehnquist relied on TRW, arguing that Congress had simply determined that public funds should not be used to subsidize noncommercial, educational broadcasting that engages in editorializing.

In a case that involved access to the ballot, he dissented from the Court's decision holding unconstitutional Ohio's statute providing an early filing deadline for independent candidates for president (Anderson v. Celebrezze, 460 U.S. 780 [1983]). He objected that the law did not infringe on any constitutional protections because it did not interfere with independent candidates' attempts to run for office.

In each of the cases discussed above, beginning with *Mayor of Oradell* and including *Anderson v. Celebrezze*, Rehnquist rejected a claim, based on the First Amendment, that clearly involved speech of a political nature. His decision making strongly suggests that he does not consider the protection of even "high value" speech to prevail over regulations that are reasonable, even in a situation in which, presumably, the First Amendment applies with full force because federal regulations are the object of the challenge. Moreover, he has expressly and repeatedly maintained that regulations that infringe only indirectly on an individual's or an organization's ability to communicate in the political realm do not violate the First Amendment.

THE FIRST AMENDMENT IN SPECIAL CONTEXTS

A theory of freedom of expression that accords more protection to speech of a political nature than to other types of speech seemed, at first glance, to help explain Rehnquist's decision making. His statements in the commercial speech cases, for example, suggest that he considers political speech to be more valuable than expression concerning brands of shampoo or requests for financial contributions. As the discussion proceeded from cases involving commercial speech to those concerned with speech of a political nature, however, it became plain that he does not offer any particular protection to speech of that nature either. Thus, while the distinction between political and nonpolitical speech offers some insight into Rehnquist's theory of freedom of expression, that distinction falls far short of providing a full explanation of the principles of his decision making.

He has outlined another set of distinctions, however, that, considered with the preeminent value he places on federalism, are much more useful in explaining his approach to freedom of expression. I have characterized this set of distinctions as Rehnquist's contextual approach to freedom of expression. It is at this point, moreover, that the meaning of the title of this chapter begins to take form: in certain contexts, "[t]he First Amendment may speak with a different voice" (Board of Education v. Pico, 457 U.S. 853, 908 [1982]).

Rehnquist set forth the dimensions of his contextual approach most clearly in an opinion he wrote in 1976. He stated that "the limits imposed by the First and Fourteenth Amendments on governmental action may vary in their stringency depending on the capacity in which the government is acting" (*Buckley*, 424 U.S. at 290). He went on to assert that the government as proprietor is permitted to affect protected interests in ways that it might not do if it was simply proscribing conduct across the board. Similarly, he explained, the government as employer may specify conditions of employment that might be in violation of the Constitution if they were enacted into rules applicable to the entire citizenry. The nature of the protections offered by the First Amendment therefore depends upon whether the government is acting as sovereign, or lawmaker, enacting criminal laws that apply to the population in general; or whether it is acting in a proprietary capacity. When that distinction is combined with Rehnquist's federalism, the principle emerges that interests protected by the First Amendment are at their strongest when a federal law is challenged and when that law directly prohibits speech. Those interests are at their weakest when a state law is challenged and when the government acts as property owner or employer to regulate speech.

Rehnquist has applied his distinction in a variety of situations. For example, he discussed the powers of the government to regulate expression in its capacity as property owner when the Court found that a municipal board's denial of the use of a city-leased theater for a showing of the musical *Hair* was a prior restraint that violated the First Amendment. He contended in his dissenting opinion that a public auditorium is not the same as public streets and parks for communicative purposes and that a city should be able to control its own property (Southeastern Promotions, Ltd. v. Conrad, 420 U.S. 546 [1975]).

Similarly, he has applied his distinction between sovereign and proprietor to cases in which he has found the government to be acting in the capacity of employer. He has argued on several occasions that conditions of public employment do not violate the First Amendment. Regulations imposing such conditions, he has maintained, should be subject only to a test of reasonableness. He joined the dissent when the Court held that patronage dismissals violate the First Amendment (Elrod v. Burns, 427 U.S. 347 [1976]) and affirmed that position when the Court held that public employees cannot be compelled to contribute to a union if they disagree with its political activities (Abood v. Detroit Board of Education, 431 U.S. 209 [1977]).

When the government acts as school administrator it performs a proprietary function; thus, for Rehnquist, the First Amendment carries less weight in such a context than when the government acts as sovereign. In 1972 the Court held that a state-supported school violated the constitutional rights of students by denying recognition to Students for a Democratic Society. Rehnquist wrote a concurring opinion in which he referred to the distinction between government as college administrator and government acting as sovereign to enforce criminal laws: "The government as employer or school administrator may impose upon employees and students reasonable regulations that would be impermissible if imposed by the government upon all citizens" (Healy v. James, 408 U.S. 169, 203 [1972]). He also referred to "a constitutional distinction" between criminal punishment and "milder" administrative or disciplinary sanctions "even though the same First Amendment interest is implicated by each" (ibid., 203).

Rehnquist dissented when the Court held that a university student could not be expelled for distributing campus newspapers containing a picture of police officers raping the Statue of Liberty and Goddess of Justice and an article entitled "Motherfucker Acquitted" (Papish v. Board of Curators of the University of Missouri, 410 U.S. 667 [1973]). He objected that, although the student could not have been criminally prosecuted for her conduct, she could have been expelled without abridging her rights of free speech: "[A] wooden insistence on equating, for constitutional purposes, the authority of the State to criminally punish with its authority to exercise even a modicum of control over the university which it operates, serves neither the Constitution nor public education well" (*Papish*, 410 U.S. at 677).

Finally, Rehnquist objected when the majority held that the First Amendment limits school board discretion to remove library books from high school and junior high school libraries. He again referred to the distinction: "[G]overnment may act in other capacities than as sovereign, and when it does the First Amendment may speak with a different voice" (*Pico*, 457 U.S. at 908).

In a similar fashion, he has supported regulations for prisoners against challenges based on the First Amendment on the grounds that the government functions in a proprietary capacity when it acts as prison administrator. In an opinion for the majority upholding restrictions on prisoners' union activities, Rehnquist reasoned that rights protected by the First Amendment are curtailed in prison (Jones v. North Carolina Prisoners' Labor Union Inc., 433 U.S. 119 [1977]). He held that the restrictions were reasonable and consistent with inmates' status as prisoners and with legitimate operational considerations of the institution. Further, he suggested that rights of prisoners under the First Amendment include only the right to communicate grievances to correctional officials.

In 1979, again writing for a majority, he upheld the "publishers only" rule whereby pretrial detainees in a federal custodial facility were prohibited from receiving books that were not mailed directly from a publisher or a book club (Bell v. Wolfish, 441 U.S. 520 [1979]). He noted that the rule operated in a neutral fashion without regard to content of expression.

Rehnquist has also applied his distinction to regulations imposed by the military. In 1972 the Court reversed a conviction for distributing peace leaflets on a street within the boundaries of an army base (Flower v. United States, 407 U.S. 197). The majority reasoned that if the public was not excluded from the area, then the military could be considered to have abandoned any claim of special interest in who distributed leaflets there. Rehnquist contended in dissent that the reasonableness standard, properly applied, would result in upholding the conviction because of the "unique requirements of military morale and security" (*Flower*, 407 U.S. at 200).[28] In another case he used the reasonableness

---

[28] The Court interpreted *Flower* narrowly in Greer v. Spock (424 U.S. 828 [1976]) when it upheld regulations at Fort Dix that barred political activities on

standard to uphold the court martial of an army captain for "conduct unbecoming an officer and a gentleman," emphasizing the differences between military and civilian commmunities and military law and civilian law (Parker v. Levy, 417 U.S. 733 [1974]).

In sum, the distinction that is based upon the capacity in which the government is acting when it regulates expression appears to be of major importance to Rehnquist, particularly when it is combined with the high value he places on federalism. Rehnquist would be most likely to vote to invalidate a federal law that directly abridged expression by prohibiting the citizenry at large from engaging in it—assuming, of course that the type of speech fell into a category that he considers to be protected.

CONCLUSION

The analysis of Rehnquist's decision making in the realm of freedom of expression has demonstrated how decisively he has chosen federalism over individual rights. It also has suggested that property rights, though higher on the scale of values than individual rights, occupy a subordinate position to federalism. The keys to understanding his approach to freedom of expression are found in the preeminent value that he places on federalism, plus the principle that the force of the First Amendment depends on the context of a government regulation of expression.

The paramount value that Rehnquist assigns to federalism is evidenced by his endorsement of expansive state power to regulate expression. His position is consistent with his democratic model insofar as he would allow majorities to regulate and limit expression with only minimal constraints from the Constitution. But the fact that he places no particular value on political as opposed to other types of expression suggests that the notion that the communication of political ideas helps the democratic process to function properly is not of major importance to him. Allowing government to "abridge" freedom of speech, however, ap-

---

the base including speeches and demonstrations of a partisan political nature and distibution of literature without prior approval of the base commander. Justice Stewart, in an opinion for the Court, distinguished *Flower*: "[T]he street there was not any different from all other public thoroughfares in San Antonio and the military had abandoned any right to exclude leafleteers. But that did not mean that whenever the public is allowed to visit a place that it becomes a public forum."

pears to contradict both his moral relativism (which would be consistent with his respect for the values that have been enacted into the positive law—the First Amendment) and his approach to constitutional interpretation (which includes limiting the meaning of the Constitution to its text). Although Rehnquist's moral relativism and his approach to constitutional interpretation would seem to require him to follow the First Amendment's explicit prohibition on abridgment of speech, he has steadfastly maintained that the amendment does not apply to the states. Thus, the states may regulate speech without confronting the First Amendment. Furthermore, when federal regulations of speech have been challenged, he has been most willing to rely on his distinction between the actions of government as sovereign and as proprietor to reject a claim of an infringement on freedom of speech. When the government acts as proprietor, it merely regulates rather than abridges speech.

The contextual approach is essential to Rehnquist's jurisprudence of freedom of expression. In the contexts in which the government acts as property owner, employer, or administrator, or if the claim is raised in the area of military regulations, the First Amendment speaks to Rehnquist with a fainter voice than when the government acts as lawmaker. Furthermore, and of fundamental importance, when it is the state that regulates speech, the First Amendment speaks with a voice so faint that Rehnquist fails to hear it.

Literalism is the technique that dominates Rehnquist's opinions in the area of freedom of expression. He has used that technique to construct a doctrine that posits essentially the following: The First Amendment protects freedom of speech, *but* its provisions apply only to the federal government; the protection the amendment offers depends on the type of expression, the source of expression, and the context in which the government seeks to regulate the expression. In short, Rehnquist's approach to constitutional interpretation and the technique he has utilized have taken him in the opposite direction from what might be expected. He has adapted his technique of literalism so that the First Amendment, surprisingly, is not an absolute ban on abridgment of freedom of expression. It is, instead, a rule dominated by its exceptions.

PART THREE

Property Rights

FIVE

Nontraditional Property:
The Bitter-Sweet Denial

During the hearings of the Senate Judiciary Committee on Rehnquist's confirmation in 1971, Sen. John Tunney queried the nominee as to whether he placed a higher value on property rights than individual freedoms. He responded as follows:

> I certainly am not prepared to say, as a matter of personal philosophy, that property rights are necessarily at the bottom of the scale. Justice Jackson, . . . commented shortly before his death that the framers had chosen to join together life, liberty, and property, and he did not feel they should be separated. I think property rights are actually a very important form of individual rights. On the other hand, I am by no means prepared to say that a property right must not on some occasion—and I am again speaking personally and not in any sense of the Constitution or statutory construction—but certainly when a legislative decision is made that a property right must give way to what may be called a human right or an individual right, that may frequently be the correct choice. (U.S. Congress 1971a, 77)

With his disclaimer, his suggestion that property rights are not separable from individual rights, plus his double negative, the nominee's answer shed very little light on the positions of property rights and individual rights in his ordering of values. His record as a Phoenix attorney and as assistant attorney general had made it clear that he was no avid supporter of individual rights and, indeed, suggested that he valued property rights highly.[1] But even the most insightful analyst in 1971 could not have predicted that Rehnquist's judicial decision making would include a

An earlier version of part of chapter 5 appeared in "Federalism and Property Rights: An Examination of Justice Rehnquist's Legal Positivism," *Western Political Quarterly* 39, no. 2 (1986): 250–64.

[1] See, for example, his comments regarding his opposition to the Phoenix public accommodations ordinance, which are discussed in chapter 1.

scheme of values that would subordinate both individual rights and property rights to states' rights.

In this chapter I examine Rehnquist's view of a particular type of property, variously referred to as nontraditional property, the "new property," and, occasionally, intangible property. Not only the relationship between his values of federalism and property rights but also his views regarding the nature of the rights of property should become increasingly clear as the discussion of his opinions proceeds.

BACKGROUND

In 1964 the *Yale Law Journal* published an article entitled "The New Property," that asserted that in modern America one's personal security depends on the "wealth" that government dispenses, much as such security once depended on the ownership of property. Charles Reich, the author of the article, described the individual's relationship to the government as the "new feudalism"—a system in which "[w]ealth is not 'owned,' or 'vested' in the holders. Instead, it is held conditionally, the conditions being ones which seek to ensure the fulfillment of obligations imposed by the state. Just as the feudal system linked lord and vassal through a system of mutual dependence, obligation, and loyalty, so government largess binds man to the state" (1964, 769–70). Characterizing governmental benefits such as jobs, occupational licenses, payments, and contracts as the "new property," Reich asserted that because such benefits are crucial to one's security, well-being, and autonomy, they ought to be protected by the principles of due process.

A year later Reich published a second article in the *Yale Law Journal* in which he advocated that due process principles be applied to the administration of the welfare system. Society is obligated to provide support for those with insufficient resources, and the individual is entitled to that support "as of right," he argued. It followed that "objective eligibility safeguards against revocation or loss of benefits [were required], and . . . the individual's rights, . . . should be known to him and enforceable through law" (1965, 1256).

Government employment—one of the governmental benefits that concerned Reich—was traditionally treated not as a property right but as a privilege that the government could confer and withdraw without constitutional constraint. Because there was no right to a job, it could be withdrawn or denied for any reason. Oliver Wendell Holmes, Jr., writing in 1892, captured the essence of the "right-privilege" distinction:

> The petitioner may have a constitutional right to talk politics, but he has no constitutional right to be a policeman. There are few employments for hire in which the servant does not agree to suspend his constitutional rights of free speech, as well as of idleness by the implied terms of his contract. The servant cannot complain, as he takes the employment on the terms which are offered him.[2]

The "right-privilege" distinction was still a part of the law in 1954. In that year the Supreme Court upheld the suspension of a physician's license to practice medicine. The state had suspended the license after the doctor was convicted of contempt of Congress. The opinion for the majority reiterated the distinction, noting that the practice of medicine "is a privilege granted by the State" (Barsky v. Board of Regents, 347 U.S. 442, 451).

The right-privilege distinction was destined to fall into disrepute. Of course, it became unfashionable during the era of the Warren Court; but, more important, justices saw with increasing clarity that the distinction, carried to its logical conclusion, amounted to an assertion that the government may infringe individual rights without constitutional problems—that a state may, contrary to what the Constitution provides, deprive people of life, liberty, or property without due process of law. It was, therefore, not at all surprising that during the late 1950s and the 1960s the Court gradually chipped away at the distinction until by 1970 it had completely repudiated it.[3]

In Goldberg v. Kelly (397 U.S. 254 [1970]), the Court held that the due process clause requires that welfare recipients be afforded a hearing before the termination of benefits. Justice Brennan, in an opinion for the majority, made it clear that the due process clause applied to welfare benefits. He stated that "[s]uch benefits are a matter of statutory entitlement for persons qualified to re-

[2] McAuliffe v. Mayor of New Bedford, 155 Mass. 216, 220, 29 N.E. 517, 517–18 (1892). As chief judge of the Massachusetts Supreme Judicial Court, Holmes made the statement when he rejected a policeman's claim for reinstatement to his job, which he had lost for violating a regulation of the police department that forbade political comment even during nonworking hours.

[3] Van Alstyne (1968) provided an overview of the demise of the right-privilege distinction as well as an analysis of its logical flaws.

ceive them" (*Goldberg*, 397 U.S. at 262). In a footnote he elaborated: "It may be realistic today to regard welfare entitlements as more like 'property' than a 'gratuity.' Much of the existing wealth in the country takes the form of rights that do not fall within traditional common-law concepts of property" (ibid., n.8). He went on to quote extensively from Reich's second article.

Goldberg signaled the Court's recognition of property interests in governmental benefits. During the next several years, rights of due process were held to apply to licensed automobile drivers (Bell v. Burson, 402 U.S. 535 [1971]), prisoners (Wolff v. McDonnel, 418 U.S. 539 [1974]), and parolees (Morissey v. Brewer, 408 U.S. 593 [1972]). In 1976 the Court held that dismissal of patronage employees for partisan reasons violated the First and Fourteenth amendments. Justice Brennan, writing for the majority in that case, summarized the demise of the right-privilege distinction:

> [D]enial of a public benefit may not be used by the Government for the purpose of creating an incentive enabling it to achieve what it may not command directly. . . . "[T]his Court now has rejected the concept that constitutional rights turn upon whether a governmental benefit is characterized as a 'right' or as a 'privilege.' " (Elrod v. Burns, 427 U.S. 347, 361 [1976], citations omitted)

The death of the right-privilege distinction and the Court's willingness to view governmental benefits as property protected by the due process clause did not mean that the Court embraced Justice Marshall's argument that "every citizen who applies for a government job is entitled to it unless the government can establish some reason for denying the employment" (Board of Regents v. Roth, 408 U.S. 564 [1972]). The Court's recognition of the "new property" meant only that one could bring a claim that he or she had been denied a property right by the withdrawal of a job or other governmental benefit. One could litigate an objection to the government's action, but that did not guarantee victory on the merits. Indeed, in the cases in which the Court considered the rights of the new property it developed a two-stage analysis. It would ask, first, whether the claimant had a property interest in the benefit that had been withdrawn. If so, it would advance to the second stage and determine whether the procedures used to take away that benefit were suitable.[4]

---

[4] Tushnet (1975) examined the problems with the Supreme Court's two-stage

In 1972 the Court decided two cases that involved college professors' property interests in continuing employment at state colleges (Board of Regents v. Roth, and Perry v. Sinderman, 408 U.S. 593). Justice Stewart provided the framework for the subsequent development of the doctrine of the new property in his majority opinions in both cases. In the first case the Court held that a political science professor, hired on a one-year contract at the University of Wisconsin, Oshkosh, had no right to a hearing when his contract was not renewed. While Stewart recognized that the principles of due process may extend to intangible property, he also noted that property interests in governmental benefits are conditional:

> To have a property interest in a benefit, a person clearly must have more than an abstract need or desire for it. He must have a legitimate claim of entitlement to it. It is a purpose of the ancient institution of property to protect those claims upon which people rely in their daily lives, reliance that must not be arbitrarily undermined. It is a purpose of the constitutional right to a hearing to provide an opportunity for a person to vindicate those claims. (*Roth*, 408 U.S. at 577).

As Stewart further underlined the conditional nature of intangible property, he suggested that although property interests are created by state law, an entitlement may exist by virtue of implicit "understandings" in the law:

> Property interests, of course, are not created by the Constitution. Rather, they are created and their dimensions are defined by existing rules or understandings that stem from an independent source such as state law—rules or understandings that secure certain benefits and that support claims of entitlement of those benefits. (Ibid., 577)

He noted that welfare recipients' property interests in their benefits were created by the state law defining eligibility; similarly, a property interest in employment could be created by a contract and defined by the terms of appointment. The employment con-

---

analysis. Van Alstyne pointed out that there were several important things that the demise of the right-privilege distinction did not do. The essence of the problem as he saw it was that the Fourteenth Amendment does not provide a substantive constitutional right to procedural due process—that is, the Fourteenth Amendment does not provide that "[n]o State shall deprive any person of life, liberty, or property, or due process of law, without due process of law" (1977, 451).

tract at issue here created a property interest, Stewart held, but only for one year.

In the second case, the Court held that a teacher, dismissed after he had been employed for ten years in a junior college system that had a de facto tenure system,[5] had the right to an opportunity to prove the legitimacy of his claim of entitlement. Stewart wrote that "[a] person's interest in a benefit is a 'property interest' for due process purposes if there are such rules or mutually explicit understandings that support his claim of entitlement of the benefit and that he may invoke at a hearing" (*Sinderman*, 408 U.S. at 601). In sum, Stewart's opinions affirmed that constitutional protections extend to intangible property; however, in order for those protections to apply, it must be established that a property interest exists in that intangible item. The existence of a property interest can be established by virtue of a statutory provision that has created the interest, if not explicitly, at least by implicit understanding. Thus, a property interest in a governmental benefit or other intangible property exists only if it has been provided for in the law.

REHNQUIST'S ANALYSIS OF THE NEW PROPERTY: TAKING THE BITTER WITH THE SWEET

Rehnquist's opinions in two new property cases, in particular, reveal his conception of the nature and source of property rights. Additionally, the two opinions illustrate the way the three components of his judicial philosophy—his democratic model, his moral relativism, and his approach to constitutional interpretation—interact with his ordering of values. By placing major emphasis on the conditional nature of property interests, he has taken the position that states may define, regulate, and take away property so long as they employ the correct procedures— procedures the states themselves have provided.

A case in which a discharged federal employee argued that he had a right to a hearing even though there was no statutory provision for it gave Rehnquist his first opportunity to explain his view of the new property. When Wayne Kennedy, a nonproba-

[5] There was no formal tenure system, but the *Faculty Guide* stated that "[t]he Administration of the College wishes the faculty member to feel that he has permanent tenure as long as his teaching services are satisfactory and as long as he displays a cooperative attitude toward his co-workers and his superiors, and as long as he is happy in his work" (quoted in *Sinderman*, 408 U.S. at 600).

tionary civil servant, was discharged for publicly accusing a colleague of bribery, he argued that he had a property interest in his continued employment and, therefore, had a right to a trial-type hearing conducted by an impartial hearing officer before he could be removed from his position. He argued that the statute that provided the procedures for removal of federal civil service employees denied him due process because it created a property interest in continuing employment by stipulating that an employee could be removed only for "cause," but then failed to require a full adversary hearing for the determination of that "cause."[6]

In Arnett v. Kennedy (416 U.S. 134 [1974]) the Court held that the discharge did not conflict with the constitutional guarantee of due process. Rehnquist wrote a plurality opinion for himself, Stewart, and Chief Justice Burger in which he noted that the statute created an "expectancy" that an employee would not be removed except for "such cause as will promote the efficiency of [the] service" (quoted in Arnett, 416 U.S. at 151–52). He emphasized that the same section of the statute provided for procedures to determine the cause for removal. A trial-type hearing was not included among those procedures. Thus, the statute created the property interest and defined the procedures for the removal of that interest; such a scheme did not create a constitutional problem, as Rehnquist explained: "[W]here the grant of a substantive right is inextricably intertwined with the limitations on the procedures which are to be employed in determining that right, a litigant in the position of appellee must take the bitter with the sweet" (ibid., 153–54). He admonished the Court not to restrain Congress from enacting a legislative compromise that granted

---

[6] The Lloyd–La Follette Act (5 U.S.C. 7501) provides that "[a]n individual in the competitive service may be removed or suspended without pay only for such cause as will promote the efficiency of the service." The procedures established for removal are as follows:
"An individual in the competitive service whose removal or suspension without pay is sought is entitled to reasons in writing and to—
"(1) notice of the action sought and of any charges preferred against him;
"(2) a copy of the charges;
"(3) a reasonable time for filing a written answer to the charges, with affidavits; and
"(4) a written decision on the answer at the earliest practicable date."
Additionally, the statute provides that "[e]xamination of witnesses, trial, or hearing is not required but may be provided in the discretion of the individual directing the removal or suspension without pay" (quoted in Arnett v. Kennedy, 416 U.S. 134, 140).

governmental employees security against being dismissed without cause. Further, he noted that the protection offered by the due process clause varies widely according to the interest involved: "Here the property interest which appellee had in his employment was itself conditioned by the procedural limitations which had accompanied the grant of that interest" (ibid., 155).

He argued that his analysis of the new property was consistent with the principles set out in Stewart's earlier assertion that property interests are not created by the Constitution but by existing rules or understandings that stem from the law. In fact, although Rehnquist built upon the earlier analysis, his opinion diverged widely from the thrust of Stewart's new property opinions.[7] Stewart had strongly suggested that once a property interest is created by a statutory provision, constitutional requirements of due process are brought into play. The benefit cannot be removed except through proper procedures, which presumably would include a hearing. In short, once Congress or a state creates a substantive right, such as a property interest in employment, principles of procedural due process will apply, and regardless of whether the law has provided for it, a hearing will be required.

Rehnquist's opinion, in contrast, came quite close to asserting that when lawmakers create a property interest in the form of an expectation of continuing employment, they may choose the procedures for the removal of that interest. Since they will not be limited by constitutional principles of due process, they may elect not to provide for any procedures at all. Rehnquist's analysis of the new property in *Arnett* suggested that because property interests are created by law, they may be limited and even obliterated by law. All that due process requires is that the procedures defined in the law be followed.

---

[7] Justice Powell's concurring opinion in which Justice Blackmun joined asserted that Rehnquist's opinion was incompatible with Stewart's earlier opinions. Rehnquist's opinion would, Powell argued, "lead directly to the conclusion that whatever the nature of an individual's statutorily created property interest, deprivation of that interest could be accomplished without notice or a hearing at any time" (*Arnett*, 416 U.S. at 167). Powell's dissent in Goss v. Lopez (419 U.S. 565 [1975]), however, suggested that his approach was akin to Rehnquist's: "Thus the very legislation which 'defines' the 'dimension' of the student's entitlement, while providing a right to education generally, does not establish this right free of discipline imposed in accord with Ohio law. Rather, the right is encompassed in the entire package of statutory provisions governing education in Ohio—of which the power to suspend is one" (ibid., 586–87).

In 1976, Rehnquist, writing for a five-person majority, held that damage to one's reputation does not constitute a deprivation of any interest protected by the due process clause of the Fourteenth Amendment (Paul v. Davis, 424 U.S. 693). In that case the Louisville, Kentucky, police chief had distributed eight hundred flyers to local merchants identifying active shoplifters. The flyers contained the name and photograph of Edward Davis, who had never been convicted of shoplifting. Davis brought suit under 42 U.S.C. Section 1983, claiming that he had been deprived "under color of law" of a right secured by the due process clause of the Fourteenth Amendment.[8] Rehnquist found that since state law did not extend a legal guarantee of enjoyment of reputation, there was no right to reputation protected by due process. Consequently, there could be no cause of action under Section 1983.

The opinions he wrote in *Paul v. Davis* and *Arnett v. Kennedy* highlight the three components of Rehnquist's judicial philosophy. First, his democratic model was readily apparent in his assertion that property interests are created by statutory provisions. Property rights come into existence by virtue of legislative enactment. Second, his moral relativism was plain in his contention that property rights are totally dependent on their enactment into the positive law; they have no value, indeed, no existence, outside of legislative enactment. The combination of the democratic model and moral relativism support the position that the procedures required by due process include only those that the lawmakers have provided. Finally, Rehnquist's approach to constitutional interpretation and his use of literalism as a technique of analysis were implicit in the two opinions. The words of the due process clauses in the Constitution, in his view, mean that although a person may not be deprived of property without due process of law, he or she may be deprived of property *with* due process of law—that is, through the proper procedures. Due process, a procedural guarantee in Rehnquist's view, does not include any substantive element; due process conveys nothing more than the words stated in the text.

His opinions in both cases indicated his preference for legisla-

---

[8] Section 1983 provides: "Every person who, under color of any statute, ordinance, regulation, custom, or usage, of any State or Territory, subjects, or causes to be subjected, any citizen of the United States or person within the jurisdiction thereof to the deprivation of any rights, privileges, or immunities secured by the Constitution and laws, shall be liable to the party injured in an action at law, suit in equity, or other proper proceeding for redress."

tive definitions of property rights. But whereas *Arnett* involved a provision in the federal law, *Paul v. Davis* involved a suit against state officials. Federalism issues thus came into play, and Rehnquist's opinion reflected clearly the preeminent value he places on state interests. He made plain that he considered that the power to establish a property right resides with the state. He also expressed his concern that Section 1983 could interfere with the states' ability to manage their own criminal justice systems when he stated that

> [r]espondent's construction would seem almost necessarily to result in every legally cognizable injury which may have been inflicted by a state official acting under "color of law" establishing a violation of the Fourteenth Amendment. We think it would come as a great surprise to those who drafted and shepherded the adoption of that Amendment to learn that it worked such a result. (*Paul*, 424 U.S. at 699)

His approach would allow states to make their own rules regarding the rights of the new property. The states would create such rights and could remove them so long as they followed the rules they had provided. In short, the states would define "property" and "due process of law."

THE NEW PROPERTY ACCORDING TO THE MAJORITY

Although Rehnquist's "bitter-sweet" analysis commanded only a three-person plurality in *Arnett*, Justice Stevens's opinion in Bishop v. Wood (426 U.S. 341 [1976]) suggested that five members of the Court, at least for the moment, were willing to go along with Rehnquist's analysis of the new property. In *Bishop*, the Court held that a police officer who was classified by a city ordinance as a permanent employee was not deprived of a property interest protected by the due process clause when he was discharged without a hearing. Like Rehnquist's opinion in *Arnett*, Stevens's opinion in *Bishop* emphasized that property interests are created and defined by statutory provisions. Stevens conceded that a property interest in employment could have been created by the ordinance defining the terms of the officer's employment. His examination of the ordinance, however, revealed that while it could be construed as conferring a guarantee of continuing employment, it could also be read as simply conditioning an employee's removal on compliance with certain specified procedures. The district court had held that under state law the employee "held his position at the will and pleasure of the city" (quoted in *Bishop*, 426 U.S. at 345) and the court of appeals had agreed. Consequently, the police officer's discharge did not violate any property interest protected by the due process clause.[9] Indeed, he had no property interest in his job because none had been created by state law. All that was required was that the procedures for removal specified in the ordinance be followed.

There were additional indications of agreement on the part of other justices with Rehnquist's approach to the new property.[10] Several decisions between 1975 and 1980 either questioned the existence of a property right in a particular governmental benefit or held that the process that provided for the benefit's withdrawal was all that was due. In its treatment of the new property the Court, albeit with some exceptions,[11] appeared to follow Rehnquist's line of reasoning.[12] In his 1977 analysis of the status of the new property, William Van Alstyne characterized the "land of 'due process of law' " as a "veritable desert" (1977, 470).

Subsequently, a majority of the Court explicitly rejected the "bitter-sweet" approach. In 1982 the Court held that a discharged employee had a property interest in having a state Fair Employment Practices Commission consider charges of employment discrimination (Logan v. Zimmerman Brush Company, 455 U.S. 422). Justice Blackmun, speaking for the majority, asserted:

> Each of our due process cases has recognized, either explicitly or implicitly, that because "minimum [procedural] requirements [are] a matter of federal law, they are not dimin-

[9] The police officer had been told that he was dismissed for failure to follow orders and for poor attendance at training classes. The evidence showed that these charges were false, but the Court chose not to become involved: "The Due Process Clause . . . is not a guarantee against incorrect or ill-advised personnel decisions" (*Bishop*, 426 U.S. at 350).

[10] For example, see Powell's statement in Goss v. Lopez, note 7 above.

[11] See, for example, Memphis Light, Gas and Water Divison v. Craft (436 U.S. 1 [1978]). Holding that a property interest exists in continued utility service, Justice Powell stated: "Although the underlying substantive interest is created by 'an independent source such as state law,' federal constitutional law determines whether that interest rises to the level of a 'legitimate claim of entitlement' protected by the due process clause" (*Craft*, 436 U.S. at 9).

[12] For example, in Mathews v. Eldridge (424 U.S. 319 [1976]), the Court held that an evidentiary hearing is not required prior to termination of Social Security disability payments. In Board of Curators of the University of Missouri v. Horowitz (435 U.S. 78 [1978]), Rehnquist, speaking for the majority, held that assuming the existence of a liberty or property interest in continuing as a medical student, a student dismissed for academic reasons was not entitled to a hearing.

ished by the fact that the State may have specified its own procedures that it may deem adequate for determining the preconditions to adverse official action." Indeed, any other conclusion would allow the State to destroy at will virtually any state-created property interest. (*Logan*, 455 U.S. at 432, citations omitted)

In 1985 the Court held that school district employees who had been terminated were entitled to a pre-termination opportunity to respond and post-termination administrative procedures as provided by the state law (Cleveland Board of Education v. Loudermill, 470 U.S. 532, 105 S.Ct. 1487). Justice White, writing for the majority, reiterated the Court's rejection of Rehnquist's approach:

In light of [previous cases] it is settled that the "bitter with the sweet" approach misconceives the constitutional guarantee. If a clearer holding is needed, we provide it today. The point is straightforward: the Due Process Clause provides that certain substantive rights—life, liberty, and property—cannot be deprived except pursuant to constitutionally adequate procedures. The categories of substance and procedure are distinct. Were the rule otherwise, the Clause would be reduced to a mere tautology. "Property" cannot be defined by the procedures provided for its deprivation any more than can life or liberty. (*Loudermill*, 105 S.Ct. at 1493)

In that case Rehnquist remained loyal to his bitter-sweet approach, but he was alone. In dissent, he denied that the state statute bestowed a property right on the discharged employees. He found the statute to be similar to the one in *Arnett* insofar as it conferred upon civil service employees a form of tenure during good behavior and then prescribed the procedures by which that tenure could be terminated. The majority, he remonstrated, had "seiz[ed] upon one of several paragraphs in a unitary statute to proclaim that in that paragraph the State has inexorably conferred upon a civil service employee something which it is powerless under the United States Constitution to qualify in the next paragraph of the statute" (ibid., 1502). He asserted that the Court had departed from the principle that property interests are not created by the Constitution but stem from other sources such as state law. He evoked memories of "the right-privilege" distinction by admonishing the Court to decide future "new property" cases on the basis of the "bitter-sweet" approach: "[O]ne who avails himself of government entitlements accepts the grant of tenure along with its inherent limitations" (ibid., 1504).

In the face of the majority's unequivocal rejection of his "bitter-sweet" analysis in favor of an approach that offers more protection to the "new property," Rehnquist has steadfastly adhered to the proposition that the property rights that are protected by the due process clause are created by the law—state or federal—not the Constitution. Because those rights are legislatively created, legislatures may prescribe the procedures for their removal. As long as those rules are followed—whatever they may be—the requirements of due process have been fulfilled.

OTHER "PROPERTY"

Two additional cases,[13] both of which involved property of a different and somewhat more traditional nature, further illustrate Rehnquist's conception of property rights in relation to the statutory law and the Constitution. In Duke Power Co. v. Carolina Environmental Study Group, Inc. (438 U.S. 59 [1978]) the Supreme Court was asked to consider a due process challenge to the Price-Anderson Act (42 U.S.C. Section 2210), which limits liability for a nuclear incident to $560 million. Two organizations and forty individuals who lived near planned nuclear power plants brought suit against the Nuclear Regulatory Commission and Duke Power Company claiming that the Price-Anderson Act's limits on recovery constituted arbitrary governmental action adversely affecting their property rights in violation of the due process clause of the Fifth Amendment. Further, they alleged that in the event of a nuclear accident their property would be "taken" without any assurance of just compensation and that the act was the instrument of the taking because without it "there would be no power plants and no possibility of an accident" (Duke Power, 438 U.S. at 69).

Chief Justice Burger, in an opinion for himself and five of the other justices, held that the $560 million ceiling was a reasonable

[13] Tribe (1985a, 171–74) analyzed the two cases discussed in this section to support his argument that the Court takes a narrow view of nontraditional property claims: "For although the Supreme Court has effectively enshrined traditional property rights that seem to it obvious, rendering them practically impervious to the vicissitudes of positive law, the Court has been reluctant to grant any degree of constitutional protection to less conventional property claims" (p. 171).

method of encouraging the private development of the production of electric energy through nuclear power, considering "the extremely remote possiblity of an accident where the liability would exceed the limitation and Congress' . . . [and the] statutory commitment to 'take whatever action is deemed necessary and appropriate to protect the public from the consequences of' such disaster" (ibid., 86, citation omitted). Thus, the act did not violate the due process clause.

Before reaching the merits, Burger considered three preliminary issues: whether the district court had jurisdiction, whether the plaintiffs had standing, and whether the case was ripe. He resolved all three in the affirmative. When he considered the threshold issue, Burger found that the cause of action against the Nuclear Regulatory Commission was based directly on the Constitution and that the action was not patently without merit; the allegations were sufficient to sustain jurisdiction.

Rehnquist wrote an opinion concurring in the judgment in which he argued that the district court had no jurisdiction. He disagreed with Burger's assessment that the complaint stated a claim under the Constitution. Instead, Rehnquist read the complaint as stating a claim under North Carolina law providing a right of action. Under this reading, the question of the constitutionality of the Price-Anderson Act would arise only if Duke Power were to invoke the act as a defense to a suit for recovery based on the state right of action. Consequently, the district court had no jurisdiction, for "mere anticipation of a possible federal defense to a state cause of action is not sufficient to invoke the federal question jurisdiction of the district courts" (ibid., 97).

Burger's analysis on the merits may have been dubious, and it is possible that the best explanation of the Court's decision can be found in Laurence Tribe's comment that the decision reflected "a judgment by the Court that the 'property' of which plaintiffs claimed to have been deprived simply did not look like anything the Court was prepared to call property; it was far too problematic" (1985, 173). At any rate, Rehnquist refrained from any consideration of the property issue, focusing solely on the jurisdictional question. He thereby took a position that would have precluded any judicial consideration of an alleged interference with property rights.

In Dames & Moore v. Regan (453 U.S. 654 [1981]), Rehnquist authored an opinion for the Court in which he more directly indicated his view of property rights. In response to the Iranian hostage crisis, President Carter, pursuant to the International Emergency Economic Powers Act, blocked the removal or transfer of all Iranian assets within the jurisdiction of the United States. After the American hostages were released pursuant to an agreement with Iran, President Carter issued a series of executive orders to implement the terms of the agreement. The orders revoked all licenses to attach Iranian funds and ordered that all Iranian assets be transferred to the Federal Reserve Bank of New York for eventual transfer to Iran. The result was that creditors such as Dames & Moore, a company that had a contract with the Atomic Energy Organization of Iran under which it was owed $3,436,694.30 plus interest for services performed, had no way to satisfy its claims. Dames & Moore filed an action in district court subsequent to the freezing of assets but prior to the president's issuing of executive orders and was awarded the amount claimed. The district court, however, vacated its judgment in light of the executive orders. Dames & Moore then filed another action in the district court, alleging that the actions of the president exceeded his statutory and constitutional powers and were unconstitutional to the extent that they adversely affected Dames & Moore's ability to recover the funds.

In his opinion for the Court, Rehnquist held that the president had the authority to settle the claims against Iran. Rejecting Dames & Moore's claim that the president's order nullifying the attachments of Iranian assets amounted to an unconstitutional taking of property, he noted that the attachments were " 'revocable,' 'contingent,' and in 'every sense subordinate to the President's power' . . . [B]ecause of the President's authority to prevent or condition attachments, and because of the orders he issued to this effect, petitioner did not acquire any 'property' interest in its attachments of the sort that would support a constitutional claim for compensation" (*Dames & Moore*, 453 U.S. at 674, n. 6). Rehnquist concluded that Dames & Moore still had the opportunity to bring suit against the United States in the Court of Claims on the grounds that the suspension of the claim constituted an unconstitutional taking of property. Still, the thrust of his opinion was clear: property rights are contingent upon the positive (statutory) law. The guarantees of due process in the Constitution provide only minimal protection against violation of procedural rules, and there are no substantive constraints on the content of those rules.

Conclusion

If property interests can be defined by federal or state procedural guidelines in a statute, an entitlement can be withdrawn at any time without constraint from the due process clauses. Rehnquist's approach to the new property would minimize judicial review of federal laws as well as administrative actions. Moreover, when state laws and state administrative acts are challenged on due process grounds, the bitter-sweet approach would severely curtail federal judicial intervention and would deprive the due process clause of the power to protect citizens against arbitrary and unfair official state activity. In short, his approach suggests the preeminent value he places on federalism insofar as it would protect state autonomy at the expense of property rights.

Rehnquist's approach to the new property also reflects the legal positivism in his judicial philosophy. The bitter-sweet approach consistently asserts that property rights are created, defined, and limited by statutory provisions. Additionally, his opinions have underlined the constancy of his belief that beyond the rights granted by express statutory or constitutional provisions, no rights of property exist. Not only are property interests created by law, but so are the procedures for taking away such interests. Thus, principles of due process are satisfied so long as provisions in the law are followed. The meaning of due process is, thereby, reduced to "due process of those laws which the legislature provided . . . what you get is what you see" (Van Alstyne 1977, 469).

The present chapter has been limited to an analysis of Rehnquist's treatment of nontraditional property. In the following chapter, in which I examine his decision making in cases that have involved the rights of traditional property, I show that although he has been more supportive of such rights than of nontraditional property rights,[14] both categories of property, in Rehnquist's view, are created, defined, and limited by the positive law.

[14] One commentator has argued that Rehnquist accords more protection to property under the just compensation clause than to property under the due process clause ("Justice Rehnquist's Theory," 1984). I do not dispute that contention but, rather, make the point that Rehnquist offers neither type of property protection beyond that prescribed in the positive law.

SIX

The Rights of Traditional Property

Justice Robert H. Jackson captured the essence of the legal positivist's view of property rights when he stated that "not all economic interests are 'property rights'; only those economic advantages are 'rights' which have the law back of them, and only when they are so recognized may courts compel others to forbear from interfering with them or to compensate for their invasion" (U.S. v. Willow River Power Co., 324 U.S. 499, 502 [1945]). The preceding chapter examined Rehnquist's treatment of nontraditional property, demonstrating that he values federalism over such rights and, indeed, that he finds scant constitutional protection for the new property. In the present chapter I analyze his treatment of traditional property rights.

A legal positivist would not accord property rights—of either type—any protection beyond that provided in the positive law and would be likely to construe the states' authority to regulate property broadly. The present chapter shows that Rehnquist's judicial philosophy, with its three components of the democratic model, moral relativism, and his approach to constitutional interpretation, entails a positivist conception of traditional property rights. Additionally, this chapter illustrates that when traditional property rights have clashed with federalism, the latter has prevailed, with rare exception.[1]

An earlier version of part of chapter 6 appeared in "Federalism and Property Rights: An Examination of Justice Rehnquist's Legal Positivism," *Western Political Quarterly* 39, no. 2 (1986): 250–64.

[1] Owen Fiss and Charles Krauthammer (1982, 21) have argued that Rehnquist places a high value on federalism because it is "consonant with classical laissez faire theory which reduces the function of government to protecting private exchanges and the aim of the Constitution to protecting the rights and expectations of property holders." Their assertion, in essence, is that for Rehnquist, property rights constitute the controlling value and federalism is a means of protecting that value. Further, it has been argued that Rehnquist accords less constitutional protection to nontraditional property under the due process clause, discussed in the previous chapter, than he does to traditional property under the just compensation and contract clauses ("Rediscovering the Contract Clause," 1984). See also Denvir (1983), who argues that Rehnquist votes to expand the protection of indi-

The due process clauses of the Fifth and Fourteenth amendments prohibit the federal government and the states from depriving persons of "life, liberty, or property, without due process of law." Two additional constitutional provisions that protect the rights of private property are the just compensation clause of the Fifth Amendment,[2] which prohibits the taking of property for public use without just compensation, and the contract clause of Article I, Section 10, which forbids states from passing any "[l]aw impairing the Obligation of Contracts."

I begin this chapter with a consideration of Rehnquist's opinions in cases in which the Court has heard challenges to governmental action under the just compensation clause and then proceed to an analysis of several cases in which state or local laws that threatened property were challenged on other grounds. Additionally, I have included an examination of the implications of Rehnquist's votes in several cases that have involved the contract clause.

LEGISLATIVE DETERMINATIONS OF PUBLIC USE

The language of the just compensation clause of the Fifth Amendment suggests a strict prohibition on the taking of property for private use. Since the 1920s, however, the Supreme Court has regularly allowed legislatures to decide what constitutes public use.

In 1984 the Court reaffirmed its deference to legislative determinations of public use when it unanimously upheld the Hawaii Land Reform Act (Hawaii Housing Authority v. Midkiff, 467 U.S. 229 [1984]). In order to redress problems created by concentrated land ownership, the act set up a condemnation scheme whereby long-term renters of certain designated property could ask the Hawaii Housing Authority to require owners to sell their land to them. In her opinion for the Court, Justice O'Connor noted that the exercise of the power of eminent domain need only be ration-

---

vidual rights in the areas of the contract and takings clauses and that his record is best explained by his model of constitutional interpretation, based on a social ideal of individualism and rejection of paternalism. In that view, the law, for Rehnquist, must protect property that was lawfully acquired and ensure the existence of a framework for contractual exchange.

[2] The Fifth Amendment is addressed to the federal government rather than the states; however, the just compensation clause applies to the states through the due process clause of the Fourteenth Amendment (see Chicago, Burlington and Quincy Railroad v. Chicago, 166 U.S. 226 [1897]).

ally related to a conceivable public purpose. By enacting the law, the Hawaii legislature had attempted to reduce the social and economic evils of land concentration and had adopted a rational approach in doing so. Rehnquist joined the Court in a decision that strongly supported extensive state power to regulate property rights.

When Regulation Becomes a Taking

The just compensation clause prohibits the actual physical takeover by the government of private property without just compensation. One commentator succinctly summarized that requirement as follows: "If the government wants to convert a private house into a post office, or run a new highway through a farm, or build a dam which will flood nearby land, it is going to have to compensate the losses sustained as a result of these activities" (Sax 1964, 36).

One of the major questions raised by the clause is, What actually constitutes a taking? Generally, the Supreme Court's pronouncements have established that governmental regulation of property may constitute a taking for which compensation is required if the regulation prevents the use of the property so that its value is virtually destroyed (Tribe 1978, 460). But if a regulation is an exercise of the police power undertaken to protect the health, safety, and morals of the community, the resultant economic loss to the property owner will not be considered a taking and compensation will not be required.

The Supreme Court's efforts to distinguish between an exercise of the police power and a taking for which compensation is required began in the late nineteenth century (Mugler v. Kansas, 123 U.S. 623 [1887]) and have yielded results that commentators have referred to as a "crazy-quilt pattern of Supreme Court doctrine" (Dunham 1962, 63) and as "ethically unsatisfying" (Michelman 1967).[3] Laurence Tribe (1985a) objected to what he found to be ad hoc decisions by the Burger Court defining the taking of property, which "perpetuate . . . the myth that the just compensation clause is a template that judges may simply lay atop the facts so as to detect a taking if any rough pieces are seen to pro-

[3] See Sax (1964, 1971) for an overview and criticism of the Supreme Court's doctrine in the area of the just compensation clause and suggestions for improvement. See Ackerman (1977, 88–167) for a helpful "ordinary observer," or layman's, explanation of the problem.

115

trude beyond the edges" (p. 179). In short, the Supreme Court has not made it clear when a regulation becomes a taking.

A consistent willingness to agree with property owners that a regulation on their property amounts to a taking would be a strong indication of support for property rights over federalism. On the other hand, opinions that only rarely acknowledge that a regulation constitutes a taking would suggest support for federalism over property rights. Unfortunately, Rehnquist has not made his position regarding the distinction between a regulation and a taking completely clear.[4] He has joined decisions that have had the effect of protecting property rights and has written both majority and dissenting opinions that elevate property rights above the positive law. In the following analysis, I nevertheless seek to demonstrate that Rehnquist places federalism in a higher position than property rights in his scheme of values.

In 1978 a six-member majority held that the application of New York City's Landmarks Preservation Law to prohibit the construction of a fifty-three-story office building on top of Grand Central Station was not a taking for which compensation was required (Penn Central Transportation Co. v. New York City, 438 U.S. 104). Justice Brennan, the author of the majority opinion, affirmed that laws that seek to preserve structures and areas with special historical architectural or cultural significance are permissible. He noted that although some owners are burdened by such laws more than others, the Court would not reject the city council's judgment that "the preservation of landmarks benefits all New York citizens and structures, both economically and by improving the quality of life in the city as a whole" (Penn Central, 438 U.S. at 134). Reasoning that the Landmarks Law did not interfere with the uses of the building as a railroad terminal with office space and concessions, and that not all development was

---

[4] For example, when the Court held that interest earned on private funds deposited in a court in an interpleader action is an unconstitutional taking and that the interest must follow the principle to be distributed among creditors, the decision was unanimous (Webb's Fabulous Pharmacies Inc. v. Beckworth, 449 U.S. 155 [1980]). Rehnquist joined Justice Marshall's majority opinion in Loretto v. Teleprompter Manhatten CATV (458 U.S. 419 [1982]), which held that a permanent physical invasion of real property sanctioned by law constitutes a taking. On the other hand, Rehnquist joined Brennan's majority opinion when he held that the application of the Migratory Bird Treaty Act to prohibit the sale of feathers from birds killed before they came under the protection of the act did not constitute a taking: "[T]he denial of one traditional property right does not always amount to a taking" (Andrus v. Allard, 444 U.S. 51 [1979]).

prohibited, he concluded that the restrictions were "substantially related to the general welfare and permit reasonable beneficial use of the landmark site" (ibid., 138).

Rehnquist dissented, arguing that the law did, indeed, constitute a taking. Objecting that "[i]n a very literal sense," the actions of the city violated the just compensation clause (ibid., 142), he explained that the application of the Landmarks Law did not fall within either of the exceptions to the rule that taking property requires just compensation. First, the application of the law to Grand Central Station would not constitute a taking if the proposed addition would be dangerous to the health, safety, or morals of the community. The proposed office building, however, was in full compliance with zoning and other legal requirements. Rehnquist found an example of his second exception to the requirement of just compensation in zoning laws that "at times reduce . . . individual property values, [but] the burden is shared relatively evenly and . . . it was reasonable to conclude that on the whole an individual who is harmed by one aspect of the zoning will be benefited by another" (ibid., 147).

He found that, unlike a zoning restriction, the Landmarks Law imposed a multimillion dollar loss that was not offset by the preservation of the other landmarks of the city. The financial burden imposed by the application of the Landmarks Law fell disproportionately on Penn Central. In short, not only did the law not fall within the police power exception to the requirement of just compensation, but it unfairly required Penn Central to bear the burden of the cost of the landmark preservation. Moreover, he did not find convincing New York City's argument that there was no taking involved because Penn Central was not deprived of all reasonable value of its property: "A taking does not become a noncompensable exercise of police power simply because the government in its grace allows the owner to make some 'reasonable' use of his property" (ibid., 149). For Rehnquist, in short, the character of the invasion was sufficient to render it a taking.

Rehnquist's analysis in *Penn Central* was marked by its literalism; nevertheless, his opinion suggested that, in his view, zoning ordinances do not constitute takings so long as they distribute the burden relatively evenly and if it is reasonable to conclude that an individual who is harmed by one aspect of the zoning will benefit by another. When the Court upheld a zoning ordinance that restricted building, Rehnquist joined the other members of the Court (Agins v. City of Tiburon, 447 U.S. 255

[1980]). The appellants had acquired five acres of land for residential development. The city then modified its zoning ordinances to restrict building on the land to five single-family residences. Justice Powell, speaking for the unanimous Court, held that the zoning ordinances did not constitute a taking because they substantially advanced legitimate governmental interests in protecting the residents from the ill effects of urbanization. In addition, the use of the land was not completely denied, and appellants would share with other landowners the benefits and burdens of the city's exercise of its police power.

In *Penn Central* Rehnquist voted to invalidate the city's attempt to preserve historic landmarks and to protect Penn Central's freedom to use its land and air rights in the most profitable manner. In *Agins* he voted to uphold zoning ordinances that limited the ability of developers to make a profit by restricting the number of houses that could be built on their land. The positions he took in the two cases, at first glance, appear to be inconsistent. On careful examination, however, it is possible to discern a factual difference between the cases that revolved around the distinction between zoning laws—reasonable exercises of the police powers—and a landmark preservation law that imposed additional restrictions on selected property.

Rehnquist's distinction between the Landmarks Law and a zoning ordinance appears to be based on some notion of fairness: zoning laws treat all owners within a designated area the same "not only for the benefit of the municipality as a whole but also for the common benefit of one another" (*Penn Central*, 438 U.S. at 141). In contrast, under the Landmarks Law "a relatively few individual buildings, all separated from one another, are singled out and treated differently from surrounding buildings" (ibid., 140). Thus, Rehnquist's dissenting opinion in *Penn Central* considered with his vote in *Agins* suggests that he finds a limit on state regulation of property where such regulation goes beyond zoning for the public's benefit and becomes arbitrary and unfair. Although the exact location of the line that he draws to distinguish between a regulation and a taking is far from clear, he plainly seems to have found some limits to a state's authority to regulate property. The source of those limits is the just compensation clause of the Fifth Amendment.

In *Agins* the Court left open the question of whether landowners may recover damages when they have been deprived of the use of their property by a regulatory ordinance.[5] The following term, confronted with that question, the majority refrained from answering it by finding that the Court did not have jurisdiction to review a case because of the lack of a final judgment from the lower court (San Diego Gas and Electric Co. v. City of San Diego, 450 U.S. 621 [1981]). In that case the owners of a 214-acre parcel of land sought damages from the city claiming that the city's rezoning of their land and its adoption of an open space plan constituted a taking. Rehnquist agreed with the decision to dismiss the appeal. He stated in a concurring opinion, however, that if there had been a final judgment by the court below, he would have had little difficulty in agreeing with much of what Justice Brennan said in his dissenting opinion that reached the merits of the appellants' claim. Brennan would have ruled that damages could be awarded for a regulatory taking.

Rehnquist's opinion in *Penn Central* and his statement in *San Diego Gas and Electric* might suggest that he values property rights over federalism. Similarly, his opinion for the majority in United States v. Security Industrial Bank (459 U.S. 70 [1982]) might be construed as evidence of a propensity to elevate the protection of property rights above the positive law. At issue in that case was a provision in the Bankruptcy Reform Act of 1978 permitting individual debtors in bankruptcy proceedings to avoid liens on certain property. In a series of bankruptcy cases, small loan companies claimed that application of the statute to liens acquired before its enactment would constitute a taking in violation of the Fifth Amendment. Rehnquist wrote an opinion for the Court in which he held that the statute was not intended to be applied retroactively to destroy property rights. Although he based his decision on construction of the statute, in dicta, he suggested that the lien avoidance statute would constitute a taking. He expressed doubt that retroactive destruction of the liens comported with the Fifth Amendment insofar as the statute involved

[5] The challengers sought a damage award for inverse condemnation—"a shorthand description of the manner in which a landowner recovers just compensation for taking of his property when condemnation proceedings have not been instituted" (United States v. Clarke, 445 U.S. 253, 257 [1980]). The California Supreme Court held that the sole remedies for such a taking under California law were mandamus and declaratory judgment. Appellants could not recover damages for inverse condemnation even if the zoning ordinance constituted a taking. The United States Supreme Court left open the question of whether a state may limit the remedies available to a person whose land has been taken without just compensation because it found that there had been no taking.

the complete destruction of the property rights of secured creditors and was inconsistent with the characterizations in the state law of what constitutes property. Although Rehnquist's opinion suggests his support for the property interests of the loan companies, it is important to emphasize that it was a federal law—the Bankruptcy Reform Act—that operated to modify the property rights created by the state. The ordering of values actually suggested by Rehnquist's opinion is one of a preference for state autonomy over federal regulation rather than for property rights over state law.

The Right to Exclude

In Kaiser Aetna v. United States (444 U.S. 164 [1979]) the Court considered the extent to which a fishpond—private property under Hawaii law—became subject to federal regulation as a result of its development into a marina connected to a bay and to the Pacific Ocean. Rehnquist, writing for a six-person majority, held that the marina was subject to regulation by the Corps of Engineers as a navigable water of the United States. Although such "navigational servitude" did not constitute a compensable taking, he held, the government's attempt to require a public right of access to the marina did amount to a taking. He asserted that "[t]he 'right to exclude,' so universally held to be a fundamental element of the property right, falls within this category of interests that the Government cannot take without compensation" (Kaiser Aetna, 444 U.S. at 180). He went on to note that a right of access would constitute an actual physical invasion of the privately owned marina. An important factor in his decision, he indicated, was that the marina had been constructed by private means with the expectation of remaining private. The owner of the pond, Rehnquist noted, invested substantial amounts of money in making improvements and "[t]he Government contends that as a result of one of these improvements, . . . the owner has somehow lost one of the most essential sticks in the bundle of rights that are commonly characterized as property—the right to exclude others" (ibid., 176).

In Kaiser Aetna Rehnquist protected property rights from governmental interference. His opinion was, however, consistent with his positivist view of property and with the high value he places on federalism. It is important to point out that the property at stake, the marina, was private under state law, and he denied the federal government the power to require a right of access to that property. Thus, his opinion indicates his preference not for the abstract rights of property but for those which are created by state law. Moreover, his opinion not only manifests his desire to prevent the federal government from snatching sticks out of the bundle of property rights but also from interfering with the state governmental process.

Rehnquist's majority opinion in Pruneyard Shopping Center v. Robins (447 U.S. 74 [1980]), which involved the right of access to a privately owned shopping center for expressive purposes, provides perhaps the clearest illustration of the value he places on federalism over property rights. Although the Supreme Court has ruled that the First Amendment does not guarantee the right to freedom of expression in privately owned shopping centers (Lloyd v. Tanner, 407 U.S. 551 [1972]), nothing in that decision, Rehnquist asserted, limited "the authority of the State to exercise its police power or its sovereign right to adopt in its own Constitution individual liberties more expansive than those conferred by the Federal Constitution" (Pruneyard, 447 U.S. at 81).

The owners of the shopping center claimed that California's constitutional provision that protects the right of free speech in privately owned shopping centers amounted to a taking of property in violation of the Fifth Amendment. Rejecting that claim, Rehnquist supported the state's broad authority to regulate property. He reasoned that although there "has literally been a 'taking' ... 'not every destruction or injury to property by governmental action has been held to be a "taking" in the constitutional sense'" (ibid., 82, quoting Armstrong v. United States, 364 U.S. 40). He found that neither the value nor the use of the property as a shopping center was impaired, since the right to exclude people who wished to express their views was not essential to the use or the economic value of the property. Distinguishing *Kaiser Aetna*, he noted that in that case the government's attempt to create a public right of access to the marina interfered with the owner's expectations that the pond would remain private, "[n]or as a general proposition is the United States, as opposed to the several States, possessed of residual authority that enables it to define 'property' in the first instance" (*Pruneyard*, 447 U.S. at 84). Although Rehnquist did not address the question of what constraints the Constitution imposes on a state's authority to define the rights of property, he suggested that the states' power in this area is extensive. His opinion inspired four of the other justices to write concurring opinions in which they stressed the importance of defining the limits on state power to regulate property.[6]

DETERMINING WHAT IS JUST: THE POSITIVIST'S APPROACH

A major question that arises in challenges to regulations under the just compensation clause, in cases in which it has been determined that there has been a taking of property, is how much compensation is "just." Faced with such an issue, a judge who subscribes to the principles of positivism could be expected to defer to the government's determination regarding the proper amount of compensation, whereas a judge who considers property rights to exist independently of the positive law would support the property owner's attempts to obtain as much compensation as possible.

Two of Rehnquist's early opinions, both of which involved the problem of how much compensation is "just," illustrate his positivism. In a 5-to-4 decision in 1973 the Court held that the concept of "just compensation" is measured by what a willing buyer would have paid for improvements, taking into account the possibility that the lease might be renewed (Almota Farmers Elevator and Warehouse Co. v. United States, 409 U.S. 470). In a dissenting opinion Rehnquist objected that the majority had departed from settled doctrine by requiring that compensation be computed in part on an expectancy that was not part of the property taken. He noted that prior cases have established "that the Fifth Amendment does not require, on a taking of property interest, compensation for mere expectancies of profit, or for the frustration of licenses or contractual rights that pertain to the land, but that are not specifically taken and that are not vested property interests" (Almota, 409 U.S. at 482, citations omitted).

In another decision in 1973 Rehnquist wrote for a five-member majority (United States v. Fuller, 409 U.S. 488). At the trial for

---

[6] Justices Blackmun, Marshall, White, and Powell all wrote concurring opinions. Justice Marshall, for example, stated: "I do not understand the Court to suggest that rights of property are to be defined solely by state law, or that there is no federal constitutional barrier to the abrogation of common-law rights by Congress or a state government—the constitutional terms 'life, liberty, and property' do not derive their meaning solely from the positive law" (Pruneyard, 447 U.S. at 93).

the purpose of fixing just compensation for 920 acres of land condemned by the United States, disagreement had arisen over the
question of whether the jury could consider additional value of
the land.[7] The Supreme Court held that the Fifth Amendment
does not require the government to pay for the enhanced value of
the land based on the use of "government permit" land. Rehnquist found that previous cases "go far toward establishing the
general principle that the Government as condemnor may not be
required to compensate a condemnee for elements of value that
the Government has created, or that it might have destroyed"
(Fuller, 409 U.S. at 492).

The positions that Rehnquist took in the two cases might be
construed simply as an indication that when there is a conflict,
he supports the interests of government over those of individuals.[8] Still, his votes, which favored governmental determination
of what is "just" compensation, are clearly consistent with a positivistic conception of property rights.

Some Other Interferences with Property

The positions that Rehnquist took in four cases in which state or
local laws limited property rights further attest to the positivism
that informs his views regarding such rights. The following also
suggests the extent to which he values federalism.

In 1973 he was a member of the majority when the Court upheld a village ordinance that limited the use of land to one-family
dwellings and occupancy of those dwellings to no more than two
unrelated persons. The Court found no infringement of equal
protection or due process in the restriction (Village of Belle Terre
v. Boraas, 416 U.S. 1). Subsequently, the Court invalidated a city
housing ordinance that limited occupancy to single families in
such a way as to prohibit a woman from living with her two
grandsons who were not brothers but cousins (Moore v. City of
East Cleveland, 431 U.S. 494 [1977]). In that case the majority

[7] The owners argued that as a result of the use of the land in combination with
adjoining federal lands for which they held a permit to graze livestock, additional
value of the land should be considered.

[8] One of Shapiro's (1976) propositions regarding Rehnquist's decision making
was that conflicts between an individual and the government should, whenever
possible, be resolved against the individual. His other two propositions were that
conflicts between state and federal authority should be resolved in favor of the
states, and questions of the exercise of federal jurisdiction should be resolved
against such exercise (p. 294).

found only a tenuous relationship between the ordinance and the objectives of the city. It also noted that the usual judicial deference is not appropriate when legislation intrudes on choices concerning family living arrangements. Rehnquist joined Stewart's dissent, which contended that the "city has undisputed power to ordain single-family residential occupancy. And that power plainly carries with it the power to say what a 'family' is" (*Moore*, 431 U.S. at 538–39, citation omitted). While it is possible that Rehnquist's votes to uphold restrictions on nontraditional living arrangements reflect a bias against the poor or a distaste for alternative life-styles—"hippy communes" or unmarried couples living together—his support for the restrictions that clearly constituted intrusions on property rights evidence his positivistic view that local governments have the power to define such rights.

The high value he places on federalism was clear in his votes in the two cases just discussed; that value was also strongly suggested in his dissent in a case in which six members of the Court held that the federal law that provided for retirement pay for army officers precluded a state court from dividing that pay pursuant to state community property laws (McCarty v. McCarty, 453 U.S. 210 [1981]). One might argue that community property laws interfere with private property because they mandate the division of property between a divorced couple. In this case the property to be split was military retirement pay—money a man had earned that could be construed as rightfully his to dispose of as he wished. If Rehnquist subscribed to such a view, it is likely that he would have agreed with the decision of the Court that the military retirement pay law preempted the state community property law. Instead, he accused the majority of misconstruing and misapplying the prior cases that involved federal preemption of state community property law and reiterated his view that property law is a matter of local concern and should be governed by state, not federal, law.

In 1982, the Court invalidated a state law that regulated the withdrawal of groundwater for use in an adjoining state for the reason that the law imposed an impermissible burden on commerce (Sporehase v. Nebraska, 458 U.S. 941). The state law infringed on property rights insofar as it limited a landowner's right to pump water from his or her land across state lines to irrigate his or her own land in an adjoining state. Rehnquist voted to uphold the law; he maintained that a state may regulate natural resources and, thereby, preclude those resources from attaining the status of articles of commerce. If state law does not recognize possession of an item, he argued, it cannot be part of commerce: " 'Commerce' cannot exist in a natural resource that cannot be sold, rented, traded, or transferred, but only used" (*Sporehase*, 458 U.S. at 963). According to Rehnquist, groundwater did not constitute private property because the state did not recognize an ownership interest in it and granted landowners only a right to use it on the land from which it had been extracted. His contention that the states have the authority to define property rights in natural resources—in effect, that the right is contingent upon the state's willingness to grant it—presents yet another indication of his positivistic view of property rights as well as the preeminent value he places on federalism.

In the groundwater case as well as the military pension case, concerns other than those of federalism may have influenced Rehnquist's votes. For example, community property laws may be viewed as protective of traditional family values, and the groundwater law, as protective of natural resources. Such concerns may have combined with the high regard in which Rehnquist holds federalism to lead him to support the challenged state regulations. At any rate, in both cases Rehnquist did, in fact, support state regulations over rights of private property.

The Contract Clause

The contract clause is an explicit constitutional protection of property rights against state infringement. Although the purpose of the clause was to prohibit state legislatures from passing laws postponing or canceling debts and was aimed at private contracts, the Court's earliest pronouncements extended its application to public grants and contracts (Fletcher v. Peck, 6 Cranch 87 [1810], and Dartmouth College v. Woodward, 4 Wheat. 518 [1819]).

The contract clause was the major constitutional provision for the protection of economic rights against state impairment throughout the nineteenth century and the early years of the twentieth (see Hale 1944a, 1944b, 1944c). Its function, however, was superseded by the due process clause of the Fourteenth Amendment.[9] After the Supreme Court in 1934 upheld the Min-

---

[9] Hale (1944c, 890–91) noted that the contract clause and the due process clause tend to coalesce, and the courts might reach the same results "if the contract clause were dropped out of the Constitution."

nesota Mortgage Moratorium Law, which authorized local courts to extend the period of redemption from foreclosure sales (Home Building and Loan Association v. Blaisdell, 290 U.S. 398 [1934]), the clause began to fall into disuse. In that case Chief Justice Hughes stated that "the prohibition is not an absolute one and is not to be read with literal exactness like a mathematical formula" (*Home Building and Loan*, 428). Instead, contract clause analysis must balance the authority of the state "to safeguard the vital interests of its people" with the constitutional limitation on the impairment of contracts. Thus, contracts could be modified to protect the public welfare. Moreover, the Court expanded the notion of the public welfare to include economic needs. The Court increasingly deferred to state legislation and, in fact, seemed to abandon the contract clause as a limitation on the states.

In 1965 Justice Black, in a dissenting opinion, complained that the Court had "balanced away" the limitation on state action imposed by the contract clause (El Paso v. Simmons, 379 U.S. 497, 515). As Laurence Tribe (1985a, 180) noted, "The Court seemed to have adopted the view that contract rights had no special constitutional status, and that statutes impairing contractual obligations would generally be upheld on a rationality test if they arguably promoted the economic welfare of the general public."

In the late 1970s, however, two decisions of the Court appeared to signal a revival of the clause. Although Rehnquist did not write an opinion in either case, he joined majorities in invalidating state laws on the ground that they impaired the obligation of a contract. The two cases are discussed briefly here for two reasons. First, they reflect the three components of his judicial philosophy—particularly his approach to constitutional interpretation. Second, his votes, which at first glance appear to favor property rights at the expense of federalism, need to be explained. If Rehnquist values federalism over property rights he could be expected to take a position in favor of state power by upholding state laws against challenges that they violate the contract clause. But, in fact, he has not done so consistently.

In 1977 he joined the majority when, by a vote of 4 to 3, the Court relied on the contract clause for the first time in almost forty years to invalidate a state law (United States Trust Co. v. New Jersey, 431 U.S. 1).[10] At issue was the constitutionality of a

---

[10] Justice Blackmun wrote the plurality opinion; Burger filed a concurring state-

retroactive repeal of a 1962 statutory covenant that limited the ability of the Port Authority of New York and New Jersey to subsidize rail passenger transportation from revenues and reserves. The port authority was largely financed by bonds sold to the public. The covenant constituted a promise to investors "that revenues and reserves securing the bonds would not be depleted by the Port Authority's operation of deficit-producing passenger railroads beyond the level of 'permitted deficits' " (*United States Trust*, 431 U.S. at 26). Prompted by the energy crisis, the two states enacted statutes in 1974 to repeal the covenant. The repeal made it possible for the states to raise bridge and tunnel tolls and to use the revenue to subsidize improved commuter railroad service. The New Jersey courts found that the repeal was a valid exercise of the state's police power insofar as the repeal of the covenant served important public interests in mass transportation, energy conservation, and environmental protection.

Justice Blackmun, the author of the Supreme Court's plurality opinion, announced that legislation by which a state impairs the obligation of its own contract is subject to more careful judicial scrutiny than a law that interferes with private contracts. A less deferential standard of review is necessary when public contracts are involved because the state's self-interest is at stake. Thus, Blackmun formulated the rule that in order to withstand a contract clause challenge, a law that impairs the obligation of a public contract must be both reasonable and necessary to serve the purposes claimed by the state. The repeal of the covenant, Blackmun held, was neither necessary to the achievement of the states' plan for encouraging the use of public transportation nor was it reasonable in light of the circumstances.

A year later Rehnquist again joined the majority when the Court invalidated, as a violation of the contract clause, a Minnesota statute that required businesses that either terminated their pension plans or moved out of the state to contribute to a pension fund for former employees (Allied Structural Steel Co. v. Spannaus, 438 U.S. 234 [1978]). Justice Stewart, who wrote for the five person majority,[11] noted that "[i]f the Contract Clause is to retain any meaning at all, . . . it must be understood to impose some limits upon the power of a State to abridge existing con-

---

ment. Brennan wrote a dissenting opinion in which Marshall and White joined. Justices Powell and Stewart took no part in the case.

[11] Justice Blackmun did not participate. Justice Brennan wrote a dissenting opinion in which White and Marshall joined.

tractual relationships, even in the exercise of its otherwise legitimate police power" (*Allied Structural Steel*, 438 U.S. at 242). Stewart did not apply the more deferential standard that Blackmun had announced in *United States Trust*. Instead, he asserted that the severity of the impairment is a crucial factor in contract clause analysis. The more severe the impairment, the more careful the Court should be in examining the legislation. The effect of the law on Allied Structural Steel's contractual obligations was clearly severe: it resulted in an assessment of an immediate charge of approximately $185,000 when the company closed its office in Minnesota—a move that had been planned before the passage of the act. The law, in fact, nullified the express terms of the company's contractual obligations and imposed a completely unexpected liability. Moreover, unlike legislation that the Court has upheld against contract clause challenges in the past, the Pension Benefits Protection Act was not enacted in response to a social or economic problem.[12]

In both cases Justice Brennan wrote extensive dissents contending that the Court had extended and distorted the meaning of the contract clause. In *Allied Structural Steel* he voiced his concern that the result of such decisions would be "to vest judges with broad subjective discretion to protect property interests that happen to appeal to them" (ibid., 261).

In 1983 the Court appeared to withdraw from its rejuvenated analysis of the contract clause when it rejected two challenges that involved private contracts (Exxon Corp. v. Eagerton, 462 U.S. 176, and Energy Reserves Group v. Kansas Power and Light Co., 459 U.S. 400). Both decisions were unanimous.[13]

---

[12] Some commentators have argued that *Allied Structural Steel* and *United States Trust* are inconsistent, particularly in that the Court applied a more exacting standard of review in *Allied Structural Steel* than it suggested in *United States Trust* would be appropriate for private contracts. See, for example, "A Process Oriented Approach," 1980, and "Revival of the Contract Clause," 1979.

[13] In *Kansas Power and Light* the Court declined to use the test of reasonableness and necessity announced in *United States Trust*, and instead stated that the impairment need only be prompted by some legitimate state interest. In *Exxon Corp. v. Eagerton* the Court suggested that the judiciary should generally defer to the legislature when reviewing a regulatory scheme that imposes a "generally applicable rule of conduct designed to advance a 'broad societal interest'" that only incidentally disrupts existing contractual relationships (462 U.S. 176, 191, citation omitted). The Court distinguished *United States Trust* and *Allied Structural Steel*, noting that the exacting judicial scrutiny used in those cases applied only to legislation whose "sole effect [is] to alter contractual obligations," not to

Any attempt to interpret Rehnquist's votes in these cases in terms of his support for property rights cannot go much beyond mere speculation. The four cases strongly suggest that the Court's attitude toward the contract clause is uncertain and shifting, and possibly inconsistent.[14] Rehnquist silently agreed with the majority in three of the cases and joined a concurring opinion in the fourth.[15] As a result, the following interpretation of his votes is, by necessity, tentative.

His votes to invalidate laws on contract clause grounds seem to belie the assertion that federalism is his preeminent value. Fiss and Krauthammer (1982), in fact, cited two of the cases discussed above (*United States Trust* and *Allied Structural Steel*) to support their assertion that Rehnquist is primarily concerned with protecting property. Indeed, the two votes seem to support their contention that when the states threaten property, Rehnquist "sometimes is prepared to sacrifice state autonomy" (1982, 21). Further, his apparent agreement with Blackmun's assertion of the need for heightened judicial scrutiny when the state's interest is at stake and with Stewart's comments emphasizing the need for careful judicial examination of severe impairments appear to conflict with opinions in which he has construed state power broadly and has advocated judicial deference to state legislative decisions.

I offer an alternative analysis of the justice's decision making. Rehnquist's votes are illustrative of his judicial philosophy and, moreover, do not compromise the preeminent value he places on federalism. Certainly he has found limits on state power to regulate property; those limits exist by virtue of the positive law—in this context, the Constitution. Although federalism takes precedence over property rights, states are limited by express provisions in the Constitution, such as the contract clause. It is possible that, in his view, the contract clause, which is an express limit on the states, provides a clearer restriction on state action

---

legislation that "impose[s] a generally applicable rule of conduct" (*Eagerton*, 462 U.S. at 192).

[14] "These decisions are inconsistent and do not accord with either past rulings on the contract clause or the constitutionality of economic regulation under the due process clause" ("Revival of the Contract Clause," 1979, 395).

[15] In *Kansas Power and Light* Justice Powell, joined by Rehnquist and the chief justice, declined to join the part of the majority opinion that held that an impairment need only further significant and legitimate state interests. It was not necessary, they maintained, to go so far, since the Court held that no reasonable expectations were impaired by the state law.

129

than either the just compensation clause, which is not addressed explicitly to the states, or the due process clause, which is limited to procedural requirements that the states themselves may define.

According to Rehnquist's approach to constitutional interpretation—one of the components of his judicial philosophy—the Constitution is limited to the text and the intent of the framers; its meaning is fixed; and it constitutes a set of rules rather than a statement of aspirations or goals for society. It is from such a perspective that he has used the technique of literalism in his opinions to emphasize that the contract clause provides an express limitation on the states. States may not impair private contracts, and when public contracts are involved, the states are required to keep their word. While the Court, particularly since the 1920s, has not construed the clause as an absolute ban on state interference with contracts, it nevertheless has steadfastly maintained that there are certain laws that the states may not pass. The contract clause, in short, constitutes an exception to the broad authority the Constitution gives to the states. Such an interpretation is consistent with Rehnquist's understanding of the Constitution. He has construed other provisions, such as the Fourteenth Amendment, in much the same fashion.[16] Notwithstanding Brennan's criticism that the Court had dusted off the contract clause and "fundamentally misconceived its nature" (*United States Trust*, 431 U.S. at 46), Rehnquist may, indeed, have believed that the Court correctly interpreted that clause.

CONCLUSION

Rehnquist's opinions and votes in the cases analyzed in this chapter do not demonstrate that he has taken an indisputably unwavering position in support of federalism when state laws interfere with property rights. In the context of the just compensation clause, his dissent in *Penn Central* and his concurring opinion in *San Diego Gas and Electric* are difficult to reconcile with the thesis that he values federalism more than property rights. Still, in both cases he found that the challenged laws transgressed the limit, explicit in the just compensation clause of the Fifth Amendment, of state power to regulate property. Rehnquist's position in those cases may therefore be interpreted as the result of

[16] See the discussion of the Fourteenth Amendment in chapter 3.

searching for a boundary, in clearest possible constitutional terms, beyond which the state may not go, rather than an indication that he values property rights over federalism.

Additionally, it is only in the exceptional case that he would conclude that a state has gone beyond the limits of its power. In cases in which federal laws were involved, he unequivocally supported the authority of the states to regulate property. In the context of the contract clause, although his views are not clear due to the dearth of opinions, it is reasonable to infer that his approach to interpreting the Constitution leads him to construe the clause as an exception to the otherwise extensive power of the states.

For Rehnquist, property rights exist within the domain of state law. The states have extensive authority to regulate those rights while the federal government has only minimal power to alter them. The states' power to create, define, and regulate property is broad regardless of whether the property consists of land or governmental benefits. Limits to the state's power, however, are found in the contract clause and the just compensation clause. Thus, although federalism occupies a higher position than property rights in Rehnquist's scheme of values, he would not allow the states the absolute authority to define property rights. The states are limited by the positive law—the Constitution—which by its express terms protects property rights.

Constitutional provisions such as the due process clauses, the just compensation clause, and the contract clause offer a modicum of protection to property rights, in Rehnquist's view. But the Constitution offers only a minimum of protection for individual rights. In the justice's view, federalism is the central value that the Consitution protects. The next three chapters will explore the nature of that value.

PART FOUR

Federalism

SEVEN

Federalism I: Congressional Power and State Sovereignty

For over thirty years prior to Rehnquist's appointment as an associate justice, the Supreme Court construed the powers of Congress with respect to the states broadly. Indeed, from 1937 until the early 1970s, concerns about autonomy appeared to have a negligible impact on constitutional law.[1] And when Rehnquist took his position on the Court in 1972, it was generally accepted that the federal courts had little role to play when federal power was challenged on behalf of state autonomy because the states were adequately protected by the political process.[2]

The Court's expansive interpretation of Congress's power under the commerce clause beginning in 1937 provided the constitutional justification for the regulation of activities that formerly had been considered to be properly state concerns, such as labor relations (NLRB v. Jones and Laughlin Steel Corp., 301 U.S. 1 [1937]), wages and hours (U.S. v. Darby, 312 U.S. 100 [1941]), farm production for home consumption (Wickard v. Filburn, 317 U.S. 111 [1942]), and the prohibition of racial discrimination in public accommodations (Heart of Atlanta Motel v. U.S., 379 U.S. 241 [1964]). Several developments during the Warren Court era contributed further to the trend of increasing federal power. One of those developments was the Court's construal of Congress's au-

---

[1] Tribe (1978, 300), for example, wrote: "[T]he conventional wisdom was that, since 1937, there have been no judicially enforceable limits on congressional power which derive from considerations of federalism. The sole protections for the states, it was said, were political."

[2] For example, Herbert Wechsler (1954, 544) wrote that "[t]he actual extent of central intervention in the governance of our affairs is determined far less by the formal power distribution than by the sheer existence of the states and their political power to influence the action of the national authority." Calling for judicial restraint in this area he asserted that "the Court is on weakest ground when it opposes its interpretation of the Constitution to that of Congress in the interest of the states, whose representatives control the legislative process and, by hypothesis, have broadly acquiesced in sanctioning the challenged Act of Congress" (ibid., 559).

thority under Section 5 of the Fourteeenth Amendment to enforce the equal protection clause in the context of voting rights (Katzenbach v. Morgan, 384 U.S. 641 [1966]).

Rehnquist became an associate justice of a Supreme Court that had, to all appearances, concluded the debate regarding the extent of Congress's power and had moved on to other issues.[3] He played an important role in the revival of that debate and the restoration of issues concerning state autonomy to constitutional law. He created his own doctrine of state sovereignty[4] that he applied to protect his federalism—the state-centered federalism that occupies the highest position in his hierarchy of values.

Rehnquist's treatment of individual rights and property rights, examined in the preceding four chapters, attests to the subordinate position those rights occupy in his ordering of values and suggests the preeminent value he places on federalism. In the present chapter I elaborate on the federalism that he values so highly by examining a number of his opinions in which he has articulated his views regarding Congress's power vis-à-vis the states. I consider at length his interpretation of the extent of Congress's power to "regulate Commerce . . . among the several States" (Article I, Section 8) and his construal of Congress's power under Section 5 of the Fourteenth Amendment. First, however, I examine Rehnquist's opinions in cases in which state regulations have been challenged on the ground that they interfere with interstate commerce.

The Negative Side of the Commerce Clause

When state legislation has been challenged on the ground that it conflicts with a federal law or that it interferes with interstate commerce, Rehnquist has demonstrated his willingness to construe state authority broadly. In fact, he has taken an extremely deferential posture toward state regulations and has urged the other members of the Court to do the same.

When the federal preemption issue has been raised to challenge

[3] One of the classics of constitutional scholarship, Robert G. McCloskey's *The American Supreme Court* (1960), identifies three periods in the history of the Supreme Court. Each period was dominated by one concern. McCloskey identified the first period, from 1789 until the Civil War, as the one during which the dominant interest of the Court was the nature of the nation-state relationship.

[4] Powell (1982, 1328) referred to Rehnquist's doctrine of state sovereignty as a specific elaboration of his theory of federalism.

a state law under the supremacy clause of the Constitution, he has advocated a most lenient standard of review of state legislation. In essence, he has argued that if the Court cannot find a direct, explicit conflict between the federal and state laws, the latter should be upheld. For example, when the Court held that the Fair Packing and Labeling Act implicitly preempted the California law regulating weight variations in the labeling of flour packages, he objected that the majority had seriously misconceived the doctrine of preemption in not requiring a showing of conflict between the state and federal laws (Jones v. Rath Packing Co., 430 U.S. 519 [1977]). In another case the Court held that Virginia statutes that limited the right of nonresidents to catch fish in the waters of the state were preempted by the federal enrollment and licensing laws (Douglas v. Seacoast Products, Inc., 431 U.S. 265 [1977]). Rehnquist concurred but asserted that the majority opinion "cut a somewhat broader swath than is justifiable" and did not give adequate "shrift" to the issue of state regulation (Douglas, 431 U.S. at 287–88). He pointed to the states' substantial interests in the conservation of fish and game:

> The range of regulations which a State may invoke under these circumstances is extremely broad. Neither mere displeasure with the asymmetry of the pattern of state regulation, nor a sensed tension with a federal statute will suffice to override a state enactment affecting exploitation of such a resource. Barring constitutional infirmities only a direct conflict with the operation of federal law—such as exists here—will bar the state regulatory action. (Ibid., 288, citations omitted)

In a third case, the Court held that the New Mexico energy tax was invalid because it conflicted with the Tax Reform Act of 1976 (Arizona Public Service Co. v. Snead, 441 U.S. 141 [1979]). Rehnquist wrote a concurring opinion to express his view that the conflict between the state and federal laws was not as clear as the majority implied.

When state laws have been challenged on the ground that they interfere with interstate commerce, and there is no relevant federal legislation to raise the issue of preemption, Rehnquist has urged the Court to take a deferential attitude. In 1978 the Court invalidated a New Jersey statute that prohibited the importation of waste from out of state (City of Philadelphia v. New Jersey, 437 U.S. 617). Justice Stewart, writing for seven members of the

Court, found that the law discriminated against articles of commerce coming from out of state and constituted an "illegitimate means of isolating the State from the national economy" (*City of Philadelphia*, 437 U.S. at 627). In his dissenting opinion, Rehnquist argued that the state statute should have been treated as a quarantine law; New Jersey should have been allowed to try to cope with the health and safety problems posed by the importation of solid waste.

In Hughes v. Oklahoma (441 U.S. 322 [1979]) the Court held that the Oklahoma statute that prohibited transporting minnows out of the state for sale was inconsistent with the commerce clause. Justice Brennan, writing for a seven-person majority, articulated the general rule for determining whether a state law imposed an impermissible burden on commerce. The proper inquiry, he stated, is

1) whether the challenged statute regulates evenhandedly with only "incidental" effects on interstate commerce, or discriminates against interstate commerce either on its face or in practical effect; 2) whether the statute serves a legitimate local purpose; and, if so, 3) whether alternative means could promote this local purpose as well without discriminating against interstate commerce. (*Hughes*, 441 U.S. at 336)

Rehnquist's much more deferential approach presents a clear contrast. In his dissenting opinion he argued that the Court should only ask whether

the regulation directly conflicts with a federal statute or treaty; allocates access in a manner that violates the Fourteenth Amendment; or represents a naked attempt to discriminate against out-of-state enterprises in favor of in-state businesses unrelated to any purpose of conservation, [if not,] the State's special interest in preserving its wildlife should prevail. (Ibid., 342)

When the Court held that Iowa's limitation on truck lengths constituted an impermissible burden on interstate commerce, Rehnquist objected that the majority had "seriously intrude[d] upon the fundamental right of the States to pass laws to secure the safety of their citizens" (Kassel v. Consolidated Freightways Corp., 450 U.S. 662, 687 [1981]). A valid safety regulation, he asserted, is entitled to the "strongest presumption of validity" (ibid., 693). He dissented when the majority held that West Virginia's gross receipts tax, which provided an exemption for in-state business, had a discriminatory effect on interstate commerce. He contended that a state tax that does not actually grant a direct commercial advantage to in-state businesses should be upheld against a challenge that it discriminates against interstate commerce. According to his analysis, the Court should have upheld the tax because the Ohio corporation that challenged the provision did not demonstrate that it actually paid higher taxes on the same goods than in-state manufacturer-wholesalers (Armco Inc. v. Hardesty, 467 U.S. 638 [1984]).

In White v. Massachusetts Council of Construction Employers (460 U.S. 204 [1983]), Rehnquist wrote an opinion for the Court holding that the commerce clause did not prohibit the Boston mayor's executive order requiring that at least half of the work force on all construction projects funded either by city money or by a combination of city and federal funds was to be composed of city residents. He relied on a distinction between state or local government as market regulator and as participant in the market. It is only when the state operates as a regulator that the commerce clause acts as a restraint; when the state or local government participates in the market—as buyer, seller, contractor, or employer—it is not subject to the limitations of the commerce clause.[5] Rehnquist found that the city was acting as a participant in the market rather than as a regulator. Therefore, there was no need to determine whether the order had any impact on out-of-state residents. Regarding the application of the mayor's order to projects supported in part with federal funds, Rehnquist found that the relevant federal regulations permitted the restrictions. Since the order was, in effect, approved by Congress, there was no conflict between the order and the commerce clause.

Rehnquist has complained that "the jurisprudence of the 'negative side' of the commerce clause remains hopelessly confused" (Kassel, 450 U.S. at 706). His opinions, which manifest an ex-

---

[5] Rehnquist referred to two cases in which the Court used the regulator-participant distinction: Hughes v. Alexandria Scrap Corp., 426 U.S. 794 (1976), and Reeves v. Stake, 447 U.S. 429 (1980). In the latter case the Court upheld South Dakota's policy of restricting the sale of its state-operated cement plant to state residents. In that case Rehnquist joined the majority opinion, which stated in part: "There is no indication of a constitutional plan to limit the ability of the States themselves to operate freely in the free market" (Reeves, 447 U.S. at 436–37).

tremely deferential attitude toward state (and local) policy, afford an important hint of the theme that dominates his judicial decision making: deference to state governmental processes.

Substantial Effects: A Tougher Test

In the early 1930s the Court struck down major federal legislation that regulated business practices (Schechter Poultry Corp. v. United States, 295 U.S. 495 [1935]), labor relations (Carter v. Carter Coal, 298 U.S. 238 [1936]), and agricultural production (United States v. Butler, 297 U.S. 1 [1936]). To reach such conclusions the Court deemed activities that were not part of interstate commerce and, thus, had only an "indirect effect" on it to be beyond Congress's powers under the commerce clause; furthermore, that such activities were reserved to the states, the Court proclaimed, was ensured by the Tenth Amendment. Formulae based upon distinctions between "direct" and "indirect" effects on interstate commerce have been thoroughly discredited (*Wickard v. Filburn*), and Rehnquist has not attempted to resurrect them. Additionally, he ostensibly has conceded that Congress's power under the commerce clause is plenary.[6] Nevertheless, his opinions indicate that he does not concur with the post-1936 Court's broad construal of Congress's commerce power.

In Hodel v. Virginia Surface Mining and Reclamation Association (452 U.S. 264 [1981]), the Supreme Court reversed a federal district court's holding that the Surface Mining Control and Reclamation Act of 1977 violated the limits imposed by the Tenth Amendment on the commerce power. In a concurring opinion, Rehnquist stated that although Congress's regulation of surface mining "has stretched its authority to the 'nth degree,' our prior precedents compel me to agree with the Court's conclusion" (*Hodel*, 452 U.S. at 311). Remonstrating that "one could easily get the sense from this Court's opinions that the federal system exists only at the sufferance of Congress" (ibid., 308), he took the opportunity to clarify his disagreement with the modern Court's construal of the commerce clause.

He maintained that although the majority opinions in prior cases supported the result in *Hodel*, they contained implicit limits on Congress's power. The Court, he asserted, has consistently

---

[6] "It is established beyond per adventure that the commerce clause of Art. I of the Constitution is a grant of plenary authority to Congress" (National League of Cities v. Usery, 426 U.S. 833, 840 [1976]).

found that a mere effect on commerce is not sufficient to justify federal regulation; a regulated activity must have a *substantial* effect on interstate commerce. He noted further that precedent has established the requirement that Congress have a rational basis for finding that a regulation has a substantial effect and that such a finding is reviewable by the courts. Because the Court's use of the rational basis test nearly always results in a decision to uphold a challenged law, the enthusiasm with which Rehnquist endorsed that test suggested that he would like to see the Court refashion it as a tool for invalidating federal laws.

By contrasting state and federal power, he also found support for his argument that there are constitutional limits on Congress's authority: "[U]nlike the reserved police powers of the States, which are plenary unless challenged as violating some specific provision of the Constitution, the connection with interstate commerce is itself a jurisdictional prerequisite for any substantive legislation by Congress under the commerce clause" (ibid., 311).

THE LIMITS: TRADITIONAL STATE FUNCTIONS

Rehnquist has not merely advocated a "substantial effects" requirement and a tougher version of the rational basis test when a federal law is challenged on the ground that it does not fall within the realm of the commerce clause. He has gone further, to formulate a doctrine of state sovereignty that posits that even when Congress acts under the authority of the commerce clause, such action may constitute a violation of the constitutional protection provided to the states by the principles of federalism. According to that doctrine, Congress would be prohibited from regulating activities even in areas concededly within the realm of the commerce power when such regulation interfered with a state's governmental functions. He alluded to such a limit on Congress's power when he stated:

> We have repeatedly recognized that there are attributes of sovereignty attaching to every state government which may not be impaired by Congress not because Congress may lack an affirmative grant of legislative authority to reach the matter, but because the Constitution prohibits it from exercising the authority in that manner. (National League of Cities v. Usery, 426 U.S. 833, 845 [1976])

The proposition that Congress may not regulate the states in such a way as to intrude on state governmental functions is the most general statement of Rehnquist's doctrine of state sovereignty. It is helpful to explain the doctrine by breaking it into two parts. The first part is the distinction between private activities that Congress may regulate and governmental activities that Congress must leave alone. The second part asserts that there is an "inherent affirmative constitutional limitation on congressional power" (Fry v. United States, 421 U.S. 542, 553 [1975]).

The two parts of the doctrine of state sovereignty are particularly apparent in Rehnquist's dissenting opinion in *Fry v. United States*. In that case the Court upheld the application to state employees of emergency federal wage and salary controls under the Economic Stabilization Act of 1970. The majority found Maryland v. Wirtz (392 U.S. 183 [1968]), in which the Court upheld the application of the Fair Labor Standards Act to state-run schools and hospitals, to be controlling. It therefore rejected the state's argument that the application of the wage controls to state employees interfered with sovereign state functions in violation of the Tenth Amendment.

In his dissenting opinion Rehnquist characterized the Court's decisions in the area as a manifest danger to the federal system.[7] He emphasized the first part of his doctrine of state sovereignty—the state-private distinction—when he noted that "[the] well-recognized principle of the Supremacy Clause [of federal preemption when both state and federal governments are considered competent to act] is traditionally associated with federal regulation of persons or enterprises, rather than with federal regulation of the State itself" (*Fry*, 421 U.S. at 552). Thus, he posited that the boundary beyond which Congress's power may not reach is drawn by the distinction between activities that are like business and subject to federal regulation and activities that are "sufficiently closely allied with traditional state functions" (ibid., 558). The latter are beyond Congress's power to regulate.

He described the second part of his doctrine of state sovereignty—that there is an affirmative constitutional limit on congressional power—by analogizing the state and an individual. An individual who challenges an act of Congress on the ground

[7] He was referring to the Court's decision in *Fry*, considered with its decisions in *Maryland v. Wirtz* and *United States v. California* (297 U.S. 175 [1936]). In the latter case the Court held that the Federal Safety Appliance Act applied to a state-run railroad.

that it is not within the bounds of the commerce clause asserts a claim that Congress lacks legislative power. If, however, an individual alleges that an act of Congress that is clearly justified under the commerce clause interferes with rights that are protected by the First or Fifth Amendment, he or she asserts an affirmative constitutional defense that can limit the exercise of power expressly delegated to Congress. Analogously, Rehnquist noted that in *Fry* the state did not simply assert an absence of congressional legislative authority but, rather, an affirmative constitutional right inherent in its capacity as a state, based on the Tenth Amendment, to be free from such congressionally asserted authority. Thus, he strongly hinted that, in his conception, states' rights are guaranteed by the Tenth Amendment just as the rights of individuals are protected by the Bill of Rights against governmental infringement.

In his dissent in *Fry*, Rehnquist outlined the basic components of his doctrine of state sovereignty. In his majority opinion a year later in *National League of Cities v. Usery*, he provided a further elaboration of that doctrine. He led a five-person majority to strike down the 1974 amendments to the Fair Labor Standards Act, which extended minimum wage and maximum hours regulations to state and local government employees. He proposed a substantive constitutional limitation on Congress's commerce power based on the distinction between regulation of private entities and regulation that interferes with the states' ability to function within the federal system. In addition, he elaborated on his conviction that the states are protected from federal interference with their ability to function as governing bodies. His opinion has been severely criticized by scholars (see especially Tribe 1978; Michelman 1977; Barber 1976; Cox 1978). The decision has, in fact, been overruled (Garcia v. San Antonio Metropolitan Transit Authority, 469 U.S. 528 [1985]). Nevertheless, Rehnquist's opinion provides valuable illumination of his doctrine of state sovereignty.[8]

In support of his assertion that the Court has always recognized limits on Congress's power even when the latter acts under powers enumerated in Article I, Rehnquist pointed to the majority's statement in *Wirtz* that the Court has "ample power to prevent . . . the utter destruction of the State as a sovereign political

---

[8] H. Jefferson Powell (1982, 1325) referred to Rehnquist's opinion in *Usery* as the "centerpiece" of his theory of federalism.

entity" (392 U.S. at 196, quoted in *Usery*, 426 U.S. at 842). He also noted that in *Fry* the majority opinion recognized that an express declaration of a limitation on Congress exists in the Tenth Amendment: "The Amendment expressly declares the constitutional policy that Congress may not exercise power in a fashion that impairs the States' integrity or their ability to function effectively in a federal system" (*Fry*, 421 U.S. at 547, n.7, quoted in *Usery*, 426 U.S. at 852). Such statements, he argued, attest to the fact that the Constitution provides protection for the states in the federal system.

It remained for Rehnquist to delineate that constitutional protection. In doing so he utilized and elaborated on his public-private distinction:

> It is one thing to recognize the authority of Congress to enact laws regulating individual businesses necessarily subject to the dual sovereignty of the government of the Nation and of the State in which they reside. It is quite another to uphold a similar exercise of congressional authority directed, not to private citizens but to the States as States. (*Usery*, 426 U.S. at 845).

There are "attributes of sovereignty" in every state government that Congress may not impair. An example of such an attribute is the state's power to locate its seat of government (Coyle v. Oklahoma, 221 U.S. 559 [1911]). Another attribute of state sovereignty, Rehnquist admonished, is the state's power to determine the wages, hours, and overtime compensation that it pays to people it employs to carry out its governmental functions. Congress may not hinder the states' ability to make determinations regarding "functions essential to [their] separate and independent existence" *Usery*, 426 U.S. at 845, quoting *Coyle*, 221 U.S. at 565, quoting Lane County v. Oregon, 7 Wall. at 76).

The justice analyzed the effects of the minimum wage and overtime requirements on state services and on state policies concerning the manner in which states structure delivery of governmental services. He found that the federal requirements restricted state policy choices regarding the structuring of pay scales. Because states were forbidden to pay their employees less than the federal minimum wage, they were constrained in the type of people they could hire.[9] Furthermore, the states' choices

---

[9] Rehnquist explained that "[t]he state might wish to employ persons with lit-

were restricted insofar as the state could not devise its own methods for saving money; it could not simply decide to pay its employees less, so in order to save money, it would have to reduce the number of people it employed. An examination of the overtime requirements of the act convinced Rehnquist that they also interfered with traditional aspects of state sovereignty insofar as they displaced state decisions and might force states to substantially restructure long-accepted employment practices such as the work periods for police and fire fighters. In sum, he found that the federal minimum wage and overtime provisions impermissibly interfered with the integral governmental functions of states.

There was some disagreement between the parties concerning the exact effect of the application of the federal provisions, as Rehnquist noted. But he denied that assessments of the actual impact of those provisions were crucial to the outcome of the case. Regardless of their specific effect, he held, the application of the amendments would significantly alter or displace the states' abilities to structure employer-employee relationships in activities that are "typical of those performed by state and local governments in discharging their dual functions of administering the public law and furnishing public services. . . . it is functions such as these which governments are created to provide, services such as these which the States have traditionally afforded their citizens" (*Usery*, 426 U.S. at 851). The application of the federal minimum wage and hours regulations to state employees, in short, impaired the states' "ability to function effectively in a federal system," and such use of Congress's power is inconsistent with the federal system of government provided by the Constitution (ibid., 852).

In *Usery*, as in *Fry*, the distinction between federal regulation of private entities and those which are governmental helped to provide the basis for Rehnquist's elaboration of the tenet that federal regulations that displace the states' freedom to structure their essential operations for what are considered to be traditional governmental functions are consitutitonally unacceptable.

---

tle or no training, or those who wish to work on a casual basis, or those who for some other reason do not possess minimum employment requirements, and pay them less than the federally prescribed minimum wage. I may wish to offer part-time employment to teenagers at a figure less than the minimum wage, and if unable to do so may decline to offer such employment at all" (*Usery*, 426 U.S. at 848).

His opinion in *Usery* manifests most clearly his conviction that the Constitution protects the states in the exercise of their governmental functions.[10]

Rehnquist's doctrine of state sovereignty serves as a means of defining the limits of Congress's enumerated powers—specifically, the commerce power—by prohibiting Congress from interfering with the states' ability to carry out their governmental functions. The principle that the Constitution protects the states from federal intrusion is a central theme that runs throughout his opinions. Moreover, it is his firm belief that it is the duty of the Supreme Court to protect the states by carefully scrutinizing and invalidating federal legislation that interferes with state autonomy. The protection of the federalism that occupies a position at the top of Rehnquist's hierarchy of values must not be left to the political process.

SECTION 5 OF THE FOURTEENTH AMENDMENT

The Fourteenth Amendment, Rehnquist has conceded, was "strong medicine" that "sharply altered the balance of power between the Federal and State Governments" (Trimble v. Gordon, 430 U.S. 762, 779 [1977]). He held for a unanimous Court that the Eleventh Amendment, which protects the states from lawsuits under certain circumstances, is limited by the Fourteenth Amendment (Fitzpatrick v. Bitzer, 427 U.S. 445 [1976]).[11] Nevertheless, he has argued that the amendment must be interpreted consistently with the intent of the framers—and not only the framers of the Civil War amendments, who, Rehnquist has suggested, designed those amendments in order "to prevent from ever recurring abuses in which the states had engaged prior to that time" (1976a, 700). He has asserted that the amendments must also be understood in light of the intent of the framers of the original Constitution, who

adopted a system of checks and balances conveniently lumped under the descriptive head of "federalism," whereby all power was originally presumed to reside in the people of the states who adopted the Constitution. The Constitution delegated some authority to the federal executive, some to

[10] But see Tribe (1978) who argued that Rehnquist's opinion could be read to suggest the existence of protected rights to basic governmental services.
[11] The Eleventh Amendment is discussed at length in chapter 8.

146

the federal legislature, some to the federal judiciary, and reserved the remaining authority normally associated with sovereignty to the states and to the people in the states. (*Trimble*, 430 U.S. at 779)

Section 5 of the Fourteenth Amendment gives Congress the power to enforce the other provisions of the amendment "by appropriate legislation." In 1980 when the Court upheld the application of the Voting Rights Act of 1965 to prevent changes in voting practices that allegedly would have had the effect of diluting the black vote in Rome, Georgia, Rehnquist dissented (City of Rome v. United States, 446 U.S. 156 [1980]). He wrote an opinion that provides a telling example of his restrictive view of Congress's power pursuant to Section 5.

A consideration of the majority and the dissenting opinions in Katzenbach v. Morgan (384 U.S. 641 [1966]) should provide the necessary background for an examination of Rehnquist's opinion in *City of Rome*. In *Morgan*, the Court upheld a provision of the Voting Rights Act of 1965 that prohibited states from denying the right to vote to any person who had completed the sixth grade in the United States or Puerto Rico. The effect of the Court's decision in that case was to render unenforceable New York's English literacy requirement. Justice Brennan, writing for the majority, based the Court's holding on two rationales. First, Congress might have found that the state had discriminated against Puerto Ricans in the furnishing of governmental services. If so, Congress's extension of the right to vote would be a remedial measure designed to cure discrimination and, thus, would be clearly reasonable as a means of enforcing the equal protection clause. Second, Congress might have made its own determination that the state's literacy requirement was a violation of equal protection. The second rationale impliedly gave to Congress the authority to interpret the equal protection clause insofar as it imparted to the legislative branch the authority to decide that a particular practice may be violative of the clause even when the Court has determined that such a practice does not amount to a constitutional violation.[12] In *Morgan*, Justice Brennan invented his much criticized "ratchet theory," according to which Congress may expand but not dilute the protections offered by the

[12] The Supreme Court held in 1959 (Lassiter v. Northampton Election Board, 360 U.S. 45) that literacy tests, unless applied in a discriminatory manner, do not violate the equal protection clause.

Fourteenth Amendment pursuant to Section 5.[13] By allowing Congress to interpret the Fourteenth Amendment, Justice Harlan objected in his dissent, the Court allowed state laws that did not violate any constitutional provision to be invalidated, in effect, by Congress. According to Harlan, the majority not only violated the principles of the separation of powers by allowing Congress to interpret the Fourteenth Amendment, but also contravened the principles of federalism by allowing federal intervention into state legislative processes absent any constitutional violation.

In his dissenting opinion in *City of Rome*, Rehnquist expressed a view of Section 5 that was akin to Harlan's dissent in *Morgan*. Pursuant to Section 5, Rehnquist argued, Congress can pass legislation that is necessary to prohibit purposeful discrimination by governmental officials or to remedy prior constitutional violations, but it cannot do more. Further, Congress can legislate to invalidate a state law or state practice only if a constitutional violation has been judicially determined. For Rehnquist, such an interpretation of Congress's power under Section 5 is the only one that is consistent with the intent of the framers of the Civil War amendments and with the understanding of the relationship between the states and the federal government in the original Constitution.

Rehnquist's position in regard to the limits on Congress pursuant to Section 5 paralleled his opinions regarding the commerce clause insofar as he posited that Congress contravenes its constitutional limits when it intrudes upon state governmental functions. Furthermore, it is the Court's duty to exercise its power to scrutinize such legislation in order to protect the states. In his dissent in *City of Rome*, for example, he made a statement that was strongly reminiscent of his *Usery* opinion: "[It is necessary] for this Court to carefully scrutinize the alleged source of congressional power to intrude so deeply in the governmental structure of the municipal corporations created by some of the 50 States" (446 U.S. at 209).

In short, the effect of the Fourteenth Amendment on the nation-state relationship is minimal. The "strong medicine" of the Civil War amendments is virtually a placebo when administered by Dr. Rehnquist.

[13] See, for example, Cohen 1975 for a sample of the criticism of Brennan's "ratchet theory."

CONCLUSION: REHNQUIST'S FEDERALISM AND HIS JUDICIAL PHILOSOPHY

The federalism that Rehnquist places at the apex of his hierarchy of values entails a vision of the relationship between the federal government and the states that is fundamentally at odds with the view that prevailed on the Court from the late 1930s until the mid-1970s. A commitment to shift power away from the federal government toward more extensive, independent authority for the states underlies Rehnquist's decision making. In his endeavors to promote his version of federalism he has adopted an extremely deferential stance toward the states in cases in which state laws have been challenged either on the ground that they are preempted by federal law or on the basis of their alleged interference with interstate commerce. In addition, when federal legislation has been challenged on the ground that it interferes with state autonomy, Rehnquist has advocated the use of a strengthened rational basis test to protect the states from federal intrusion. He has also objected to the Court's acceptance of extensive congressional power under Section 5 of the Fourteenth Amendment, and he has made clear his belief that Section 5 does not give Congress the power to prohibit state practices unless it has been judicially determined that such practices violate the Constitution.

The principle that the Constitution forbids Congress from acting pursuant to its enumerated powers when it acts "directly to displace the States' freedom to structure integral operations in areas of traditional governmental functions" (*Usery*, 426 U.S. at 852) is at the center of Rehnquist's doctrine of state sovereignty. His opinions in the cases discussed in the present chapter indicate that he has developed his own doctrine to limit Congress's power when state governmental functions are involved. Not only has he interpreted Congress's enumerated powers in a restricted way, but he has also maintained that even when Congress acts pursuant to its enumerated powers, it transgresses its constitutional limits when it infringes on state autonomy.

What is the source of the federalism that Rehnquist values so highly? Given his approach to constitutional interpretation, the justice might be expected to ground his principles of federalism firmly in the text of the Constitution or in long-established precedent and to avoid relying on principles that are not found within the confines of the document. He might well use a historical mode of interpretation, looking to the past for answers to questions about the nature of the relationship between the national government and the states. It would also be reasonable to expect him to utilize techniques of literalism and "intent of the Framers," just as he has in cases that have involved individual and property rights.

Contrary to expectations, however, the opinions discussed in the present chapter are marked by a structural mode of analysis that is commonly associated with an approach to constitutional interpretation fundamentally different from Rehnquist's—one based on an understanding of the Constitution as consisting of more than the text, as an evolving rather than a static document, and as representing the goals of a good society rather than simply as a set of rules limiting governmental powers.

Structuralism as an interpretive mode looks to the whole document, at times beyond the document itself, and to the relationship between the clauses rather than to the specific language of particular provisions.[14] Possibly, Rehnquist has adopted structuralism as a mode of analysis out of necessity, since there are no constitutional provisions that explicitly protect state autonomy.

His departure from the expected historical mode of interpretation and the techniques of literalism and stare decisis was particularly manifest in his opinions in both *Fry* and *Usery*. At the point in his dissent in *Fry* at which one might expect to find references to prior cases in which states that asserted rights were vindicated by the Court, there appears, instead, a brief discussion of intergovernmental tax immunity with a reference to Chief Justice Stone's concurring opinion in a 1946 case. Stone stated that "a federal tax which is not discriminatory as to the subject matter may nevertheless so affect the State, merely because it is a State that is being taxed, as to interfere unduly with the State's performance of its sovereign functions of government" (New York v. United States, 326 U.S. 572, 587). In his opinion in *Fry*, Rehnquist asserted that six members of the Court in the case quoted above believed that "the principles of federalism reflected in the Tenth Amendment to the Constitution did not stop with merely prohibiting Congress from discriminating between States and other taxable entities in the exercise of its taxing power"

[14] See, Murphy, Fleming, and Harris (1986, ch. 10). See also Black (1965, 93), characterizing structuralism as "the method of inference from structures, status, and relationship[s]."

(421 U.S. at 556). He noted also that Justice Douglas, dissenting in *Maryland v. Wirtz*, relied on the Tenth Amendment when he stated: "If all this can be done, then the National Government could devour the essentials of state sovereignty, though that sovereignty is attested by the Tenth Amendment" (392 U.S. at 205, quoted in *Fry*, 421 U.S. at 551). In short, confronted by a paucity of precedent, the justice seemed to grasp at all that was available.

In *Fry* he also departed from the technique of literalism that has been so prevalent in his opinions in other areas. Indeed, in his dissent in that case he declined to rely expressly on any particular constitutional provision:

> [I]t is *not* the Tenth Amendment by its terms that prohibits congressional action which sets a mandatory ceiling on the wages of all state employees. Both [the Tenth and the Eleventh] Amendments are simply examples of the understanding of those who drafted and ratified the Constitution that the States were sovereign in many respects, and that although their legislative authority could be superseded by Congress in many areas where Congress was competent to act, Congress was nonetheless not free to deal with a State as if it were just another individual or business enterprise subject to regulation. (421 U.S. at 557, emphasis mine)

Similarly, in his opinion in *Usery*, Rehnquist declined to ground his support for federalism on any particular constitutional provision and relied instead on general statements about federal principles contained within the structure of the Constitution: "[The state] is itself a coordinate element in the system established by the Framers for governing our Federal Union" (426 U.S. at 849). Thus, in both opinions he adopted a structural mode of analysis that liberated him from the language of the text.[15]

Rehnquist has supported his federalism by adopting a mode of analysis and techniques of interpretation that differ from those that were so apparent in his opinions in the areas of individual and property rights. That shift brings the consistency of his fundamental understanding of the Constitution into question. When

[15] Justice Brennan stated in his dissent in *Usery*: "My Brethren thus have today manufactured an abstraction without substance, founded neither in the words of the Constitution nor on precedent" (426 U.S. at 860). Powell (1982, 1329) alleged that Rehnquist's failure to link his federalism to the Tenth Amendment or any other constitutional provision may increase the credibility of Brennan's criticism and may, indeed, leave the doctrine of state sovereignty "floating in mid-air."

individual rights and property rights have been involved, he has been steadfast in his view that the Constitution includes only its text, to be understood by discerning the meaning of the words and the intent of the framers, while his opinions concerning federalism suggest that he may lean toward a view that the Constitution includes more than that. However, he has remained faithful to the understanding that the Constitution is unchanging and that its meaning should be discovered in history. And so it is still by turning to the intent of the framers that he finds the grand design of the federal system and the implicit protection guaranteed to the states against incursion by the national government.

Rehnquist's federalism is more clearly consistent with the other two components of his judicial philosophy. Indeed, his democratic model, his moral relativism, and his federalism form a triad of mutually supportive elements. His democratic model strongly emphasizes majority rule as the basic principle of governmental policy making, while his moral relativism holds that no value is more legitimate than any other until it is enacted into the positive law. Because the laws derive their authority from the fact of their enactment by legislative bodies that represent the will of the majority, the laws that are most clearly the product of the will of the majority are the most legitimate. Rehnquist apparently looks to the states—the units of government close to the people—as the governing entitites that will be more likely to reflect the will of the majority. Consequently, federalism, in Rehnquist's view, is a means of protecting the democratic process—a means of ensuring that the will of the majority prevails. For Rehnquist, federalism is part of the positive law; it was enacted into law by the framers of the Constitution, and therefore it is more than an abstract principle: it is a legal fact.

EIGHT

Federalism II:
Protecting the States from the Federal Courts

Judicial federalism refers to the relationship between the state and federal judicial systems—a relationship of major importance that has never been precisely defined. Although the framers of the Constitution provided in Article III that the federal courts would have jurisdiction in cases involving the federal law or the Constitution, they left Congress the discretion to establish "inferior Courts" that would share the judicial power with the Supreme Court. Pursuant to that power, Congress has provided for a system of lower federal courts,[1] and for judicial review of state court decisions.[2] Still, Congress has never drawn a firm line between the jurisdiction of the state and federal judicial systems. Consequently, since the days of Chief Justice John Marshall, the Supreme Court has frequently been confronted with questions involving the division of power between the state and federal judiciaries.

From a historical perspective, the Supreme Court has only rarely deviated from a steady course of expanding federal jurisdiction.[3] Several developments during the 1960s, in particular, resulted in the significant expansion of federal court power. The incorporation of nearly all of the provisions in the Bill of Rights into the due process clause of the Fourteenth Amendment

---

[1] Congress created the federal district courts in the Judiciary Act of 1789 and the circuit courts of appeals in the Judiciary Act of 1891.

[2] Section 25 of the Judiciary Act of 1789 provided the statutory basis for judicial review of state court decisions. Congress also defined federal judicial power in the context of civil rights in post–Civil War legislation that included the Civil Rights Acts of 1866 (now 42 U.S.C. sections 1981 and 1982) and the Ku Klux Klan Act of 1871 (now 42 U.S.C. sections 1983 and 1985); additionally, Congress bestowed jurisdiction on the federal courts in the Civil Rights Act of 1964.

[3] Some of the Supreme Court's early opinions that established federal judicial power were Martin v. Hunters Lessee, 14 U.S. 304 (1816); Gibbons v. Ogden, 22 U.S. 1 (1824); Abelman v. Booth, 62 U.S. 506 (1859). Also see *Ex Parte Young*, 209 U.S. 123 (1908); Dombrowski v. Pfister, 380 U.S. 479 (1965); Flast v. Cohen, 392 U.S. 83 (1968).

brought state criminal proceedings under federal judicial supervision. Voting rights and legislative apportionment also became subject to federal judicial review. Additionally, decisions of the Warren Court eased access to the federal courts for the protection of individual rights by relaxing standing requirements (for example, in *Flast v. Cohen*, 392 U.S. 83 [1968]). The civil rights era revealed the insensitivity and weaknesses of state courts to the entire nation. As individuals and groups increasingly turned away from state courts for redress of their grievances, the federal judiciary came to be widely regarded as the superior forum for constitutional litigation (see, for example, Neuborne 1977).

In the present chapter, I continue to explore the nature of the federalism that Rehnquist values so highly by examining his attempts to limit the jurisdiction of the federal courts. He has taken an active role in the decisions of the Supreme Court in the area of judicial federalism and has persistently expressed his belief that the tradition of expanding federal judicial power constitutes a series of unwarranted intrusions into areas of decision making that properly belong to the states. I analyze his opinions in three areas: the Eleventh Amendment, federal suits against state officials for deprivation of constitutional rights "under color of law" under 42 U.S.C. Section 1983,[4] and habeas corpus. The decisions of the Court in all three areas have had a significant, if not always obvious, impact on the power of the federal judiciary. The constant theme in Rehnquist's decision making is one of a thoroughgoing commitment to protecting the states from what he perceives to be unnecessary, burdensome, and constitutionally inappropriate intrusion by the federal courts. My analysis in the following pages will depict the means he has used to undercut—in gradual, subtle, and, at times, even covert ways—the basis for federal judicial power.

Buttressing the Eleventh Amendment

Although the Eleventh Amendment by its express terms prohibits federal suits against a state by citizens of another state,[5] in

---

[4] 42 U.S.C. 1983 provides that "[e]very person who, under color of any statute, ordinance, regulation, custom, or usage, of any State or Territory, subjects, or causes to be subjected, any citizen of the United States or other person within the jurisdiction thereof to the deprivation of any rights, privileges, or immunities secured by the Constitution and laws, shall be liable to the party injured in an action at law, suit in equity, or other proper proceeding for redress."

[5] The Eleventh Amendment reads: "The Judicial power of the United States

1890 the Supreme Court held that the amendment prohibits a person from bringing a federal suit against his or her own state.[6] Much of the scholarship on the Eleventh Amendment has examined the original understanding of the amendment and has asserted that the intent was much narrower and, furthermore, that "the broad constitutional prohibition against suing states in federal court is unworkable in a federal system premised in important part on controlling state behavior by federal law in order to protect private individuals" (Fletcher 1983, 1040–41).[7] Nevertheless, the Court has continued to interpret the Eleventh Amendment as a prohibition against citizens taking their states to federal court.

The Court has developed two major exceptions to the prohibition on federal suits against states. First, in *Ex Parte Young* (209 U.S. 123 [1908]), the Court held that, the Eleventh Amendment notwithstanding, it is permissible to bring a federal suit to enjoin state officers from enforcing an allegedly unconstitutional state law. In order to justify such an exception, the Court established the fiction that a state official who acts illegally is stripped of the

---

shall not be construed to extend to any suit in law or equity, commenced or prosecuted against one of the United States by Citizens of another State, or by Citizens or Subjects of any foreign state."

[6] Hans v. Louisiana, 134 U.S. 1 (1890), is the case commonly cited for the extension of the Eleventh Amendment to bar suits by citizens against their own states. In that case the Court held that a Louisiana citizen could not sue Louisiana in federal court for failing to pay off state bonds in violation of the federal contract clause. The Court did not actually hold that the Eleventh Amendment, by its own terms, forbade such suits. Instead, Justice Bradley stated: "Can we suppose that, whan the Eleventh Amendment was adopted, it was understood to be left open for citizens of a State to sue their own state in the federal courts, whilst the idea of suits by citizens of other states, or of foreign states, was indignantly repelled? Suppose that Congress, when proposing the Eleventh Amendment, had appended to it a proviso that nothing therein contained should prevent a State from being sued by its own citizens in cases arising under the constitution or laws of the United States: can we imagine that it would have been adopted by the States? The supposition that it would is almost an absurdity on its face" (*Hans*, 134 U.S. at 5). Justice Brennan, in his dissent in Employees v. Department of Public Health and Welfare of Missouri, 411 U.S. 279, 313–14 (1973), argued that *Hans* held that it was not the Eleventh Amendment that barred a suit against a state by citizens of that state, but the doctrine of sovereign immunity. (Some articles that examine the Supreme Court's development of Eleventh Amendment case law are Shapiro 1984; Fletcher 1983; Baker 1977.)

[7] Fletcher (1983) argued extensively that the intent of the Eleventh Amendment was merely to require that the state-citizen diversity clause of Article III be construed to confer party-based jurisdiction only when a state sued an out-of-state citizen. See also Shapiro 1984.

authority of the state and is, therefore, acting as an individual. The second exception to the prohibition on federal suits against states is waiver of the state's immunity, which may take place either by state statute, by agreement in an individual case, or by a federal statute.

Rehnquist has written several opinions that indicate that he construes the two exceptions narrowly and that he favors expanding the scope of the Eleventh Amendment to protect states from federal suits. Moreover, in two cases in which he did not write opinions, he agreed with the majority's broad construal of the amendment.

In Employees v. Department of Public Health and Welfare of Missouri (411 U.S. 279 [1973]), he joined Justice Douglas's majority opinion holding that the Federal Labor Standards Act did not constitute waiver of the sovereign immunity of the states; thus, state employees could not recover damages from the state of Missouri for its failure to pay overtime compensation required by the law. Congress, the Court held, does not lift the states' immunity from federal suit merely by regulating overtime compensation. Neither is a state considered to have waived its immunity merely by continuing to operate facilities that are regulated by Congress. The employees could recover damages only if Congress had abrogated the states' constitutional immunity by clear language.

During the Court's succeeding term Rehnquist wrote an opinion for a five-member majority in Edelman v. Jordan (415 U.S. 651 [1974]), holding that the Eleventh Amendment bars federal courts from ordering retroactive relief against state governments. The case arose out of a suit that alleged that state officials were administering federal programs of aid to the aged, blind, or disabled in a way that was inconsistent with the federal regulations and with the Fourteenth Amendment. The district court found that benefits had been wrongfully withheld, issued an injunction requiring state officials to comply with federal regulations, and ordered the state officials to pay the benefits that had been withheld. The suit, brought against state officials alleging that they had violated the federal law, appeared to be within the exception specified in Ex Parte Young. Rehnquist, however, held that because the funds to be paid would come from the general revenues of the state, the award "resemble[d] far more closely the monetary award against the State itself, . . . than it d[id] the prospective injunctive relief awarded in Ex Parte Young" (Edelman, 414 U.S. at 665, citation omitted). Although in several previous cases the Court had upheld retroactive federal court relief, the justice expressly disavowed those holdings and referred to the tradition whereby the Court is less constrained by precedent when it addresses constitutional questions than when it engages in statutory construction.

His opinion in *Edelman* indicated that he would construe the *Ex Parte Young* exception to the prohibition on federal suits against states so that only actions for injunctive relief would be allowed under the Eleventh Amendment. Additionally, his opinion suggested that he would consider only the most explicit statements from Congress to constitute waiver of state immunity. He noted that Congress could not have waived the state's immunity because the federal laws governing the welfare program did not create a cause of action against the state. He rejected the findings of the court of appeals that Section 1983 was intended to create a waiver and that the state had "constructively consented" to suit by participating in the federal program. Tightening the "clear language" requirement, which the Court used in *Employees*, Rehnquist made it clear that the Court would consider a state to have waived its protection under the Eleventh Amendment "only where stated 'by the most express language or by such overwhelming implications from the text as [will] leave no room for any other reasonable construction' " (ibid., 673, citation omitted).

In two subsequent cases, Justice Powell, writing for five-person majorities, further extended the reach of the Eleventh Amendment as a bar to federal adjudication. The first case began in 1974 when a resident of Pennhurst State School and Hospital, a state institution for the mentally retarded in Pennsylvania, filed a complaint in federal district court against the institution and various state officials. The suit alleged that conditions violated federal statutory and constitutional requirements and state law. After a lengthy trial, the district court held that mentally retarded individuals who were cared for by the state were entitled to live in the least restrictive setting consistent with their needs (Halderman v. Pennhurst State School and Hospital, 446 F.Supp. 1295 E.D. Pa. [1977]). The court's conclusion was based on both state law and constitutional requirements of due process. The court ordered the defendants to remove the retarded residents from Pennhurst and to provide suitable community living arrangements for them. The court of appeals upheld the decision but relied entirely on a federal statute: the Developmentally Disabled Assistance and Bill of Rights Act, particularly 42 U.S.C. Section 6010. The Supreme Court reversed, holding that Section 6010 did not create any substantive rights to appropriate treatment in the least restrictive environment (Pennhurst v. Halderman, 451 U.S. 1 [1981]). On remand, the court of appeals held that the least restrictive environment was required by state law. In 1984 the Supreme Court again reversed the decision of the court of appeals and held that the Eleventh Amendment prohibited the federal courts from ordering state officials to conform their conduct to state law (Pennhurst v. Halderman, 465 U.S. 89 [1984]). Rehnquist was a member of the five-person majority. Justice Powell reasoned that the claim that state officials violated state law in carrying out their official duties at Pennhurst was one against the state, and therefore the claim was barred by the Eleventh Amendment. The doctrine of *Ex Parte Young*, he held, applies only when officials are alleged to be acting in violation of federal constitutional law. He stated that "it is difficult to think of a greater intrusion on state sovereignty than when a federal court instructs state officials on how to conform their conduct to state law. Such a result conflicts directly with the principles of federalism that underlie the Eleventh Amendment" (*Pennhurst*, 465 U.S. at 101). Thus, in *Pennhurst* the Court limited the exception to the prohibition on suits against state officials and, thereby, narrowed the conditions under which such officials may be sued in federal court.

In a second case the Court built further on the "clear language" rule that Rehnquist had stiffened in *Edelman*. Atascadero State Hospital v. Scanlon (473 U.S. 234 [1985]) originated in an action filed in federal district court alleging that the state hospital's denial of employment to a man with impaired vision was discrimination in violation of a federal statute. Section 504 of the Rehabilitation Act of 1973 prohibits discrimination on the sole basis of handicap by any program receiving federal financial assistance under the act. Powell, who wrote the majority opinion, found that the state constitutional provision, which specified that "[s]uits may be brought against the State in such manner and in such courts as shall be directed by law" (*Atascadero State Hospital*, 473 U.S. at 241), did not constitute waiver of the state's immunity from suit. The state, Justice Powell held, must specify its intention to subject itself to suit in federal court. Similarly, Powell found no waiver of the state's immunity in Section 504 of the Rehabilitation Act because Congress did not make "its intention . . . in unmistakably clear language in the statute itself" (ibid., 243). Finally, he noted that the state's acceptance of federal funds under the Rehabilitation Act did not constitute consent to be sued in federal court. Rehnquist was a member of the majority in that case.

In 1976 Rehnquist, in what at first glance may appear to be an opinion that belies his broad construal of the Eleventh Amendment, held that Congress had the power to authorize an award of money damages to private individuals against a state government that engaged in discrimination in violation of Title VII of the Civil Rights Act of 1964 (Fitzpatrick v. Bitzer, 427 U.S. 445). Noting that the "substantive provisions [of the Fourteenth Amendment] are by express terms directed at the States" (*Fitzpatrick*, 427 U.S. at 453), he concluded that the Eleventh Amendment is limited by the enforcement provisions of Section 5 of the Fourteenth Amendment. He therefore held that the Fourteenth Amendment limits the Eleventh Amendment's protection for states from being taken to federal court against their will. Nevertheless, in dissent in City of Rome v. United States (446 U.S. 156 [1980]), he expressed unequivocally his view that the extent of Congress's power under Section 5 of the amendment is limited to remedial action for violations of the amendment.[8]

His opinions in the context of the Eleventh Amendment and his votes in the two decisions in which the opinions were authored by Powell attest to Rehnquist's commitment to the goal of protecting the states from the federal courts. Although he has not directly attacked the doctrine of Ex Parte Young, he contributed to limiting it with his opinion in *Edelman*. And while he ostensibly supported the rule that Congress by clear language may lift the states' immunity from federal suit, he provided the basis for the subsequent strengthening of that rule by specifying that only the clearest expression of an intention to allow the states to be sued in federal court would constitute a waiver of immunity.

SECTION 1983: MERGING CONSTITUTIONAL RIGHTS WITH THE AVAILABILITY OF STATE REMEDIES

As a means of enforcing the Fourteenth Amendment, Congress, in the Civil Rights Act of 1871, provided a cause of action for the

[8] See the discussion of *City of Rome v. United States* in chapter 7.

deprivation "under color of law" of rights secured by the Constitution. As a result of the Supreme Court's restrictive interpretations of the Fourteenth Amendment in the nineteenth and early twentieth centuries, that statutory provision was rarely used.[9] In 1961, however, in its decision in Monroe v. Pape (365 U.S. 167), the Court revived the provision, which is now codified as 42 U.S.C. Section 1983. Subsequently, Section 1983 became a major source of the tremendous increase in the volume of federal suits.[10]

In *Monroe*, Justice Douglas, writing for the majority, found the following three purposes in the legislative history of Section 1983: to override discriminatory state laws, to provide a remedy when state law was inadequate, and to provide a federal remedy when the state remedy, although available in theory, was not

[9] For example, in the Slaughterhouse Cases (16 Wall. 36 [1873]) the Court severely limited the rights protected by the privileges and immunities clause and suggested a narrow view of the equal protection and due process clauses of the Fourteenth Amendment. In the Civil Rights Cases (109 U.S. 3 [1883]) the Court construed the "No state shall . . ." language of the Fourteenth Amendment in such a way as to limit strictly the notion of deprivation of rights protected by the Fourteenth Amendment by holding that a public accommodations law was beyond the power of Congress because it attempted to regulate private action. The equal protection of the laws, the Court reasoned, can only be denied by state action. Such reasoning restricted the meaning of "under color of law" to actions undertaken by the state.

[10] 18 U.S.C. Section 242 provides: "Whoever, under color of any law, statute, ordinance, regulation, or custom, willfully subjects any inhabitant of any State, Territory, or District to the deprivation of any rights, privileges, or immunities secured or protected by the [Constitution or laws], or to different punishments, pains, or penalties, on account of such inhabitant being an alien, or by reason of his color, or race, than are prescribed for the punishment of citizens, shall be fined not more than $1,000 or imprisoned not more than one year, or both; and if death results shall be subject to imprisonment for any term of years or for life." In United States v. Classic, 313 U.S. 299 (1941), and Screws v. United States, 325 U.S. 91 (1945), the Court construed "under color of law" to encompass the unauthorized and unlawful conduct of a state officer, or, as Justice Douglas stated it, the phrase "under color of law" included "under pretense of law." In *Monroe* the Court applied the same construction of under color of law to the civil context. On the increase in federal suits see, for example, Whitman (1980, 6), who reported that between 1961 and 1979, the number of federal filings under Section 1983 increased from 296 to 13,168. Civil rights petitions by state prisoners increased from 218 cases in 1966 to 11,195 in 1979. While many commentators and judges have expressed concern about the burden on the federal judiciary created by the proliferation of federal litigation, Rehnquist's primary concern lies elsewhere—in protecting state governments from interference by the federal judiciary. Still, he has commented on the problem. See, for example, Rehnquist 1973, 1974, 1976b.

available in practice. Finding that one of the purposes of Section 1983 was to provide a supplementary federal remedy, Douglas held that the state remedy "need not be first sought and refused before the federal one is invoked" (365 U.S. at 183). *Monroe* thereby established the rule that a plaintiff whose constitutional rights have been infringed by an action under color of state law may bring a federal cause of action under Section 1983 without first exhausting state remedies. Moreover, relief may be available under Section 1983 even when a state remedy exists. While Douglas based his reasoning on legislative history, Justice Harlan's concurring opinion suggested an additional justification for the Court's decision.[11] Harlan speculated that Congress in 1871 may have believed that "[a] deprivation of a constitutional right is significantly different from and more serious than a violation of a state right and therefore deserves a different remedy even though the same act may constitute both a state tort and the deprivation of a constitutional right" (ibid., 196).

Harlan's statement suggested that a federal remedy is appropriate when the interest asserted by the plaintiff is important enough to be protected by the federal Constitution. Thus, Douglas's opinion, considered in conjunction with Harlan's, came to stand for the principle that federal rights should be litigated in and protected by federal courts because "[f]ederal courts are the most appropriate place for redress of federal rights. An open federal door symbolizes the importance of those rights" (Whitman, 1980, 23).

Rehnquist has expressed his thoroughgoing disagreement with such an interpretation of Section 1983. He has engaged in several attempts to undercut the rule that the existence of a state remedy for the deprivation of a constitutional right does not preclude a Section 1983 action. Indeed, his opinions strongly suggest that he would favor the adoption of a rule under which federal courts would dismiss all Section 1983 suits, thereby relegating virtually all claims of deprivation of constitutional rights to state proceedings.

His attitude is illustrated by his majority opinions in three cases in which the Court held that a plaintiff who brought an

---

[11] Whitman (1980, 14, 15, 22) pointed out that the three aims of Section 1983 that Douglas listed in his opinion address a case like *Monroe* in which an adequate state tort remedy arguably exists. It was Justice Harlan, Whitman argued, who suggested a proper justification for providing a remedy under Section 1983 when state law provided a remedy.

action under Section 1983 against state or local officials did not have a cause of action. The plaintiffs lacked a cause of action in all three of the cases, he held, because they had not been deprived of any constitutional right. Considered together, the three opinions reveal the determination with which Rehnquist has attempted to limit the availability of a federal forum for the adjudication of federal rights.

The first case involved a Section 1983 action against the police chief in Louisville, Kentucky (Paul v. Davis, 424 U.S. 693 [1976]). Edward Davis filed suit after the police distributed a flyer to local merchants identifying him as a shoplifter although he had never been convicted of such a crime.

Rehnquist held that Davis had not been deprived of a liberty protected by the due process clause and that, therefore, there was no cause of action under Section 1983. Although it was quite probable, he reasoned, that the distribution of the flyer would provide a basis for a defamation action in state court, he denied that defamation alone deprives a person of a liberty protected by the Fourteenth Amendment. Thus, Davis had not been deprived of a constitutional right, but even if he had, Rehnquist asserted, the right could have been protected by state law.[12] He then posited that if one has not been deprived of a constitutional right, then a state remedy for any wrong that one may have suffered will be deemed adequate and there will be no cause of action under Section 1983.

Rehnquist's reasoning suggested a major departure from the principles of *Monroe*. Whereas *Monroe* established the rule that if a constitutional right is involved, a federal court must be available, Rehnquist suggested in *Davis* that if an individual is deprived of a right that is constitutionally protected, a state remedy may, nevertheless, be adequate. If so, no federal adjudication would be warranted. In fact, the existence of a state remedy would abrogate any claim of deprivation of a constitutionally protected right. Rehnquist's reasoning is actually circular in its suggestion, only implicit in *Davis*, that if a plaintiff has been deprived of a constitutional right, a state remedy may be adequate; if the state remedy is adequate, the plaintiff is not deprived of a constitutional right.

[12] Rehnquist suggested that if Davis had lost his employment as a result of the flyer, he might have had a cause of action. Nevertheless, the right to continuing employment could be protected by virtue of recognition by state law. That protection would negate the need for federal adjudication.

In the second case Rehnquist wrote an opinion for six members of the Court holding that Leonard McCollan, who spent eight days in jail as a result of Texas police officers' negligence in failing to follow proper identification procedures, did not have a cause of action under Section 1983 (Baker v. McCollan, 443 U.S. 137 [1979]). Rehnquist found no merit in the argument that the officers deprived McCollan of a liberty protected by the due process clause by wrongly imprisoning him. He held that because there had been a valid arrest warrant, which conformed to the requirements of the Fourth Amendment, there was no constitutional violation in McCollan's arrest and detention. Rehnquist reviewed the Fourth Amendment requirements for arrest—which he found the police had followed—and he failed to find the deprivation of a constitutional right. He then asserted that McCollan may well have had a remedy under the state law for any legal wrong he may have suffered—an assertion that appears in the opinion no less than four times (*McCollan*, 443 U.S. at 143–46).

It was in the third case that the circularity of Rehnquist's reasoning became most clear. In his majority opinion holding that a prison official's negligence in losing a prisoner's hobby kit was not actionable under Section 1983, he noted that although the prison officials acted "under color of law," and although the kit was property and its loss amounted to a deprivation of property, such facts did not establish a cause of action under Section 1983 (Parratt v. Taylor, 451 U.S. 527 [1981]). The due process clause, Rehnquist noted, does not protect against all deprivations of property, only deprivations "without due process of law." If due process was provided, there would be no deprivation of a constitutional right and, thus, no Section 1983 case. Rehnquist held that because the state provided the requisite due process in its tort remedies, there had been no deprivation of a constitutional right. In short, there was no deprivation of a constitutional right because the state provided a remedy. He went on to assert that although state remedies do not provide all the relief that Section 1983 does, state remedies may, nevertheless, be adequate to satisfy the requirements of due process.

Rehnquist has severely weakened the general principle of *Monroe* that a federal forum must be available for litigation involving constitutional rights. He has done so by reviving the rule that the existence of a state remedy precludes a plaintiff's access to the federal courts. With his approach, a claim of deprivation of a constititutional right would not be sufficient to get one's case into federal court, the language of Section 1983 notwithstanding.

The justice has also supported the restriction of access to the federal courts in another, closely related context. He has explicitly urged the Court to overrule the aspect of *Monroe* according to which a plaintiff need not seek a state remedy for deprivation of constitutional rights before taking action in federal court. He dissented from the Court's denial of certiorari in a case in which two police officers who, after a police hearing board upheld their dismissals from the department, took action in federal court rather than seek review in the state courts (City of Columbus v. Leonard, 443 U.S. 905 [1979]). The district court dismissed their action but the court of appeals held that the lower court should have reached the merits of the claims. Suggesting that the district court's dismissal was correct, Rehnquist argued that the Supreme Court should have granted certiorari. He stated that "the time may now be ripe for a reconsideration of the Court's conclusion in *Monroe* that the 'federal remedy is supplementary to the state remedy, and the latter need not be first sought and refused before the federal one is invoked' " (*Leonard*, 443 U.S. at 910–11, citations omitted).[13]

Rehnquist's approach to Section 1983 reveals a strategy for protecting state and local officials from being sued in federal court. He has strictly delineated the category of constitutionally protected rights and then asserted that even when there has been a deprivation of such a right, a state remedy is adequate and precludes a Section 1983 action. Because he places federalism at the top of his hierarchy of values, Rehnquist interprets Section 1983 in a way that, as he has stated, will prevent every "legally cognizable injury" inadvertently inflicted by state and local officials from becoming a federal case (*Paul v. Davis*, 424 U.S. at 699). By way of contrast, an observer who is primarily concerned with individual rights will be quick to admonish that Rehnquist's con-

---

[13] An aspect of *Monroe* that I have not included in the present discussion of Rehnquist's opinions is the Court's holding that local governments were immune from suit under Section 1983. In Monell v. New York City Department of Social Services (436 U.S. 658 [1978]), the Court overruled that aspect of *Monroe*. Rehnquist dissented, arguing that Congress did not intend to impose liability on municipal governments. He found no justification for the overruling. He joined the dissent when the Court held that a municipality may not assert the good faith of its officers as a defense to liability under Section 1983 (*Owen v. City of Independence*, 445 U.S. 622 [1980]).

strual of Section 1983 will have the effect of denying the right, clearly established in *Monroe*, of raising a federal claim in federal court.

LIMITING HABEAS CORPUS: STATE TRIALS AS THE MAIN EVENT

Federal habeas corpus provides a means by which state prisoners, who have exhausted all appeals at the state level, may take a claim to federal court that they are being detained in violation of the federal Constitution or the law.[14] During the Warren era the Supreme Court expanded the availability of habeas corpus. As a result, the writ began to function as the remedial counterpart to the Court's constitutionalization of criminal procedure.[15]

In 1963 in Fay v. Noia (372 U.S. 391 [1963]) the Court construed federal habeas corpus as a guarantee of broad independent review of state court decisions.[16] In his opinion for the majority, Justice Brennan held that federal habeas corpus cannot be precluded by state court adjudication of a federal claim.[17] He also

[14] Article I, Section 9 of the Constitution provides that the writ of habeas corpus shall not be suspended except in cases of rebellion or invasion when the public safety requires it. Habeas corpus was incorporated in the federal statutory law in the Judiciary Act of 1789. It was in the Judiciary Act of 1867, however, that the availability of the writ was extended to state prisoners. In the 1867 act, lower federal courts were given the authority to review judgments of state courts.

[15] Habeas corpus acted as the "vehicle for the reform" that the Warren Court instituted; that is, it was through the expanded availability of habeas corpus that decisions such as that in Gideon v. Wainwright (372 U.S. 335 [1963]) could be enforced. Cover and Aleinikoff (1977, 1041) explained: "Habeas corpus (like appellate review) is a remedy that acts not upon those persons whose behavior is the target of reform but upon institutional outcomes. Policemen are not penalized for illegal searches; judges are not fined for failures to appoint counsel, to empanel proper juries or to exclude illegal evidence. Rather, the defendant's release is held out as the incentive to redo the process until it is done correctly."

[16] Justice Brennan summarized the importance of habeas corpus: "Although in form the Great Writ is simply a mode of procedure, its history is inextricably intertwined with the growth of fundamental rights of personal liberty. For its function has been to provide a prompt and efficacious remedy for whatever society deems to be intolerable restraints. Its root principle is that in a civilized society, government must always be accountable to the judiciary for a man's imprisonment: if the the imprisonment cannot be shown to conform with the fundamental requirements of law, the individual is entitled to his immediate release" (*Fay*, 372 U.S. at 401–402).

[17] Brennan quoted from both Justice Reed's and Justice Frankfurter's opinions in Brown v. Allen (344 U.S. 443 [1953]). Reed stated that "the state adjudication

165

clarified the "exhaustion of state remedies" requirement when he held that federal courts have the power to grant habeas corpus in a situation involving an applicant who failed to pursue a state remedy that was not available at the time he or she applied.[18] The exhaustion requirement, therefore, would apply only to failure to exhaust state remedies that are open to the applicant at the time he or she files an application for habeas corpus in federal court. Furthermore, the doctrine according to which the Supreme Court will decline to review state court judgments that rest on independent and adequate state grounds, Brennan held, does not apply to habeas proceedings in which the state law grounds were merely procedural.[19] Brennan's opinion asserted, finally, that federal courts could use their discretion to deny relief to applicants who have "deliberately by-passed" state procedures for adjudicating their federal claims.[20] The "deliberate bypass" rule, as Brennan formulated it, specified that a court could only consider an applicant for habeas corpus to have waived his right to federal relief if he had, "after consultation with competent counsel or otherwise, understandingly and knowingly forewent the privilege of seeking

carries the weight that federal practice gives to the conclusion of a court . . . of another jurisdiction on federal constitutional issues. It is not res judicata" (*Brown*, 344 U.S. at 458, quoted in *Fay*, 372 U.S. at 423). Frankfurter stated: "The State court cannot have the last say when it, though on fair consideration and what procedurally may be deemed fairness, may have misconceived a federal constitutional right" (ibid., 508, quoted in 372 U.S. at 508).

[18] The requirement that state remedies be exhausted before habeas will be granted is found in 28 U.S.C. 2254, which reads in part:

"An application for a writ of habeas corpus in behalf of a person in custody pursuant to the judgment of a State court shall not be granted unless it appears that the applicant has exhausted the remedies available in the courts of the State, or that there is either an absence of available State corrective process or the existence of circumstances rendering such process ineffective to protect the rights of the prisoner."

"An applicant shall not be deemed to have exhausted the remedies available in the courts of the State, within the meaning of this section, if he has the right under the law of the State to raise, by an available procedure, the question presented."

[19] The adequate and independent state ground on which the state court judgment purported to rest was Noia's failure to appeal his conviction. In other words, the state argued that procedural defaults constituted an adequate and independent state ground that precluded federal relief.

[20] See also Townsend v. Sain, 372 U.S. 293 (1963). In that case the Court held that federal courts must conduct an evidentiary hearing to determine a constitutional claim if the petitioner "did not receive a full and fair evidentiary hearing in a state court" (372 U.S. at 312).

to vindicate his federal claims in the state courts . . . [it] depends on the considered choice of the petitioner" (*Fay*, 372 U.S. at 439).

Subsequently, the Burger Court launched a three-pronged attack on its predecessor's construal of the availability of habeas corpus. One method that the Court employed to limit its availability was to bar habeas corpus when a Fourth Amendment claim was made at trial and given a full hearing (Stone v. Powell, 428 U.S. 465 [1976]). In a majority opinion that Rehnquist joined, Justice Powell held that raising a federal claim in state court has a res judicata effect provided that the state court afforded the petitioner opportunity for a full and fair litigation of the claim. That decision was in direct opposition to the Court's holding in *Fay* that adjudication of a federal claim at the state level does not preclude a federal court from hearing that claim.

In the second prong of its attack on habeas corpus the Court thoroughly undermined the element of *Fay* that required "deliberate bypass" of state remedies before a federal right could be deemed to have been waived. It is in such a context that Rehnquist has written key majority opinions. In Davis v. United States (411 U.S. 233 [1973]), which involved a federal prisoner, Rehnquist held that one's failure to comply with a rule requiring pretrial objection to an indictment barred habeas review of the underlying constitutional claim unless one could show cause for the failure and actual prejudice resulting from the alleged constitutional violation. Subsequently, in an opinion written by Justice Stewart, the Court applied the "cause and prejudice" standard from *Davis* to a state prisoner who had failed to comply with a state requirement that challenges to grand jury composition be raised before trial (Francis v. Henderson, 425 U.S. 536 [1976]).

Rehnquist's attack on the deliberate bypass rule culminated in Wainwright v. Sykes (433 U.S. 72 [1977]). Sykes sought habeas corpus after he was convicted of third-degree murder in Florida. He asserted that he had not understood the *Miranda* warnings when he made statements after his arrest that were admitted as evidence at his trial. He had not raised the issue during the trial or in his first appeal. The district court held that Sykes had not lost the right to assert his claim and ordered the state to hold a hearing on whether Sykes knowingly waived his *Miranda* rights. The court of appeals, following *Fay*, held that the failure to comply with the state procedural rule requiring objection at trial would only bar review of the suppression claim if the right to object was deliberately bypassed for reasons relating to trial tactics.[21] The court concluded that Sykes's failure to object did not constitute a deliberate bypass.

Emphasizing that the deliberate bypass rule was based on Brennan's dicta in *Fay* and noting that it was limited by *Francis*, Rehnquist applied the "cause and prejudice" standard. He concluded that Sykes had not shown cause for his failure at his trial to object to the admission of his statements. Furthermore, he noted, evidence of his guilt was "substantial to a degree that would negate any possibility of actual prejudice resulting to [Sykes] from the admission of his inculpatory statement" (*Wainwright*, 433 U.S. at 91).[22] The substitution of the cause and prejudice for the deliberate bypass standard when a defendant did not comply with a state procedural rule, Rehnquist asserted, would have the effect of making "the state trial on the merits the 'main event,' . . . rather than a 'tryout on the road' for what will later be the determinative federal habeas hearing" (ibid., 90).

Although Rehnquist rejected the deliberate bypass standard and replaced it with a rule that will undoubtedly make it more difficult for a state prisoner to obtain federal habeas corpus relief, he explicitly declined to define precisely the new cause and prejudice standard. Moreover, three justices filed concurring opinions.[23] Federal habeas corpus appears to be in transition. Nevertheless, it is clear that Rehnquist has attempted to formulate a doctrine that, if accepted by a majority of the Court, would lead to significant restrictions on the availability of federal habeas re-

[21] Florida Rule Crim. Proc. 3.190(i) provides in relevant part: "The motion to suppress shall be made prior to trial unless opportunity therefore did not exist or the defendant was not aware of the grounds for the motion, but the court in its discretion may entertain the motion or an appropriate objection at the trial" (quoted in *Wainwright*, 433 U.S. at 76 n. 5).

[22] *Wainwright v. Sykes* did not actually overrule *Fay*. Rehnquist stated: "We have no occasion today to consider the *Fay* rule as applied to the facts there confronting the Court. Whether the *Francis* rule should preclude federal habeas review of claims not made in accordance with state procedure where the criminal defendant has surrendered, other than for reasons of tactical advantage, the right to have all of his claims of trial error considered by a state appellate court, we leave for another day" (*Wainwright*, 433 U.S. at 88, n. 12).

[23] Chief Justice Burger asserted that the deliberate bypass standard was inapplicable to errors alleged to have been committed during trial. It was applicable only to a defendant's decision on whether to appeal. Justice Stevens indicated that he was not satisfied with a rigid application of either the deliberate bypass standard or a cause and prejudice rule. Justice White asserted that the Court could have decided the case without considering the deliberate bypass rule; nevertheless he suggested that he would adhere to that standard.

lief for state prisoners who seek to raise federal claims in federal court.

Rehnquist launched the third prong of the Court's attack on habeas corpus when he held in Sumner v. Mata (449 U.S. 539 [1981]) that federal courts must explain their reasons for differing with the findings of a state court. After the California state courts rejected Mata's contention that pretrial photographic identification violated due process standards, he filed a habeas corpus petition in federal district court where the judge summarily denied relief. The U.S. Court of Appeals for the Ninth Circuit reviewed the state court record and found that the photographic identification procedure was impermissibly suggestive and that under the circumstances it was unnecessary. The court concluded that it violated Mata's right to due process.

The Supreme Court reversed on the grounds that the Ninth Circuit had failed to justify its findings as required by federal law. A statute, 28 U.S.C. Section 2254(d), provides for the presumption of correctness of state court factual findings except under specified circumstances.[24] The Ninth Circuit's opinion did not

[24] 28 U.S.C. Section 2254(d) provides:

"In any proceeding instituted in a Federal court by an application for a writ of habeas corpus by a person in custody pursuant to the judgment of a State court, a determination after a hearing on the merits of a factual issue, made by a State court of competent jurisdiction in a proceeding to which the applicant for the writ and the State or an officer or agent thereof were parties, evidenced by a written finding, written opinion, or other reliable and adequate written indicia, shall be presumed to be correct, unless the applicant shall establish or it shall otherwise appear, or the respondent shall admit—

"1) that the merits of the factual dispute were not resolved in the State court hearing;

"2) that the factfinding procedure employed by the State court was not adequate to afford a full and fair hearing;

"3) that the material facts were not adequately developed at the State court hearing;

"4) that the State court lacked jurisdiction of the subject matter or over the person of the applicant in the State court proceeding;

"5) that the applicant was an indigent and the State court, in deprivation of his constitutional right, failed to appoint counsel to represent him in the State court proceeding;

"6) that the applicant did not receive a full, fair, and adequate hearing in the State court proceeding; or

"7) that the applicant was otherwise denied due process of law in the State court proceeding;

"8) or unless that part of the record of the State court proceeding in which the determination of such factual issue was made, pertinent to a determina-

refer to the statute. Rehnquist, writing for a majority, held that a federal court granting habeas corpus must explain why a case falls within an exception to Section 2254(d) or what led it to conclude that the state finding was not supported by the record.

Before Congress enacted Section 2254(d) in 1966, the Supreme Court had established that federal courts should defer only to factual findings of state courts, not to legal findings or to mixed questions involving the application of law to facts (Brown v. Allen, 344 U.S. 443 [1953], and Townsend v. Sain, 372 U.S. 293 [1963]). After the enactment of Section 2254(d), the Court construed it to apply only to situations in which state and federal courts differed on matters of historical fact. Rehnquist's opinion in *Mata* extended Section 2254(d) to mixed findings that involve not only facts but also the application of law to those facts. He contended that "it is clear that in adopting [Section 2254(d) Congress] intended . . . to minimize that inevitable friction [that occurs when a federal habeas court overturns] either the factual or legal conclusions reached by the state-court system" (449 U.S. at 541).

In short, Rehnquist's opinion in *Mata* portended stringent restrictions on federal habeas corpus. The consequence of that opinion, illustrated by the resolution of the case by the Ninth Circuit after two remands,[25] was the extension of the circum-

---

tion of the sufficiency of the evidence to support such factual determination, is produced as provided for herinafter, and the Federal court on a consideration of such part of the record as a whole concludes that such factual determination is not fairly supported by the record" (quoted in *Mata*, 449 U.S. at 544). For the background of the statute and the Court's construal prior to *Mata*, see "Summer v. Mata," 1983.

[25] The Supreme Court remanded the case to the Ninth Circuit for an explanation of its holding in light of Section 2254(d). The Ninth Circuit held that the statute was inapplicable because the issue to be resolved involved both fact and law. Indeed, the Ninth Circuit had no dispute with any of the historical facts found by the California court. Thus, according to the Ninth Circuit, the California court's decision was reviewable by a federal court. The case reached the Supreme Court a second time on California's petition for certiorari. In a per curiam opinion, the Court conceded that the "ultimate question as to the constitutionality of the pretrial identification procedures used in this case is a mixed question of law and fact that is not governed by Section 2254(d)" (*Mata*, 455 U.S. 591 [1982]). Nevertheless, the Court held that "the questions of fact that underlie this ultimate conclusion are governed by the statutory presumption" (ibid., 597, emphasis in original). The Ninth Circuit on a second remand again held that the photographic identification procedures violated Mata's rights of due process. The court reached its decision by applying Section 2254(d) and concluding, after a review of the facts, that certain state court findings were not fairly supported by

stances in which a federal court must apply Section 2254(d) and justify its rejection of a state court's findings.

In his opinion in *Mata*, Rehnquist also expressed his belief that state courts should be allowed to interpret the federal law independently of federal courts: "State judges as well as federal judges swear allegiance to the Constitution of the United States, and there is no reason to think that because of their frequent differences of opinions as to how that document should be interpreted, all are not doing their mortal best to discharge their oath of office" (449 U.S. at 549).

In subsequent opinions the justice elaborated on the limits that *Mata* imposes on federal courts. For example, he suggested that it may not be sufficient under Section 2254(d) for a federal court to base its rejection of a state court's decision on its conclusion that the state court findings were not supported by the record (Marshall v. Lonberger, 459 U.S. 422 [1983]). In the *Marshall* case he found that the court of appeals did not give the state court the high measure of deference required and held that a federal habeas court must find that a state court's findings lacked even fair support in the record (see also Smith v. Phillips, 455 U.S. 209 [1982], and Wainwright v. Witt, 469 U.S. 412 [1985]).

Conclusion

Commentators and judges have often asserted that federal courts are the more appropriate forum for the protection of individual rights; Rehnquist, however, is unmoved by the possibility that a federal court is more likely to affirm individual rights.[26] He has devoted his attention to the question of whether a federal court may properly intervene in matters of state policy. And when he answers that question, it is, with rare exception, in the negative.

Rehnquist's opinions in the areas of the Eleventh Amendment, Section 1983, and habeas corpus considered together attest to the enthusiasm with which he has undertaken the task of reversing the trend of expanding federal judicial power. When his endeavors to protect the states from what he sees as the encroachment

the record and therefore did not merit the presumption of correctness required by the statute.

[26] Cover and Alienkoff (1977, 1077) explained Rehnquist's position as "a plea for certainty, finality, and efficiency understood in linear terms. The approach is content-free; it says nothing about the nature of the rights that are to exist or about their relative ordering."

of the federal judiciary have explicitly involved constitutional questions, he has employed a structural mode of analysis. For example, when he dissented from the Court's holding that the Eleventh Amendment does not afford a state immunity from suit in the courts of another state he castigated the majority for its "literalism" in interpreting the amendment:

[T]he Court should have been sensitive to the constitutional plan and avoided a result that destroys the logic of the Framers' careful allocation of responsibility among the state and federal judiciaries, and makes nonsense of the effort embodied in the Eleventh Amendment to preserve the doctrine of sovereign immunity. (Nevada v. Hall, 440 U.S. 410, 441 [1979])

In that opinion he also stated:

Concepts such as "state" and "bill of attainder" are not defined in the Constitution and demand external referents. But on a more subtle plane when the Constitution is ambiguous or silent on a particular issue, this Court has often relied on notions of a constitutional plan—implicit ordering of relationships within the federal system necessary to make the Constitution a workable governing charter and to give each provision within that document the full effect intended by the Framers. (Ibid., 433)

In a similar vein, in his dissent in *Fry v. United States* he referred to both the Tenth and Eleventh amendments as "simply examples of the understanding of those who drafted and ratified the Constitution that the States were sovereign in many respects" (421 U.S 542, 557 [1975]).

Rehnquist's willingness to utilize a structural mode of interpretation and, thereby, to suggest that his federalism depends on some notion of a "constitutional plan" rather than on explicit provisions within the text, brings into question the consistency of his fundamental understanding of the Constitution. Does it include more than the text? His opinions concerning judicial federalism, as well as his pronouncements regarding the extent of Congress's power, imply that the answer would be yes. In contrast, his opinions construing the Bill of Rights suggest that he subscribes to a textual approach to constitutional interpretation. Possible inconsistencies aside, the value that is most important to the justice is federalism.

It would, in Rehnquist's view, advance the interests of federalism and democracy—indeed, it would benefit the American constitutional system immensely—to limit the jurisdiction of the federal courts. His concern for giving proper respect to the decisions of state courts, manifested in the opinions discussed in the present chapter—particularly his opinions regarding habeas corpus—is revealed even more clearly in the context of "Our Federalism," examined in the following chapter.

NINE

Federalism III:
"Our Federalism" or Rehnquist's Federalism?

In this chapter I conclude my examination of Rehnquist's judicial federalism by discussing several of his opinions in cases in which the Supreme Court has limited the circumstances under which a federal court may issue an injunction against state officials. In Younger v. Harris (401 U.S. 37) in 1971,[1] the Court held that only under exceptional circumstances may a federal court enjoin a pending state criminal proceeding. The Court's decision created a major exception to the guarantee, which was provided in *Monroe*, of a federal forum under Section 1983. Justice Black, writing for the majority, identified two sources of the "longstanding public policy against federal court interference with state court proceedings" (*Younger*, 401 U.S. at 43). The first was the doctrine of equity jurisprudence—that courts should not act to restrain a criminal prosecution when there is an adequate remedy at law and when the claimant will not suffer injury if denied equitable relief. Second, he identified comity as a source of the policy against federal injunctions on state criminal proceedings. Black explained that comity is "a proper respect for state functions, a recognition of the fact that the entire country is made up of a Union of separate state governments, and a continuance of the belief that the National Government will fare best if the States and their institutions are left free to perform their separate functions in their separate ways" (ibid., 44).

Comity, also referred to as "Our Federalism," Black added, represents a "system in which there is sensitivity to the legitimate interests of both State and National Governments, and in which the National Government, anxious though it may be to vindicate and protect federal rights and federal interests, always endeavors to do so in ways that will not unduly interfere with the legitimate activities of the States" (ibid.).

[1] The companion cases to *Younger* were Samuels v. Mackell, 401 U.S. 66 (1971); Boyle v. Landry, 401 U.S. 77 (1971); Perez v. Ledesma, 401 U.S. 82 (1971); Dyson v. Stein, 401 U.S. 200 (1971); Byrne v. Karalexis, 401 U.S. 216 (1971).

The Court's actual holding in *Younger* was that "a federal court should not enjoin a state criminal prosecution begun prior to the institution of the federal suit except in very unusual situations where necessary to prevent immediate irreparable injury" (ibid., 69). The irreparable injury must be both "great and immediate," as demonstrated by a threat to the plaintiff's federally protected rights that cannot be eliminated by the defense of a single criminal prosecution, a showing of bad faith, harassment, or a statute that is flagrantly unconstitutional.[2] In short, Black proposed that "the normal thing to do when federal courts are asked to enjoin pending proceedings in state courts is not to issue such injunctions" (ibid., 45).

The common situation that raises questions regarding the dimensions of *Younger* is one in which a plaintiff who is involved in state criminal proceedings seeks a declaration from a federal court that the state law under which he or she is being prosecuted is invalid and asks for an injunction halting that prosecution. Thus, a federal court is asked to intervene directly into the state judicial process by forbidding the state authorities from proceeding with a criminal prosecution.

REHNQUIST AND THE YOUNGER DOCTRINE

In the years since its decision in 1971 the Court has failed to provide a clear set of rules for the application of the principles of *Younger*, possibly as a consequence of the justices' inability to agree on any coherent rationale for the doctrine.[3] In contrast,

[2] See Fiss (1977) for an analysis of Dombrowski v. Pfister (380 U.S. 479 [1965]), which provides the details of the background of *Younger*. See also Soifer and Macgill (1977) for a critique of the precedent used in *Younger*.

[3] A number of commentators have argued that the Court has not developed a consistent or coherent rationale for "*Younger* deference" and that, consequently, the post-*Younger* decisions seem to draw arbitrary distinctions between situations in which federal courts may and may not act. See, for example, Redish's (1978, 465) assertion that "[t]he Court . . . has never satisfactorily delimited the range of state 'interests' or state institutions constituting the intended beneficiaries of this considerable federalistic deference. The Court has, at times, specifically considered the nature of state interests deserving protection. But many of these statements, as well as many of the Court's actions in developing and applying the *Younger* doctrine, appear internally inconsistent or contradictory." Soifer and Macgill (1977, 1214) concluded their critical piece on the *Younger* doctrine with: "[T]he nature of the larger policy served by circumscribing the role of federal courts remains difficult to discern." Wells (1981, 85) argued that the Court has made arbitrary distinctions between cases in which comity requires restraint

Rehnquist, although he did not participate in the Court's decision in *Younger*, has played a major role in the clarification and expansion of the doctrine of that case. In fact, he has applied himself vigorously to the task of expanding the *Younger* doctrine in the cause of insulating state governments from federal judicial supervision.[4] He has consistently pointed to a concern for the protection of state decision making processes as the basis of *Younger* and has tried to transform the doctrine of that decision into a powerful tool to limit federal judicial power.

The Anti-Injunction Act prohibits federal courts from enjoining state proceedings except when expressly authorized by Congress.[5] In his opinion in *Younger*, Justice Black referred to that statute as evidence of a long-standing public policy against federal judicial interference with state court proceedings. Nevertheless, he declined to consider the question of whether relief sought under Section 1983 was within the exception to the Anti-Injunction Act. One year later, however, the Court considered the question and answered in the affirmative (Mitchum v. Foster, 407 U.S. 225 [1972]). Justice Stewart, who wrote the opinion for the Court, limited the decision, stating that it did not "question or qualify in any way the principles of equity, comity, and federalism that must restrain a federal court when asked to enjoin a state court proceeding" (*Mitchum*, 407 U.S. at 243). Thus, although Section 1983 constitutes an exception to the Anti-Injunction Act, the ability of Section 1983 to provide remedies for state denial of constitutional rights is severely limited by the *Younger* rule.[6] Rehn-

---

and those in which it does not because it is using comity to avoid a choice between two competing values: state court adjudication of constitutional challenges to state law and individual access to federal court for constitutional claims.

[4] H. Jefferson Powell (1982, 1336) stated: "To a remarkable extent, Rehnquist has carried a majority of the Court with him in his crusade to universalize *Younger*."

[5] 28 U.S.C. Section 2283 (1970) reads: "A Court of the United States may not grant an injunction to stay proceedings in a State court except as expressly authorized by Act of Congress, or where necessary in aid of its jurisdiction, or to protect or effectuate its judgments." In Atlantic Coastline R.R. v. Brotherhood of Locomotive Engineers (398 U.S. 281 [1970]), the Court held the Anti-Injunction Act to be an absolute bar to interference in all pending state cases.

[6] *Younger* and *Mitchum* have a confusing relationship. As one commentator posed the problem: "[W]hy, if Section 1983 qualifies as an express exception from the letter of the statute, [does it] not also qualify as an exception to judge-made rules derived from the statute?" ("Developments in the Law," 1977, 1289, n. 88). Weinberg (1977, 1213) explained that "the Court decided *Younger* as it did be-

quist did not participate in the decision, but he has indicated in a different context that he would construe the exceptions to the Anti-Injunction Act narrowly.[7]

Other important questions that *Younger* raised but did not resolve concerned the type of relief that federal courts were prohibited from granting and the question of whether federal relief could be obtained absent bad faith, harassment, or a flagrantly invalid state statute when there was no state prosecution in progress. In one of the companion cases to *Younger*, Justice Black stated that in unusual circumstances a declaratory judgment might be appropriate. Ordinarily, however, he maintained that the practical effect of declaratory and injunctive relief would be virtually identical, "and the basic policy against federal interference with pending state criminal prosecutions will be frustrated as much by a declaratory judgment as it would be by an injunction" (Samuels v. Mackell, 401 U.S. 66, 72).

In 1974 the Court held that although injunctive relief against future prosecutions is barred, a declaratory judgment may be issued without a finding of the special circumstances required by *Younger* (Steffel v. Thompson, 415 U.S. 452). In an opinion for the majority, Justice Brennan suggested that declaratory and injunctive relief should be treated differently: "When no state proceeding is pending and thus considerations of equity, comity, and federalism have little vitality, the propriety of granting federal declaratory relief may properly be considered independently of a request for injunctive relief" (*Steffel*, 415 U.S. at 462). Indeed, Brennan noted, in the Declaratory Judgment Act of 1934 Congress made declaratory relief available in cases in which an injunction would be inappropriate. Therefore, to require that all of the conditions for an injunction be satisfied before a declaratory judgment can be considered would defy Congress's intent.

Rehnquist wrote a concurring opinion in which he emphasized the limited scope of a declaratory judgment—"simply a statement of rights, not a binding order supplemented by continuing sanctions" (ibid., 482). He asserted that the effects of a declara-

cause *Mitchum* was waiting in the wings. After *Younger* the Court could decide *Mitchum* without fear of opening any new jurisdictional doors other than those it was prepared to open."

[7] In Vendo Company v. Lektro-Vend Corporation (433 U.S. 623 [1977]) Rehnquist wrote for a three-person plurality that Section 16 of the Clayton Act does not fall within the exception to the Anti-Injunction Act because a stay of a state action is not necessary to give Section 16 its intended scope.

tory judgment are minimal and underlined the independence of state judicial processes:

> If the federal court finds that the threatened prosecution would depend upon a statute it judges unconstitutional, the State may decide to forgo prosecution of similar conduct in the future, believing the judgment persuasive. Should the state prosecutors not find the decision persuasive enough to justify forbearance, the successful federal plaintiff will at least be able to bolster his allegations of unconstitutionality in the state trial with a decision of the federal district court in the immediate locality. The state courts may find the reasoning convincing even though the prosecutors did not. Finally, of course, the state legislature may decide, on the basis of the federal decision, that the statute would be better amended or repealed. (Ibid., 484)[8]

Rehnquist also maintained that declaratory relief could not be used as a basis for obtaining an injunction against a subsequent criminal prosecution. Moreover, he asserted that if the federal plaintiff pursues the conduct for which he was previously threatened with arrest, and is arrested, he may not return the controversy to federal court, although he may raise the issue of the federal declaratory judgment in the state court.

Thus, although he agreed with the majority that declaratory judgments against threatened prosecutions do not fall within the restrictions of *Younger*, Rehnquist was careful to delineate the extremely limited effect of such judgments. He grounded his opinion in the concern for comity underlying the *Younger* cases. Those cases, he stated, "depend upon considerations relevant to the harmonious operation of separate federal and state court systems, with a special regard for the State's interest in enforcing its own criminal laws" (ibid., 482).

In 1975 Rehnquist joined the majority when it held in a 5 to 4 decision that *Younger* applies when the state brings criminal proceedings against the federal plaintiffs after they have filed a federal complaint but before any proceedings of substance on the merits have taken place in federal court (Hicks v. Miranda 422

---

[8] Justice White concurred in order to underline his disagreement with Rehnquist. He contended that Rehnquist's interpretation of a declaratory judgment contradicted the terms of the Declaratory Judgment Act, which specifies that "[a]ny such declaration shall have the force and effect of final judgment or decree" (28 U.S.C. Section 2201, quoted in 415 U.S. at 477).

U.S. 332 [1975]). A brief summary of the facts of the case may clarify the significance of the Court's decision. The police seized copies of the film *Deep Throat* from a theater, and a misdemeanor charge was brought against theater employees. Several days later a state court viewed the film and declared it obscene. The theater owners brought suit in federal court, seeking an injunction against enforcement of the state's obscenity statute and a judgment declaring the statute unconstitutional. A three-judge federal court was convened to consider the case. Meanwhile, the county prosecutor amended the criminal complaint to include the theater owners in the state criminal proceeding—an action that the Supreme Court did not construe as harassment. The decision considerably expanded the power of the states by providing them with the opportunity to force dismissal of federal action by instituting their own proceedings.[9] As Justice Stewart pointed out in his dissenting opinion, the applicability of the *Younger* doctrine now turns solely on "the outcome of a race to the courthouse . . . [the race is one which] permits the State to leave the mark later, run a shorter course, and arrive first at the finish line" (*Hicks*, 422 U.S. at 354).

Less than a week after its decision in *Hicks v. Miranda* the Court held that no relief was available to federal plaintiffs who had been served with a state criminal summons after they instituted federal litigation but before any contested matter had been decided. The Court held, however, that other plaintiffs against whom the state had not instituted proceedings could obtain a preliminary injunction against a threatened prosecution without a finding of the special circumstances required by *Younger* (Doran v. Salem Inn, Inc., 422 U.S. 922). Rehnquist wrote the opinion for a majority in which he noted that temporary relief "seriously impairs the State's interest in enforcing its criminal laws, and implicates the concerns for federalism which lie at the heart of *Younger*" (*Doran*, 422 U.S. at 931). Nevertheless, he found that the plaintiffs had successfully met the traditional

---

[9] "[F]ederal jurisdiction may be destroyed by a state functionary even after it is properly assumed. This powerful tactical weapon is solely within the control of the state prosecutor" (Soifer and Macgill 1977, 1193). Fiss (1977, 1135) noted that the district attorney now has the power to remove a case from the federal court to the state court: "After a federal anticipatory suit is filed, the district attorney can initiate a criminal prosecution against the aggrieved citizen and by the action abort the federal suit and remit the citizen to adjudicating his claim as a defense in a criminal prosecution in the state court."

standard for obtaining a preliminary injunction—that without the relief they would suffer irreparable injury.[10]

In sum, although the Supreme Court has allowed the lower courts to operate outside the bounds of *Younger* when no state prosecution is pending and when the relief has been limited to a declaratory judgment or a preliminary injunction, Rehnquist has carefully emphasized the strictly limited nature of the relief that may be granted. Further, he joined the majority in the Court's decision that allowed states to halt a federal action simply by filing charges of their own.

Although limited federal relief is available when no state prosecution is pending, it is quite possible that such relief would be denied because the Court would find that there was no genuine case or controversy. In *Younger* Justice Black noted that those who have not actually been prosecuted and have "no fears of state prosecution except those that are imaginary or speculative, are not to be accepted as appropriate plaintiffs" (401 U.S. at 37). The result may be "[a] kind of 'catch-22.' " If a federal plaintiff has not been prosecuted by the state, there may not be a controversy; if a state prosecution is pending, the doctrine of *Younger* will probably prohibit federal relief (Redish 1980, 314). Although Rehnquist has not explicitly endorsed the "catch-22," he has emphasized the need for a "concrete case or controversy" (Moore v. Sims, 442 U.S. 415, 442 [1979]); he has underlined the limited nature of the relief that is available when no prosecution is pending; and he has reiterated that when a prosecution is pending, *Younger* usually bars a federal injunction against state criminal proceedings.

Another question that arose in the aftermath of *Younger* was whether a plaintiff must exhaust state appellate remedies before obtaining relief from a federal court. In Huffman v. Pursue (420 U.S. 592 [1975]), the federal plaintiffs argued that *Younger* was not applicable because there were no pending state proceedings.

[10] When the Court authorized the issuance of permanent injunctive relief against future prosecutions at a time when no prosecution was pending, Rehnquist dissented (Wooley v. Maynard, 430 U.S. 705 [1977]). Chief Justice Burger held that "*Younger* principles aside, a litigant is entitled to resort to a federal forum in seeking redress under 42 U.S.C. Section 1983 for an alleged deprivation of federal rights" (*Wooley*, 430 U.S. at 710). Burger then went on to hold that New Hampshire could not require an individual to display the state motto, "Live Free or Die," on automobile license plates. Rehnquist, in dissent, did not discuss the applicability of *Younger* but instead voiced his disagreement with the the Court's decision on the merits. The scope of the decision is unclear, and Burger's opinion is generally considered to border "on hopeless confusion" (Redish 1980, 312).

The proceeding for abatement of a nuisance had ended by the time the federal complaint was filed. Rehnquist emphasized federalism, rather than equity jurisprudence, as the basis of *Younger* when he held that absent a showing that irreparable injury will result, state appellate remedies must be exhausted before federal relief will be granted. Federal intervention after a state trial, he asserted, would be duplicative, would cast aspersions on the capabilities and good faith of state appellate courts, and would disrupt the state's efforts to protect important interests. He posited that if the federal courts are allowed to negate the results of state trials, the states will be deprived of their function of overseeing trial court dispositions of constitutional issues that are raised in cases in which state courts have jurisdiction.[11]

An additional question of major importance that was not resolved by *Younger* was whether the doctrine would apply to civil as well as state criminal proceedings.[12] While Rehnquist's role in the decisions discussed so far in this chapter has been far from negligible, he has played an even more prominent role in a series of decisions that have expanded the *Younger* doctrine to severely limit the availability of federal injunctions against civil proceedings.

In 1972 Rehnquist, in his capacity as circuit justice, denied a request for declaratory and injunctive relief in a case that involved the election of delegates to the Democratic National Convention. He asserted that although *Younger* and its companions involved state criminal prosecutions, "the principles of federal comity upon which it was based are enunciated in earlier decisions of this Court dealing with civil as well as criminal matters" (Cousins v. Wigoda, 409 U.S. 1201, 1205).[13]

---

[11] In 1980 in Allen v. McCurry (449 U.S. 90), a six-person majority held that res judicata and collateral estoppel are applicable to Section 1983 actions. That decision rendered the aspect of *Huffman* concerning exhaustion of state remedies irrelevant. Once state remedies are exhausted, a Section 1983 suit is precluded.

[12] The *Harvard Law Review* argued against applying *Younger* in the civil context: If the *Younger* "exceptional circumstances" rule were applied, "much of the rigidity of 2283 would be reintroduced and the significance of Mitchum for those seeking relief from state civil proceedings would largely be destroyed, and the recognition of section 1983 as an exception to the Anti Injunction Statute would have been a Pyrrhic victory" ("The Supreme Court, 1971 Term," 1972, 217–18). Justice Brennan has adhered to the view that *Younger* should not apply to civil proceedings (Huffman v. Pursue, 420 U.S. 592 [1975], dissenting opinion, and Juidice v. Vail, 430 U.S. 327 [1977], dissenting opinion). See Fiss 1977.

[13] Soifer and Macgill (1977, 1179 n. 156) noted that the cases that Rehnquist cited to support his assertion all involved criminal sanctions.

In *Huffman*, Rehnquist, speaking for a six-person majority, held the principles of *Younger* applicable to a civil proceeding. It appeared that an important factor in the decision was that the civil proceeding involved was "a state proceeding which in important respects is more akin to a criminal prosecution than are most civil cases" (420 U.S. at 604). The similarities grew out of the state's interest in the litigation: not only was the state a party but the proceeding was

> both in aid of and closely related to criminal statutes. . . . Thus, an offense to the State's interest in the nuisance litigation is likely to be every bit as great as it would be were this a criminal proceeding. . . . Similarly, . . . the District Court's injunction . . . has disrupted the state's efforts to protect the very interests which underlie its criminal laws and to obtain compliance with precisely the standards which are embodied in its criminal laws. (Ibid., 604–5, citations omitted)

Rehnquist's opinion, nevertheless, strongly suggested that those similarities were not crucial. Indeed, he noted at the outset that for many years the Court has recognized the seriousness of federal judicial interference with state civil functions. Additionally, he reiterated the concern for federalism underlying *Younger*: intervention in state judicial proceedings prevents the state from effectuating its substantive policies and from providing a forum to vindicate constitutional objections to those policies; it results in duplicative legal proceedings, and may reflect negatively upon the state court's ability to enforce constitutional principles.

He went further by distinguishing the rationale for *Younger* based upon "Our Federalism" from the rationale that was based on equity jurisprudence, or "the traditional reluctance of courts . . . to interfere with a criminal prosecution" (ibid.).[14] That distinction was important for the following reason: If *Younger* was based entirely on the need to preserve Our Federalism, the principle of the decision would be equally applicable to a civil or criminal proceeding. *Younger's* foundations in equity jurisprudence, however, would suggest that the doctrine should be limited to criminal proceedings. Thus, if one could successfully

[14] Earlier in his opinion he stated that the Court has "consistently required that when federal courts are confronted with requests for such relief, they should abide by standards of restraint that go well beyond those of private equity jurisprudence" (420 U.S. at 603).

182

ground *Younger* in Our Federalism concerns and sever its connections to equity jurisprudence, the doctrine would be fully applicable to civil proceedings. Rehnquist utilized such a strategy in *Huffman* to pave the way for the expansion of *Younger*. He de-emphasized *Younger*'s roots in equity jurisprudence and accentuated concerns for federalism by addressing the importance of the state's interest in its judicial proceedings.

Two years after *Huffman*, Rehnquist authored an opinion for the majority in which he applied the *Younger* doctrine to state civil contempt proceedings (Juidice v. Vail, 430 U.S. 327 [1977]). The similarity between certain types of civil proceedings and a criminal prosecution was even less important to the decision than it was in *Huffman*. Asserting that in *Huffman* the applicability of *Younger* to civil cases generally had been reserved, Rehnquist held that the principles of *Younger* and *Huffman* are not confined solely to the types of state actions that were sought to be enjoined in those cases. He indicated that *Younger* applied to a civil contempt process not because it was similar to a criminal prosecution but because the state's interests were involved:

> A State's interest in the contempt process, through which it vindicates the regular operation of its judicial system, . . . is surely an important interest. Perhaps it is not quite as important as is the State's interest in the enforcement of its criminal laws, . . . or even its interest in the maintenance of a quasi-criminal proceeding such as was involved in *Huffman*. But we think it is of sufficiently great import to require application of the principles of those cases. The contempt power lies at the core of the administration of a State's judicial system. (*Juidice*, 430 U.S. at 335, citations omitted)

In Trainor v. Hernandez (431 U.S. 441 [977]), Rehnquist joined the majority in its decision to apply *Younger* to a civil proceeding brought by the state seeking to recover welfare benefits allegedly obtained by fraud and that included the attachment of defendants' savings. Justice White's opinion for the majority extended *Younger* to the type of civil action involved in *Trainor* not on the grounds that it resembled a criminal proceeding but because the state had the choice of bringing a criminal action in this case although it chose a civil remedy. White also focused on the concerns of federalism and noted that the action was brought by the state in its sovereign capacity: "Both the suit and the accompanying writ of attachment were brought to vindicate important state policies such as safeguarding the fiscal integrity of those programs" (*Trainor*, 431 U.S. at 443). The Court's further movement away from equity jurisprudence as a basis for *Younger*, which Rehnquist began in *Huffman*, is evidenced in White's conclusion that "the interests of comity and federalism on which *Younger . . . primarily* rest apply in full force here" (ibid., 447, emphasis mine).

In Moore v. Sims (442 U.S. 415 [1979]) Rehnquist spoke for the majority when the Court applied the principle of *Younger* to a child custody proceeding. References to similarities between the type of civil proceeding involved and a criminal prosecution were notably absent from his opinion. He asserted that the "basic concern—that threat to our federal system posed by displacement of state courts by those of the National Government—is also fully applicable to civil proceedings in which important state interests are involved" (*Moore*, 442 U.S. at 423). Thus, the presence of important state interests had become crucial to the decision to prohibit injunctions against civil proceedings; the similarity between the civil proceeding and a criminal prosecution was negligible. The justice prepared the way for such a change in previous opinions in which he emphasized federalism as the basis for *Younger* while he largely ignored its foundations in equity jurisprudence.

In 1982 the Court held the principles of *Younger* to be applicable to state bar disciplinary proceedings. Speaking for the majority, Chief Justice Burger stated that "[t]he policies underlying *Younger* are fully applicable to noncriminal judicial proceedings when important state interests are involved" (Middlesex County Ethics Committee v. Garden State Bar Association, 457 U.S. 423).[15] Burger resolved the question of whether federal relief should be granted absent the special circumstances of *Younger* in a three-part inquiry. First, did the state bar disciplinary hearings constitute an ongoing state judicial proceeding? Second, do the proceedings implicate important state interests? And, finally, is there an adequate opportunity in the state proceedings to raise constitutional challenges? Burger's opinion illustrates the way in which the Court has transformed *Younger* from a rule prohibiting federal courts from enjoining state criminal prosecutions into a doctrine that protects the states' interests in using their judicial

[15] In Zauderer v. Office of Disciplinary Counsel, 105 S.Ct. 2265, 2275–76, n. 8 (1985), Justice White wrote that "the principle [of *Younger*] is as applicable to attorney disciplinary proceedings as it is to criminal cases."

systems to enforce their public policies.[16] Rehnquist's opinions emphasizing concerns for federalism and virtually eliminating the element of equity jurisprudence underlying *Younger* were instrumental in bringing about that transformation.

State Executive Officials and the Rubric of "Our Federalism"

In 1976 the Court found that the principles of Our Federalism are not limited to state judicial proceedings but that they extend to prevent federal judicial intervention in a situation in which injunctive relief is sought "against those in charge of an executive branch of an agency of state or local government" (Rizzo v. Goode, 423 U.S. 362, 380). *Rizzo* arose out of an action under Section 1983 against the mayor and the police commissioner of Philadelphia to stop police mistreatment of minorities in the city. Although the trial court found that there had been numerous violations of citizens' civil rights, it did not find that the named defendants intended such violations. Nevertheless, the district court found that the defendants had failed to take remedial steps and issued an injunction ordering the supervising officers to revise police manuals and to draft a comprehensive program for improving the handling of citizen complaints. The court of appeals affirmed. The Supreme Court, by a vote of 5 to 3, reversed. Writing for the majority, Rehnquist based his opinion largely upon the idea that federal intervention in state governmental affairs was unnecessary and undesirable.[17]

Disputing the district court's pronouncement that its power to issue the injunction was firmly established, Rehnquist asserted that the principles of Our Federalism, which he illustrated in part

[16] The requisite extraordinary circumstances of bad faith, harassment, or a patently unconstitutional statute, at least according to Supreme Court assessments, rarely occur. See, for example, *Hicks v. Miranda*, in which the Court dismissed the lower court's finding of bad faith and harassment as "vague and conclusory" (422 U.S. at 350), and *Trainor v. Hernandez*, regarding a finding of flagrant unconstitutionality: "Even if such a finding was made below, which we doubt, it would not have been warranted in light of our cases" (437 U.S. at 447). Soifer and Macgill (1977, 1211) quipped that *"Trainor* extinguished any thought that may still have lingered that any of the exceptions to *Younger* if theoretically viable, would ever be found and sustained."

[17] The other two grounds for reversal were the absence of an actual case or controversy and the failure to show that the authorities had engaged in any action to deprive the plaintiffs of their constitutional rights.

by citing his own opinions clarifying the doctrine of *Younger*,[18] must govern the type of relief granted here. The district court, he concluded, departed from those precepts when it "injected itself by injunctive decree into the internal disciplinary affairs of this state agency" (ibid.).

Rehnquist's opinion in *Rizzo* represents the culmination of his strategic efforts to create out of *Younger* a tool for insulating state and local governments from the federal judiciary. His opinion suggested that no federal injunctive relief will be forthcoming even if no other remedy is available—a result of the severence of the ties between equity jurisprudence and Our Federalism that his analysis made complete. Similarly, his application of the presumption against federal judicial intervention to limit the actions of state executive officials freed the doctrine of *Younger* from the remaining ties to its original conception—giving respect to state judicial processes.

In Fair Assessment in Real Estate Association, Inc. v. McNary (454 U.S. 100 [1981]), the Court held that state taxpayers could not bring an action for damages to redress the allegedly unconstitutional administration of their state tax system. Again writing for the majority, Rehnquist reasoned that although "modern expressions" of comity have been limited in that they have been applied to prohibit the enjoining of state judicial proceedings, they "illustrate the principles that bar petitioner's suit" (*Fair Assessment*, 454 U.S. at 112). Although he specified that the Court was not abandoning that limit, he strongly suggested that regardless of any such constraints delineated by past cases, the principles of *Younger* are subject to extension into areas never envisioned by the justices who constituted the majority in *Younger* itself.[19] In Rehnquist's hands the doctrine of *Younger* may have no limits; he seems to have fashioned a powerful tool to limit federal judicial power.

Conclusion

Rehnquist's opinions in the area known as Our Federalism have been criticized on various grounds. For example, Justice Brennan

[18] Rehnquist quoted from his opinion in *Huffman* and cited *Doran v. Salem Inn, Inc.*

[19] H. Jefferson Powell (1982, 1338) effectively made the point that Rehnquist has made it possible for the *Younger* doctrine to function "as a freewheeling judicial metaprinciple, available to trump virtually any federal equitable intervention into the affairs of state or local governments."

has accused him of using federalism as an excuse for stripping the federal courts of the jurisdiction conferred upon them by Congress.[20] Some commentators have labeled Rehnquist as a misinterpreter of precedent who has mean-spritedly invoked principles of federalism to disguise his decisions on the merits (Soifer and Macgill 1977). Others have castigated him for using federalism to support the status quo. For example, Owen Fiss (1977, 1160–61) expressed his suspician that

> at the heart of *Rizzo*—and at the heart of the progeny of "Our Federalism"—[there] is more than a concern that federal courts should not interfere in state agencies. I suspect that at the heart of *Rizzo* there is a new version of laissez faire—one specially tailored to the welfare state. It consists of a desire to insulate the status quo from judicial interference, regardless of whether the protected institution is a judicial system, legislature or administrative agency. . . . "Federalism" is but one handle available to the Supreme Court for curbing some of the more ambitious—more idealistic—projects of its own judges.

Finally, Rehnquist has been castigated for declining to tie his expansion of Our Federalism to any particular constitutional provision (Powell 1982).[21]

In order to expand Our Federalism for the sake of protecting "His Federalism," he has found it necessary to rely on the overall design of the Constitution rather than on any specific provision. Just as he has done with regard to the areas of the law treated in the previous two chapters, in the area of Our Federalism, Rehnquist has reached beyond the text of the Constitution to a "constitutional plan" for a federalism that he discovers in the structure of the document.

His opinions construing the Eleventh Amendment, Section 1983, habeas corpus, and Our Federalism attest to the steadfast dedication with which he has pursued the goal of insulating the states from the federal courts. His majority opinions have taken

[20] For example, Brennan stated: "The increasingly talismanic use of the phrase 'comity and federalism'—itself essentially devoid of content other than in the *Younger* sense of determining the timing of federal review—has ominous portent; it has the look of an excuse being fashioned by the Court for stripping federal courts of the jurisdiction properly conferred by Congress" (Francis v. Henderson, 425 U.S. 536, 551 [1976]).

[21] See also Brennan's dissent in National League of Cities v. Usery (426 U.S. 833 [1976]).

the Court a considerable distance toward a revived and rejuvenated dual federalism in which state courts—indeed, state governments—would operate as independent, autonomous governing bodies, free from federal judicial review. His opinions limiting the reach of Section 1983 and the availability of habeas corpus strongly suggest that Rehnquist would applaud abolishing the jurisdiction of the federal courts to hear federal claims in cases that either originate in state court or that involve state interests. If a majority of the Supreme Court adopts such a position, state courts will have the final say on questions involving the protection of individual rights, and the federal courts will lose a major portion of their function as interpreters of the federal Constitution. Such a result would be entirely consistent with the justice's vision of the proper distribution of powers between the federal government and the states.

Conclusion

TEN

Legal Positivism, Federalism, and Rehnquist's Constitution

He has an agile mind but not an open mind.—*Sen. Joseph R. Biden, Jr. (D., Del.)*

On the merits, Justice Rehnquist is not mainstream but too extreme—he is too extreme on race, too extreme on women's rights, too extreme on freedom of speech, too extreme on separation of church and state, too extreme to be Chief Justice.—*Senator Edward M. Kennedy (D., Mass.)*

The [Senate Judiciary Committee] hearings showed who the extremists really are.—*Senator Orrin G. Hatch (R., Utah)*

On June 17, 1986, President Ronald Reagan announced his nomination of William H. Rehnquist to succeed Warren E. Burger as chief justice of the United States. The president chose Antonin Scalia, a judge on the United States Court of Appeals for the District of Columbia, to fill Rehnquist's seat as associate justice. Until Reagan's nomination of Rehnquist, only two sitting associate justices had been promoted to Chief Justice.[1] Rehnquist's record during his fourteen and a half years on the Court made him, from the perspective of the Reagan administration, an ideal choice for chief justice. His positions regarding the applicability of the Bill of Rights to the states, abortion, the rights of the accused, prayer in the schools, school busing, and affirmative action were all in accord with the policies of the Reagan administration. In addition, his voting record and his willingness to dissent alone made it seem highly unlikely that Rehnquist would disappoint President Reagan by changing his views after he became chief justice. Rehnquist's intellect and personal charm also must have have made him attractive to the administration.

The administration's determination to fill judicial vacancies with people whose views were consistent with its own policy goals was particularly apparent in the active role played by the White House in the selection process at the lower court level.[2]

---

[1] Edward D. White was promoted by President William Howard Taft in 1910, and Harlan Fiske Stone was promoted by President Franklin D. Roosevelt in 1941.

[2] By the end of Ronald Reagan's second term in office more than half of the judges in the lower courts will be Reagan appointees. See Goldman 1985.

That commitment was also clear when President Reagan nominated Sandra Day O'Connor to fill the vacancy created by Potter Stewart's retirement in 1981. By 1986, the advanced ages of five Supreme Court justices made it appear quite likely that President Reagan would have an opportunity to fill at least one additional vacancy on the Court.

The prospect of two, possibly three, Reagan appointments to the Court rekindled the debate regarding the role of the Senate in providing "advice and consent" to the president. Justice Rehnquist, in an address he delivered in October 1984, underscored the limited success that presidents have had in their attempts to "pack" the Supreme Court (1985). Laurence Tribe, concerned that such comments could serve to "lessen the Senate's vigilance, when the time came to review the next nomination," published a short book that was, in essence, a response to Rehnquist's speech.[3] Tribe (1985b, 93) argued that the Senate has an obligation to examine not only a nominee's integrity and competence but also his or her judicial philosophy. Senators have the duty to vote against the confirmation of a candidate whose views of "what the law should be, and [his or her] . . . institutional views of what role the Supreme Court should play" fall outside the circle of acceptability. If a nominee is an extremist who does not subscribe to the *American* vision . . . *our* aspirations, *our* idea of a just society," he or she should be rejected (ibid., 96, emphasis in original). An unacceptable nominee, according to Tribe, would be one who would disregard a constitutional amendment, or who believed that the Bill of Rights does not limit state action, or who would overturn the apportionment decisions, or who would construe equal protection to require the abolition of private property. Moreover, he asserted that the Senate should reject a nominee whom the administration had selected solely on the basis of his or her politically approved views on a single issue and should also consider carefully the effect confirmation of a nominee would have on the overall balance of the Court.

REHNQUIST'S CONFIRMATION

The issue of whether the Senate should probe and assess a nominee's judicial philosophy or whether it should limit its inquiry

[3] In his preface, Tribe (1985b, p. x) noted that he had actually begun work on the book long before Rehnquist's speech but accelerated its completion after hearing the speech.

to establishing the nominee's competence and character was central to the Senate's consideration of Rehnquist's nomination for chief justice. Sen. Strom Thurmond (R., S.C.) opened the Senate Judiciary Committee hearings by outlining in sweeping general terms the qualities a Supreme Court justice should possess:

[U]nquestioned integrity—honesty, incorruptibility, fairness;

Courage—the strength to render decisions in accordance with the Constitution and the will of the people as expressed in the law of Congress;

A keen knowledge and understanding;

Compassion—which recognizes both the rights of the individual and the rights of society in the quest for equal justice under law;

Proper judicial temperament—the ability to prevent the pressures of the moment from overcoming the composure and self-discipline of a well ordered mind; and

An understanding of, and appreciation for, the majesty of our system of government. (U.S. Congress 1986a, 1–2)

Thurmond's statement implied that he hoped the committee would focus on the quality of the nominee's character and not probe too deeply into his judicial philosophy. Sen. Orrin Hatch, in his opening remarks, was more direct: "Since judges are obligated to find and not make law, their personal views on the political or sociological merits of an issue have little relevance to the inquiries about judicial qualifications" (ibid., 26).

In contrast, Sen. Joseph Biden urged his colleagues to consider the nominee's "judicial philosophy and vision of the Constitution" (ibid., 5). Sen. Patrick Leahy (D., Vt.) sounded as though he might have been delving into Tribe's book when he declared that

[i]f any Senator feels that a judicial nominee is so committed to a particular agenda that the nominee would not be fair and impartial, if he or she feels that the nominee would not protect fundamental rights of Americans, if he or she believes that the nominee would fail to respect the prevailing principles of constitutional law, that Senator not only has the right, that Senator really has a sworn duty to reject the nominee. (Ibid., 30)

Rehnquist's competence as a jurist was clearly not in question. The American Bar Association's Standing Committee on Federal

Judiciary gave him its highest rating of "well qualified." His confirmation became increasingly controversial, however, during the four days of hearings as the Judiciary Committee examined a number of questions regarding his integrity and judicial ethics. There was a question of whether Rehnquist misled the Committee in 1971 when he testified that the memorandum he prepared for Justice Jackson regarding *Brown v. Board of Education* did not represent his own views (see ch. 1). Although the memorandum did not became public until after the conclusion of the hearings in 1971, Rehnquist declared in a letter to the chair of the committee that the views it presented were Jackson's rather than his own. Subsequently, conflicting accounts cast doubt on that explanation.[4] Thus, in the Hearings in 1986, several members of the committee formulated questions designed to reveal whether the nominee had, in fact, favored the doctrine of "separate-but-equal" in 1952. Rehnquist maintained that the memorandum was a summary of Jackson's views rather than his own. He testified that he could not recall what his own position was in 1952; he "saw factors on both sides" (U.S. Congress 1986a, 137), and he did not believe he had reached a conclusion. "Law clerks do not have to vote" (ibid., 138). He conceded that he may have defended *Plessy v. Ferguson* in the presence of some of his fellow clerks, but only for the purpose of presenting "arguments on the other side" (ibid., 276) that he believed should be considered.

The committee also reviewed Rehnquist's participation in *Laird v. Tatum* (408 U.S. 1), which the Court decided in 1972. In that case he provided the fifth vote for the decision that a challenge, on First Amendment grounds, of military surveillance of civilians who had been engaged in protests during the Vietnam War was nonjustifiable. The American Civil Liberties Union filed a petition for rehearing and asked that Rehnquist disqualify himself. The ACLU asserted that the justice's participation was inappropriate because he had appeared as an expert witness before a Senate committee that was investigating army activities while the case was in the lower courts and had made public statements to the effect that the case had no merit. Rehnquist subsequently explained his reasons for denying the motion to disqualify himself in a memorandum (Laird v. Tatum, 409 U.S. 824 [1972]). During the hearings in 1986 several members of the committee que-

---

[4] See, for example, Richard Klugar's (1975, 606–609) account.

ried the nominee about his refusal to recuse himself. He stood by his memorandum.[5]

Review of the allegations that he had harassed minority voters in Phoenix in the late 1950s and early 1960s occupied more of the committee's time than any other issue. Rehnquist avowed that as a participant in checking the qualifications of voters he had not harassed, intimidated, or challenged qualifications of black or Hispanic voters.[6]

[5] If Rehnquist had disqualified himself from the case, the Supreme Court's 4-to-4 vote would have affirmed the decision of the lower court and the case would have been tried on the merits. During the hearings, the Judiciary Committee attempted to obtain memorandums that Rehnquist had written while he was head of the Office of Legal Counsel, but the Justice Department invoked executive privilege. After the hearings, however, the Senate obtained a draft of a directive authored by Rehnquist that endorsed the use of military intelligence to accomplish the goals of a civil disturbance plan (U.S. Congress 1986b, 94). That memo prompted speculation that Rehnquist's involvement in plans to use military surveillance to gather information about civilians was more extensive than he had led the committee to believe (see the statements of Senators Kennedy and Metzenbaum, for example (Congressional Record, 1986, September 11, S 12388–89, S 12410–11).

Two other memos from Rehnquist's career at the Justice Department became public after the hearings. In one, Rehnquist appeared to advocate a constitutional amendment that would have made it easier for schools to remain segregated. The amendment would have allowed school boards to adopt freedom-of-choice plans and would have allowed zoning plans that were intended to keep the schools segregated. So long as "fair-minded school board members could have selected it [a zoning plan] for nonracial reasons, it [would be] valid regardless of the intent with which a particular school board may have chosen it" (Congressional Record, 1986, September 15, S 12554). The other memo summarized objections to the Equal Rights Amendment. In that memo Rehnquist stated that the amendment would be likely to have an "adverse effect on the family." He raised the question of whether most women would want to "be deprived of special protection" that they now enjoy and characterized the effect of the amendment as "the granting to women of a rigid, doctrinaire equality in all respects with men." He also depicted the movement for equal rights as one motivated by a "virtually fanatical desire to obscure . . . insofar as possible, physical distinctions between the sexes" (quoted in Congressional Record, 1986, September 15, S 12557).

[6] Five witnesses testified before the Judiciary Committee that Rehnquist had been involved in harassing voters. One witness, James Brosnahan, testified that as a federal prosecutor in Phoenix in 1962, he investigated complaints at polling places that voters were being intimidated with literacy tests. He stated that he had seen Rehnquist at a polling place where there had been complaints. Another witness, Sydney Smith, then a professor of psychology at Arizona State University, testified that in 1960 or 1962 he saw Rehnquist approach two black men at a polling place. He told the committee that Rehnquist held up a card for the men to read and said: "You have no business being in this line trying to vote. I would ask you to leave." Eight other witnesses testified that the nominee had not ha-

195

Questions of judicial ethics, credibility, and honesty threat-ened to overwhelm the hearings.[7] It was largely due to the persis-tence of the committee's Democratic members, particularly Sen-ator Biden, that substantial portions of the hearings were devoted to an examination of the nominee's judicial philosophy. Rehn-quist was asked to explain his views on such issues as constitu-tional interpretation, application of the equal protection clause to gender as well as racial discrimination, the establishment clause, the incorporation of the Bill of Rights, and the constitu-tionality of legislation that would limit the jurisdiction of the federal courts. He took the position that a justice should not be called to account for his decisions on the Court. He declined to answer questions about his past decisions in particular cases and he refrained from discussing issues that may come before the Court in the future. Essentially, he advised his questioners to read his opinions if they wished to obtain more information about his positions and his reasoning.

While Democratic senators such as Biden and Kennedy, through their questions and comments, endeavored to depict Rehnquist as a justice with extreme views, several Republican committee members, particularly Senator Hatch, defended Rehn-quist's record. Hatch contended, for example, that the justice's

---

rassed voters but that he merely offered legal advice to others involved in chal-lenging voters (U.S. Congress 1986a, 73).

[7] There were two additional issues that the Committee examined regarding Rehnquist's integrity. First, after an FBI report revealed that the deeds to Rehn-quist's houses in Phoenix and Vermont contained restrictive covenants, the com-mittee tried to ascertain whether the nominee had been aware of those provi-sions. He avowed that he had not known of their existence. Subsequently, however, an article (*Legal Times*, August 4, 1986) disclosed that Rehnquist's law-yer in the purchase of the Vermont house had sent two letters to him before the purchase advising him to read the property deed (*Congressional Record*, 1986, September 11, S 12393). That same day Rehnquist wrote a letter to the Judiciary Committee in which he stated that he had found a letter in his file notifying him that his Vermont house could not be sold to "anyone of the Hebrew race." He stated that he had undoubtedly read the letter but did not recall doing so (U.S. Congress 1986b, 31). The second issue involved a family matter that brought Rehnquist's ethics into question. On August 2, 1986, a story in the *Los Angeles Times* revealed that Rehnquist's wife's brother Harold Cornell had alleged that Rehnquist acted unethically by concealing for twenty years the existence of a trust fund set up by Mr. Cornell's father. Rehnquist had helped his father-in-law set up the $25,000 trust, the purpose of which was to provide for Harold Cornell when his multiple sclerosis made it impossible for him to support himself. Mr. Cornell's allegations raised the question of whether Rehnquist had an ethical ob-ligation to disclose the existence of the trust.

propensity to dissent alone was evidence of his courage to stand by his principles in the face of adversity—to do what he believes is correct under the Constitution—rather than of his extremism (U.S. Congress 1986a, 26–27).

The hearings in 1986 were similar to the hearings on Rehnquist's nomination in 1971 insofar as a number of people appeared before the Judiciary Committee to urge the rejection of the nominee on the basis of his political and judicial views. Representatives of groups such as the Leadership Conference on Civil Rights, National Abortion Rights Action League, National Organization for Women, Center for Constitutional Rights, National Gay and Lesbian Task Force, and People for the American Way provided lengthy testimony to demonstrate Rehnquist's lack of commitment to equal justice and his hostility to the rights of minorities. Unlike 1971, however, in 1986 Rehnquist's opponents had much more to support their arguments than his record as a former Phoenix attorney and an assistant attorney general; they could point to the record he had established as associate justice for fourteen and a half years.[8]

On August 14, 1986, the Judiciary Committee, by a vote of 13 to 5,[9] recommended that Rehnquist's nomination be confirmed. The majority, which was composed of the Republican members of the committee and three Democrats,[10] dismissed all of the questions regarding the nominee's integrity and ethics.[11] The ma-

---

[8] In 1986 Gary Orfield testified for the second time against Rehnquist's confirmation and provided a systematic review of his record on individual rights. Orfield's prepared statement warned the committee that: "the appointment of an ideological extremist is likely to either deepen polarization on the court or lead the court into a situation in which it can offer nothing but frustration to a severely divided society where governmental power is increasingly being used to deepen rather than remedy inequalities" (U.S. Congress 1986a, 741).

[9] The minority consisted of Biden (Del.), Kennedy (Mass.), Metzenbaum (Ohio), Leahy (Vt.), and Simon (Ill.), all Democrats, who asserted that "the Nation will be best served if this nomination is rejected" (U.S. Congress 1986b, 66).

[10] The Democrats who voted with the Republicans in favor of Rehnquist's confirmation were Robert C. Byrd (W.Va.), Dennis DeConcini (Ariz.), and Howell Heflin (Ala.).

[11] The majority report pointed out that there were discrepancies in the testimony of the witnesses regarding Rehnquist's alleged harassment of voters. The witnesses were unable to identify Rehnquist positively as the man whom they had seen harassing voters. The report also noted that there had been complaints about another man—Wayne Bentson—not Rehnquist. In addition, Mr. Brosnahan was not certain of the name of the precinct, and had stated that he was accompanied by an FBI agent when records showed that he was not (U.S. Congress

jority report expressed very little concern about Rehnquist's judicial philosophy.[12] The separate reports submitted by the members of the minority reflected concerns about Rehnquist's
integrity, his truthfulness before the committee, and his judicial
philosophy.[13]

1986b, 4–12). Regarding Rehnquist's participation in *Laird v. Tatum*, the majority
considered the memo he wrote at the time to be the best reply to the questions
raised. The majority dismissed the "Jackson Memo" as "totally irrelevant and
without merit" (ibid., 28). The issue of the Cornell trust, according to the majority, "apparently involves nothing more than a longstanding family dispute by an
alienated family member" (ibid., 28). The majority found the restrictive covenants irrelevant and noted that Rehnquist had taken steps to have them removed
(ibid., 30–31).

[12] The majority dismissed the issue of his extremism with this statement:
"[D]uring the last four terms of the Court, no Justice has written more opinions
of the Court than Justice Rehnquist . . . [he] has proven himself a leader of majorities, one who believes in equal justice for all, and there is no reason to think he
will not continue to do so as Chief Justice" (U.S. Congress 1986b, 30). Republican
Charles McC. Mathias (Md.), who was the only member of the majority to provide additional comments, found the allegations regarding Rehnquist's integrity
troubling. He addressed the issue of Rehnquist's judicial philosophy: "In my
view, the Nation is fortunate that some of Justice Rehnquist's opinions did not
command a majority" (U.S. Congress 1986b, 64). He noted, however, that respect
for judicial independence and the fact that Rehnquist would continue to be a
member of the Supreme Court whether or not confirmed as chief justice led him
to decline to base his vote on his "distaste for some of his opinions" (ibid., 64–
65). It is interesting to note that Mathias was one of two Republicans to vote
against Rehnquist's confirmation in the final vote in the Senate.

[13] Senators Biden, Kennedy, and Simon devoted the most attention to the nominee's judicial philosophy while the others also expressed their belief that questions regarding his integrity had not been resolved. Senator Simon's brief statement addressed Rehnquist's judicial philosophy only. Simon concluded, "The
reality is that any member of the Court can fulfill the role of Chief Justice as the
symbol of justice for all the people better than Justice Rehnquist can" (U.S. Congress 1986b, 114). Simon had previously expressed the view that since presidents
choose justices with their legal views in mind, the Senate has the right to do the
same (Roberts 1986). Senator Metzenbaum referred in his report to Rehnquist's
lack of credibility. Rehnquist had, in Metzenbaum's view, misled the committee
regarding the allegations of voter harassment and the "Jackson Memo," as well
as about his awareness of the restrictive covenant on his property in Vermont.
Metzenbaum expressed his belief that there was evidence that Rehnquist had
more extensive involvement in the development of the policy of domestic surveillance by the military than he acknowledged to the committee (U.S. Congress
1986b, 94). Metzenbaum also based his negative vote on Rehnquist's judicial philosophy: "[T]he Senate must consider how the nominee, if confirmed, may affect
fundamental constitutional values. I conclude that the confirmation of Justice
Rehnquist may threaten these values, and that he is not an appropriate choice to
lead the Court" (ibid., 100).

On the floor of the Senate the questions regarding Rehnquist's integrity were aired once again, and his judicial philosophy was discussed at length. The issue of the Senate's proper role in assessing a nominee's qualifications remained prominent in the debates. Although Senator Hatch expressed his willingness to "talk about ideology," he suggested that the emphasis on "red herrings" in the committee was based on ideological opposition to Rehnquist: "And to impugn a person because he differs with you ideologically is really stooping too low" (*Congressional Record*, 1986, September 11, S 12385, S 12386). Sen. Barry Goldwater, denouncing "Liberal Bigotry," admonished his colleagues to assess the nominee on the basis of his fitness for the office, "not the shade of [his] philosophy" (ibid., S 12415). Some went further, accusing Rehnquist's critics of intellectual dishonesty—of raising the issues of the nominee's integrity as a facade behind which they tried to hide the true basis of their opposition to his confirmation.[14]

On September 17 the Senate confirmed the nominee by a vote of 65 to 33. Although the deliberations may have appeared to be controversial, in reality Rehnquist's confirmation was never in question. The examination of Rehnquist's integrity revolved around three types of issues: first, those that were aired in 1971 and were reviewed at length in 1986, such as the allegations of voter harassment in Phoenix; second, issues that were so minor as to have no consequence, such as unenforceable restrictive covenants on the deeds to his property; and, finally, issues of major consequence that did not arouse the concern of many senators because they involved incidents that took place many years ago, such as Rehnquist's involvement in military surveillance of civilians during the Nixon administration.

Throughout the hearings and the debates, Rehnquist's critics

---

[14] For example, during the debate in the Senate, Sen. Alan K. Simpson (R., Wyo.) stated:

"[I]f you really want to be intellectually honest, just get up and say:

" 'Mr. Rehnquist, I don't like your philosophy. I don't like it at all. I think it is bad for the country. I think you are bad for the country and I will not vote for you.'

"Period, with emphasis. That would do it very nicely. Then we would not have to go through all of this remarkable posturing and watch it go on for days as it did in the committee and now hours here.

"That is the issue. 'I don't like his philosophy. I haven't the courage to say it,' and the rest of it is applesauce every foot of the way." (*Congressional Record*, 1986, September 11, S 12446)

persistently tried to focus attention on his record as an associate justice by pointing to his positions on controversial constitutional issues. His critics emphasized the important role of the chief justice, the probable length of his tenure, and the impact of his decisions on "the society that will be inhabited by our children and our children's children" (Senator Pell, *Congressional Record*, 1986, September 15, S 12572).

In sharp contrast, the justice's strongest supporters tried to minimize the importance of judicial philosophy in the confirmation process. Senator Hatch, for example, discussed Rehnquist's judicial philosophy primarily to defend the nominee against charges of extremism. During the debates Senator Hatch denounced the "ideological inquisition," and contended that "much of . . . [the information gathered by Rehnquist's opponents] can be summarized as much ado about very little. It shows little more than [that] honest people can disagree with Justice Rehnquist on his reading of the law" (ibid., S 12474, S 12383). In the end, of course, his supporters prevailed. Few senators were willing to heed the advice of Professor Tribe and Senator Biden and reject a nominee on the basis of his judicial philosophy.

THE NEW CHIEF JUSTICE AS LEADER

The chief justice has often been described as primus inter pares, "first among equals."[15] Although he has one vote, as do each of the eight associate justices, the chief justice of the United States is potentially able to shape the decisions of the Supreme Court. The realization of that potential depends, to a great extent, on the chief justice's personal characteristics, a set of qualities that combine to form "leadership." It has been said that the chief leads through "instinct, knowledge, persuasion, intelligence, craft, example, patience, inspiration and compromise."[16]

Leadership skills, both intellectual and personal, are essential to a chief justice who wishes to shape the substance of the Supreme Court's decisions. David J. Danelski (1960, 570) examined leadership in the Court's conference, distinguishing between task leadership and social leadership. A social leader attends to

[15] But see Steamer (1986, 10): "[T]he primus inter pares concept more nearly approximates the truth prior to the incumbency of William Howard Taft, and it has become totally inappropriate since the time of Charles Evans Hughes."

[16] Lance Morrow, "A Cry for Leadership," *Time*, August 6, 1979, p. 28, quoted in Steamer 1986, 19.

the emotional needs of his colleagues and concentrates on keeping the Court socially cohesive, while a task leader concentrates on the Court's decisions. If the chief justice performs both leadership roles, Danelski hypothesized, conflict among members of the Court would be minimal, cohesion would increase, satisfaction with the conference would be high, and production would increase. David M. O'Brien (1986, 233) added a third type of leader: the policy leader who persuades "others to vote in ways (in the short and long run) favorable to their policy goals."

The ability of the chief justice to lead may be constrained by personal interaction among the other justices, as well as by the organizational characteristics of the institution. The organization of the Court has been compared to nine small, independent law firms (Powell 1976, 1454).[17] Before he was nominated for chief justice, Rehnquist (1985, 328) observed that "the Supreme Court is an institution far more dominated by centrifugal forces, pushing towards individuality and independence, than it is by centripetal forces pulling for hierarchical ordering and institutional unity."

In spite of such limits on the powers of the chief justice, there are a number of instruments available that can be useful to the chief who wishes to influence the outcome of the Court's decisions. The chief justice has the opportunity to influence the outcome of cases by virtue of his personal interaction with the other justices, the leadership roles he assumes in conference, the strategy he uses in opinion assignments[18] and in circulating the "discuss list" for petitions for certiorari,[19] the quality of his own opinions, and the image he presents to the press (and, thus, the public) during oral argument.

How will Chief Justice Rehnquist lead the Court? Will he suc-

[17] Justice Blackmun commented that "[t]he Court pretty much goes its own way" (quoted in O'Brien 1986, 233) and described the justices as "prima donnas" (quoted in ibid., 123).

[18] The chief justice assigns the writing of the majority opinion to one of the other justices or to himself if he is in the majority. If the chief justice is in the minority, the most senior associate justice who is in the majority may either write the opinion or assign it to one of the others in the majority.

[19] In order for the Court to grant certiorari (to accept a case for review in its discretionary jurisdiction), four members of the Court must vote in the affirmative. The chief justice circulates a "discuss list"—a list of cases that he considers worthy of discussion in the conference. Each of the other members of the Court may add cases to that list. A case is not discussed unless it is placed on that list (Stevens 1985, 80).

ceed in persuading a majority to join him in important decisions? Will he shape the Court's decisions in accord with his own judicial values? Will he compromise in the interest of Court cohesiveness? If he does succeed in molding the Court's decisions to his own views, will he be able to maintain the integrity and prestige of the Supreme Court in the eyes of the American people?[20]

Such questions cannot be answered until Rehnquist has had sufficient time to establish the quality of his leadership as chief justice. He has the qualities of a forceful, influential leader, however. The new chief justice has "extraordinary intellectual power" (Schmidt 1986). He also has strong convictions that his answers to constitutional questions are the correct ones. Vincent Blasi commented that Rehnquist "is an excellent court infighter—certainly better than Burger and maybe even better than Earl Warren. He's an intensely political person. Some people see him sitting out there in his own world with his principles but I think he really likes to win" ("Reagan's Mr. Right," 1986, 28).

Rehnquist also has the type of personality that is essential to effective leadership. A. E. Dick Howard stated that "perhaps no justice at the Court generates more genuine warmth and regard among both his colleagues and others who work at the Court" (ibid., 47).

The last few years of the Burger Court were marked by fragmentation that was evidenced by the large number of 5 to 4 decisions. It is possible that the Court under the direction of Rehnquist will become increasingly cohesive during the next few years. Justice Scalia can be expected to join O'Connor and the new chief justice to form a strong alliance on the Court. Justice Powell's retirement at the end of the Court's 1986 term and his replacement by Anthony Kennedy may well provide Rehnquist with an additional ally. Four justices, of course, do not make a majority. Moreover, regardless of Rehnquist's skills of persuasion, Justices Brennan, Marshall, Stevens, and Blackmun are not going to be persuaded, when major issues are involved, to join their conservative brethren. The number of times that Justice White joins the "Rehnquist bloc" to make a majority may increase, however, as a result of the persuasive abilities not only of

[20] Steamer (1986, 24) suggested that part of the chief justice's effective leadership consists of convincing "the American people that what the Court decides is ethically and morally sound and legally correct, that the Court is not only conforming to the Constitution but is in tune with transcendent justice."

Rehnquist but also of O'Connor and Scalia. Additionally, it is quite likely that the Rehnquist-O'Connor-Scalia bloc may shift the boundaries of the debate among the justices to the right, and in so doing move the center of the Court accordingly.[21]

It is also possible that Rehnquist will compromise and moderate his views for the sake of presenting an image to the public of the Supreme Court as a decisive, cohesive institution.[22] In light of his record as an associate justice, however, it seems more plausible that, although he may make minor concessions in the interest of Court cohesion, he will not change his positions on specific issues. Neither his objection to the incorporation of the Bill of Rights, his interpretation of the equal protection clause,[23] nor his rejection of a constitutional right to privacy are likely to change. At the most fundamental level, he is not at all likely to retreat from his commitment to federalism. Indeed, his ordering of values and the three components of his judicial philosophy will almost certainly remain stable. He can be expected to try to persuade a majority to see things his way rather than to moderate his views.

Political developments during the last two years of the 1980s could have major repercussions on Chief Justice Rehnquist's ability to influence the decisions of the Court. If a Republican is elected to the presidency in 1988 and is as determined as Ronald Reagan has been to shape the Supreme Court, one or two new justices might join the Rehnquist-O'Connor-Scalia (and possibly Kennedy) alliance to form a majority.

In short, the mere fact of Rehnquist's elevation to chief justice is not a guarantee that he will shape the Court's decisions to conform to his judicial philosophy. His own skills as a leader; the combined persuasive abilities of Rehnquist, O'Connor, and Scalia; the positions that Kennedy takes; and the outcome of the presidential election in 1988 will converge to determine the character of the Rehnquist Court.

[21] It is also possible that O'Connor may assume a position, formerly occupied by Powell, at the center of the Court (see Coyle 1987).

[22] Such a possibility has been suggested by Laurence Tribe and Yale Kamisar ("The Rehnquist Court Still Seems an Appointment Away") and by Justice Brennan (Leeds 1986).

[23] The one area in which O'Connor and Rehnquist have disagreed has been that of sex discrimination. See Mississippi University for Women v. Hogan (458 U.S. 718 [1982]). It is possible that O'Connor may influence Rehnquist to moderate his views on the application of the equal protection clause to gender discrimination.

Rehnquist's Judicial Philosophy and
Supreme Court Doctrine

In the preceding chapters of this book I have presented an analysis of Rehnquist's work as an associate justice from the beginning of his tenure in 1972 until the end of the Court's 1985 term. I have examined his opinions in a number of areas in order to show that his decision making is based on a judicial philosophy grounded in legal positivism. That judicial philosophy, I have argued, is best understood if it is separated into its three components—the democratic model, moral relativism, and Rehnquist's approach to constitutional interpretation. I have utilized a framework consisting of those three components plus the relative weight he assigns to the values of federalism, property rights, and individual rights. The interaction between the three components and Rehnquist's ordering of values provided a useful perspective from which to view his decision making. At the top of his hierarchy of values, federalism is the guiding principle in his decision making. His federalism both shapes and is shaped by his democratic model, his moral relativism, and his basic understanding of the Constitution. Although he values property rights over individual rights, he subordinates both to federalism. Protecting the states from what he perceives to be undesirable federal intrusion is so central to Rehnquist's decision making that he has adopted those tools of constitutional interpretation which are the most useful in accomplishing his goal. While his approach to interpreting the Constitution appears to be most consistent with a historical mode of analysis and with the techniques of literalism and "intent of the framers," when a structural mode of analysis would be more helpful to the cause of federalism he has not hesitated to use it. Additionally, he has adapted the "intent of the framers" technique to his own purposes. In effect, he has posited that, regardless of the language they used, federalism was as central to the framers' vision of the American constitutional system as it is to his own.

Rehnquist's use of structural analysis to support federalism as a principle that is central to the Constitution, or, as he has phrased it, part of the "constitutional plan—implicit ordering of relationships within the federal system" (Nevada v. Hall, 440 U.S. 410, 433 [1978]), brings into question the consistency of his approach to constitutional interpretation. His construal of certain constitutional provisions, such as the Bill of Rights and the

Fourteenth Amendment, manifests a particular understanding of the Constitution according to which that document is limited to its text, is unchanging, and provides a set of rules rather than goals or aspirations for a good society. Moreover, his public statements have also suggested such an understanding of the Constitution (1976a, 1980). In contrast, when the justice has engaged in constitutional interpretation in such contexts as Congress's power vis-à-vis the states and the jurisdiction of the federal courts, his mode of analysis has suggested that he perceives the Constitution to include more than its text, such as implicit understandings of the framers regarding a constitutional plan for protecting the position of the states in the American political system. In short, while he has denied that the Constitution includes more than the text, he has been willing to admit extratextual principles in order to protect the federalism that he places at the apex of his hierarchy of values. The federalism that has provided Rehnquist's motivating force is, in his perception, a central principle of the Constitution.

Throughout this book I have focused primarily on the processes of Justice Rehnquist's decision making. That focus was consistent with my goal of providing a basis for understanding the values and the judicial philosophy that supply the motivation for his opinions and votes. Still, it is important to consider the results, in addition to the processes, of his decision making. If Rehnquist's judicial philosophy and his ordering of values were accepted by a majority of the Supreme Court, there would be a profound change in the distribution of power between the federal government and the states that would have a major impact on the American political system. The emphasis on state autonomy would have profound implications for civil liberties.

If Rehnquist was to lead a majority, the Court would overrule a large body of precedent in order to "unincorporate" the Bill of Rights. The states would then be released from the restrictions of the Bill of Rights and would be free to define due process regarding the rights of the accused. Although they would still be required to comply with the general principles of due process, the states would be at liberty to work out the details of the administration of their criminal justice systems in their own ways. The states would no longer be constitutionally required, for example, to provide all indigents with free counsel, to exclude evidence seized in violation of the prohibition against unreasonable searches and seizures, or to provide a person accused of a crime with the "Right to remain silent . . ." As a result, huge disparities between the states in the protection of rights of those accused of crimes would, most likely, emerge within a few years. Some states might provide free counsel for an indigent accused of a crime while others would not; some states would allow the admission of illegally seized evidence while others would require its exclusion. This sounds familiar because it is. A majority guided by Rehnquist would take the law back to the days before the incorporation of the Bill of Rights when the states were marked by a particularly unpredictable lack of uniformity regarding the protection of the rights of the accused.

Because the First Amendment would no longer apply to the states, the federal judiciary would require only that state action be reasonable even if it interfered with freedom of expression or religious freedom, or if it created an establishment of religion. Disparities between the states would, undoubtedly appear in the regulations and prohibitions on films, books, and magazines with sexual content. Some states might prohibit the distribution of literature that contained extreme political views. Moreover, some states would reinstitute school prayer and Bible reading, while public school teachers would be required by law to teach the creationist theory of the origins of human life along with the theory of evolution.

States would have extensive power to define and regulate property so long as they complied with the general principles of procedural due process. Although Hawaii might provide a means of redistributing property, other states might legislate to protect the holdings of a few wealthy landowners. While California might extend rights of freedom of expression to privately owned shopping centers, other states would be free to prohibit all activities except those related to buying and selling.

The Court, under the tutelage of Rehnquist, would construe the equal protection clause as a prohibition on official discrimination against blacks but would not extend the prohibition to discrimination that could not be attributed directly to official action. Black plaintiffs would be required to prove that the state had engaged in purposeful discrimination, and if they were successful, they would have the opportunity to recover only what they could show they would have had if the discrimination had not occurred. Neither would the clause be available as a tool for achieving equality between men and women. Nor would the equal protection clause protect other minorities, such as aliens.

Thus, "private" clubs could exclude racial minorities. Schools could remain segregated so long as they had no official policy of exclusion. Laws that categorize people according to sex could disadvantage women in the marketplace, at work, and at home. States would be free to prohibit noncitizens from holding jobs in both the public and private sectors. Affirmative action in education and employment, whether for the benefit of racial minorities or women, would be regarded as a violation of the principle of equal treatment without regard to color or sex and would be prohibited.

Severely restricted access to the federal courts would be an additional consequence of the Court's redefinition, at the behest of Rehnquist, of the relationship between the federal government and the states. Disputes involving federal statutes or constitutional issues would be relegated to state courts. Additionally, in view of the decisions of the Supreme Court, civil liberties–civil rights advocates would probably choose increasingly to avoid the federal courts and to devote their efforts to the development of protective doctrine based on state constitutional law. The state courts would become the "main event," without supervision from the federal judiciary.

The Supreme Court would also minimize the role of the judiciary in relation to the other institutions of government. More responsibility would be left with elected officials, particularly at the state level. As Rehnquist (1976a, 698) urged in his now well known article, "The Notion of a 'Living Constitution,' " in a democracy it must be elected officials who decide what to do about particular social problems rather than "a small group of fortunately situated people with a roving commission to second guess Congress, state legislatures, and state and federal administrative officers concerning what is best for the country."

The Court would have a less important role to play in assessing decisions made by elected officials—particularly when individual rights were involved—but it would play a more important role in defining the relationship between the national government and the states. More specifically, the Court would have the duty to protect the states in their ability to function as autonomous governmental units without interference from Congress or the federal courts.

During the consideration of Rehnquist's confirmation as chief justice, Gary Orfield warned the Judiciary Committee that with Rehnquist leading a majority "we would risk repeating one of the most disgraceful stories in our legal history, the Supreme Court's emasculation of the laws and constitutional amendments of the Reconstruction which culminated in the 1896 *Plessy* decision. . . . The specific issues would be different but the consequences would be very similar" (U.S. Congress 1986a, 770). Senator Kennedy was more expansive as he conjured up an image of Rehnquist's America:

> The schools of America would still be segregated. Millions of citizens would be denied the right to vote under scandalous malapportionment laws. Women would be condemned to second-class status as second-class Americans. Courthouses would be closed to individual challenges against police brutality and executive abuse—closed even to the press. Government would embrace religion, and the wall of separation between church and state would be in ruins. State and local majorities would tell us what we can read, how to lead our private lives, whether to bear children, how to bring them up, what kinds of people we may become. Such a result would be a radical and unacceptable retreat from the protections Americans enjoy today, and our Constitution would be a lesser document in a lesser land. (U.S. Congress 1986b, 77)

Rehnquist's judicial philosophy and his ordering of values would require the Court to reverse much of its doctrine of the past thirty years. If Rehnquist commands a majority in decisions involving the major issues the Court will face during the remainder of the twentieth century, the country is quite likely to closely resemble Kennedy's description. The Supreme Court could, as Anthony Lewis (1986) wrote, "give us a different country: one in which our freedoms were less secure, official power less restrained."

APPENDIXES

APPENDIX A

Justice Rehnquist's Opinions for the Majority, 1972–1986

Adamo Wrecking Co. v. United States, 434 U.S. 275 (1978).
Adams v. Williams, 407 U.S. 143 (1972).
Albernaz v. United States, 450 U.S. 333 (1981).
Aldinger v. Howard, 427 U.S. 1 (1976).
American Radio Assn. v. Mobile Steamship Assn., 419 U.S. 215 (1974).
Andrews v. Louisville & Nashville Railroad Co., 406 U.S. 320 (1972).
Arnett v. Kennedy, 416 U.S. 134 (1974).
Baker v. McCollan, 443 U.S. 137 (1979).
Barclay v. Florida, 463 U.S. 939 (1983).
Batson v. Kentucky, 105 S.Ct. 712 (1986).
Bell v. Wolfish, 441 U.S. 520 (1979).
Blue Chip Stamps v. Manor Drug Stores, 421 U.S. 723 (1975).
Blum v. Yaretsky, 457 U.S. 991 (1982).
Board of Curators of the University of Missouri v. Horowitz, 435 U.S. 78
  (1978).
Board of Education v. Rowley, 458 U.S. 176 (1982).
Board of Regents of the University of the State of New York v. Tomanio,
  446 U.S. 478 (1980).
Burch v. Louisiana, 441 U.S. 130 (1979).
Cady v. Dombrowski, 413 U.S. 433 (1973).
Calder v. Jones, 465 U.S. 783 (1984).
Califano v. Boles, 443 U.S. 282 (1979).
California Bankers Assn. v. Shultz, 416 U.S. 21 (1974).
California v. LaRue, 409 U.S. 109 (1972).
California v. United States, 438 U.S. 645 (1978).
Chrysler Corp. v. Brown, 441 U.S. 281 (1979).
City of Kenosha v. Bruno, 412 U.S. 507 (1973).
City of Los Angeles v. Preferred Communications, 476 U.S. 488 (1986).
City of Milwaukee v. Illinois, 451 U.S. 304 (1981).
City of Renton v. Playtime Theatres, 475 U.S. 41 (1986).
Clements v. Fashing, 457 U.S. 957 (1982).
Consumer Product Safety Commission v. GTE Sylvania, 447 U.S. 102
  (1980).
Cupp v. Naughton, 414 U.S. 141 (1973).

The lists of Rehnquist's opinions were obtained from *Lexis*.

Dames & Moore v. Regan, 453 U.S. 654 (1981).

Daniels v. Williams, 474 U.S. 327 (1986).

Davidson v. Cannon, 474 U.S. 344 (1986).

Davis v. United States, 411 U.S. 233 (1973).

Dayton Board of Education v. Brinkman, 433 U.S. 406 (1977).

Delaware v. Van Arsdall, 475 U.S. 673 (1986).

Diamond v. Diehr, 450 U.S. 175 (1981).

Dobbert v. Florida, 432 U.S. 282 (1977).

Donnelly v. DeChristoforo, 416 U.S. 637 (1974).

Donovan v. Lone Steer, 464 U.S. 408 (1984).

Doran v. Salem Inn, Inc., 422 U.S. 922 (1975).

Edelman v. Jordan, 415 U.S. 651 (1974).

Fair Assessment in Real Estate Association, Inc. v. McNary, 454 U.S. 100 (1981).

Federal Election Commission v. National Conservative Political Action Committee, 470 U.S. 480 (1985).

Federal Election Commission v. National Right to Work Committee, 459 U.S. 197 (1982).

Federated Department Stores v. Moitie, 452 U.S. 394 (1981).

First National City Bank v. Banco Nacional De Cuba, 406 U.S. 759 (1972).

Fitzpatrick v. Bitzer, 427 U.S. 445 (1976).

Flagg Bros. v. Brooks, 436 U.S. 149 (1978).

Forsham v. Harris, 445 U.S. 169 (1980).

Furnco Construction Corp. v. Waters, 438 U.S. 567 (1978).

Garcia v. United States, 469 U.S. 70 (1984).

Garrett v. United States, 471 U.S. 773 (1985).

General Building Contractors Association v. Pennsylvania, 458 U.S. 375 (1982).

General Electric Co. v. Gilbert, 429 U.S. 125 (1976).

Givhan v. Western Line Consolidated School District, 439 U.S. 410 (1979).

Goldman v. Weinberger, 475 U.S. 503 (1986).

Gooding v. United States, 416 U.S. 430 (1974).

Green v. Mansour, 474 U.S. 64 (1985).

Griffin v. Oceanic Contractors, 458 U.S. 564 (1982).

Grubbs v. General Electric Credit Corp., 405 U.S. 699 (1972).

Gustafson v. Florida, 414 U.S. 260 (1973).

Ham v. South Carolina, 409 U.S. 524 (1973).

Hamling v. United States, 418 U.S. 87 (1974).

Hampton v. United States, 425 U.S. 484 (1976).

Heckler v. Chaney, 470 U.S. 821 (1985).

Heckler v. Ringer, 466 U.S. 602 (1984).

Herweg v. Ray, 455 U.S. 265 (1982).

Hewitt v. Helms, 459 U.S. 460 (1983).

Miree v. DeKalb County, Georgia, 433 U.S. 25 (1977).

Moe v. Confederated Salish and Kootenai Tribes, 425 U.S. 463 (1976).

Moore v. Sims, 442 U.S. 415 (1979).

Moose Lodge v. Irvis, 407 U.S. 163 (1972).

Mt. Healthy City School District Board of Education v. Doyle, 429 U.S. 274 (1977).

Mueller v. Allen, 463 U.S. 388 (1983).

Nashville Gas Co. v. Satty, 434 U.S. 136 (1977).

National Labor Relations Board v. Bildisco & Bildisco, 465 U.S. 513 (1984).

National Labor Relations Board v. Boeing Co., 412 U.S. 67 (1973).

National League of Cities v. Usery, 426 U.S. 833 (1976).

Nevada v. United States, 463 U.S. 110 (1983).

New York v. P. J. Video, Inc., 475 U.S. 868 (1986).

New York v. Quarles, 467 U.S. 649 (1984).

Norfolk Redevelopment and Housing Authority v. Chesapeake & Potomac Telephone Company of Virginia, 464 U.S. 30 (1983).

Northeast Bancorp, Inc. v. Board of Governors of the Federal Reserve System, 472 U.S. 159 (1985).

Ohio v. Johnson, 467 U.S. 493 (1984).

Oklahoma City v. Tuttle, 471 U.S. 808 (1985).

Oliphant v. Suquamish Indian Tribe, 435 U.S. 191 (1978).

Oregon v. Bradshaw, 462 U.S. 1039 (1983).

Oregon v. Corvallis Sand & Gravel Co., 429 U.S. 363 (1977).

Oregon v. Kennedy, 456 U.S. 667 (1982).

Parker v. Levy, 417 U.S. 733 (1974).

Parker v. Randolph, 442 U.S. 62 (1979).

Parratt v. Taylor, 451 U.S. 527 (1981).

Parsons Steel, Inc. v. First Alabama Bank, 474 U.S. 518 (1986).

Pasadena City Board of Education v. Spangler, 427 U.S. 424 (1976).

Paul v. Davis, 424 U.S. 693 (1976).

Paulsen v. Commissioner of Internal Revenue, 469 U.S. 131 (1985).

Pennhurst State School and Hospital v. Halderman, 451 U.S. 1 (1981).

Philbrook v. Glodgett, 421 U.S. 707 (1975).

Phillips Petroleum Co. v. Shutts, 472 U.S. 797 (1985).

Ponte v. Real, 471 U.S. 491 (1985).

Portley v. Grossman, 444 U.S. 131 (1980).

Posadas de Puerto Rico Assoc. v. Tourism Co., 106 S.Ct. 2698 (1986).

Pruneyard Shopping Center v. Robins, 447 U.S. 74 (1980).

Quern v. Jordan, 440 U.S. 332 (1979).

Railway Labor Executives' Assn. v. Gibbons, 455 U.S. 457 (1982).

Rakas v. Illinois, 439 U.S. 128 (1978).

Rawlings v. Kentucky, 448 U.S. 98 (1980).

Regan v. Taxation with Representation of Washington, 461 U.S. 540 (1983).

United States Postal Service v. Council of Greenburgh Civic Associations, 453 U.S. 114 (1981).
United States Railroad Retirement Board v. Fritz, 449 U.S. 166 (1980).
United States v. Abel, 469 U.S. 45 (1984).
United States v. Allegheny-Ludlum Steel Corp., 406 U.S. 742 (1972).
United States v. Apfelbaum, 445 U.S. 115 (1980).
United States v. Bailey, 444 U.S. 394 (1980).
United States v. Ceccolini, 435 U.S. 268 (1978).
United States v. Clarke, 445 U.S. 253 (1980).
United States v. Euge, 444 U.S. 707 (1980).
United States v. Florida East Coast Railway, 410 U.S. 224 (1973).
United States v. Fuller, 409 U.S. 488 (1973).
United States v. Gouveia, 467 U.S. 180 (1984).
United States v. Jenkins, 420 U.S. 358 (1975).
United States v. Knotts, 460 U.S. 276 (1983).
United States v. MacCollom, 426 U.S. 317 (1976).
United States v. Maze, 414 U.S. 395 (1974).
United States v. Mazurie, 419 U.S. 544 (1975).
United States v. Mechanik, 475 U.S. 66 (1986).
United States v. Mendoza, 464 U.S. 154 (1984).
United States v. Montoya De Hernandez, 473 U.S. 531 (1985).
United States v. New Mexico, 438 U.S. 696 (1978).
United States v. Peltier, 422 U.S. 531 (1975).
United States v. Powell, 423 U.S. 87 (1975).
United States v. Powell, 469 U.S. 57 (1984).
United States v. Ramsey, 431 U.S. 606 (1977).
United States v. Robinson, 414 U.S. 218 (1973).
United States v. Rodgers, 466 U.S. 475 (1984).
United States v. Russell, 411 U.S. 423 (1973).
United States v. Rylander, 460 U.S. 752 (1983).
United States v. Salvucci, 448 U.S. 83 (1980).
United States v. Santana, 427 U.S. 38 (1976).
United States v. Scott, 437 U.S. 82 (1978).
United States v. Security Industrial Bank, 459 U.S. 70 (1982).
United States v. Stauffer Chemical Co., 464 U.S. 165 (1984).
United States v. Valenzuela-Bernal, 458 U.S. 858 (1982).
United States v. Villamonte-Marquez, 462 U.S. 579 (1983).
United States v. Ward, 448 U.S. 242 (1980).
Upjohn v. United States, 449 U.S. 383 (1981).
Valley Forge Christian College v. Americans United for Separation of Church and State, 454 U.S. 464 (1982).
Vendo Co. v. Lektro-Vend Corp., 433 U.S. 623 (1977).
Vermont Yankee Nuclear Power Corp. v. Natural Resources Defense Council, 435 U.S. 519 (1978).
Wainwright v. Sykes, 433 U.S. 72 (1977).

Justice Rehnquist's Concurring Opinions, 1972–1986

Abood v. Detroit Board of Education, 431 U.S. 209 (1977).
Albemarle Paper Co. v. Moody, 422 U.S. 405 (1975).
Arizona Public Service Co. v. Snead, 441 U.S. 141 (1979).
Bates v. State Bar of Arizona, 433 U.S. 350 (1977).
Bellotti v. Baird, 443 U.S. 622 (1979).
Blanding v. DuBose, 454 U.S. 393 (1982).
Bolger v. Young's Drug Products Corp., 463 U.S. 60 (1983).
Brown v. Hartlage, 456 U.S. 45 (1982).
Buckley v. Valeo, 424 U.S. 1 (1976).
Burnett v. Grattan, 468 U.S. 42 (1984).
Busic v. United States, 446 U.S. 398 (1980).
Butz v. Economou, 438 U.S. 478 (1978).
California v. Sierra Club, 451 U.S. 287 (1981).
California v. United States, 457 U.S. 273 (1982).
Cannon v. University of Chicago, 441 U.S. 677 (1979).
Central States, Southeast & Southwest Areas Pension Fund v. Central
   Transport, Inc., 472 U.S. 559 (1985).
Citizens Against Rent Control/Coalition for Fair Housing v. City of
   Berkeley, 454 U.S. 290 (1981).
City of Revere v. Massachusetts General Hospital, 463 U.S. 239 (1983).
Cousins v. Wigoda, 419 U.S. 477 (1975).
Davis v. Bandemer, 106 S.Ct. 2797 (1986).
Deposit Guaranty National Bank of Jackson, Mississippi v. Roper, 445
   U.S. 326 (1980).
Diamond v. Charles, 476 U.S. 54 (1986).
Director, Office of Workers' Compensation Programs v. Perini North
   River Associates, 459 U.S. 297 (1983).
Donovan v. Dewey, 452 U.S. 594 (1980).
Dothard v. Rawlinson, 433 U.S. 321 (1977).
Douglas Oil Company of California v. Petrol Stops Northwest, 441 U.S.
   211 (1979).
Douglas v. Seacoast Products, Inc., 431 U.S. 265 (1977).
Duke Power Co. v. Carolina Environmental Study Group, Inc., 438 U.S.
   59 (1978).
Ellis v. Dyson, 421 U.S. 426 (1975).
Estelle v. Smith, 451 U.S. 454 (1981).

Firestone Tire & Rubber Co. v. Risjord, 449 U.S. 368 (1981).

Gannett Co. v. Depasquale, 443 U.S. 368 (1979).

Gosa v. Mayden, 413 U.S. 665 (1973).

Granny Goose Foods v. Brotherhood of Teamsters & Auto Truck Drivers, 415 U.S. 423 (1974).

Guardians Association v. Civil Service Commission of the City of New York, 463 U.S. 582 (1983).

Harlow v. Fitzgerald, 457 U.S. 800 (1982).

Healy v. James, 408 U.S. 169 (1972).

Heckler v. Community Health Services of Crawford County, Inc., 467 U.S. 51 (1984).

Hodel v. Indiana, 452 U.S. 314 (1981).

Hodel v. Virginia Surface Mining and Reclamation Association, 452 U.S. 264 (1981).

Illinois State Board of Elections v. Socialist Workers Party, 440 U.S. 173 (1979).

Industrial Union, Dept., AFL-CIO v. American Petroleum, 448 U.S. 607 (1980).

International Longshoremen's Association v. Davis, 476 U.S. 380 (1986).

Inwood Laboratories v. Ives Laboratories, 456 U.S. 844 (1982).

Jones v. Rath Packing Co., 430 U.S. 519 (1977).

Lee v. United States, 432 U.S. 23 (1977).

Lehman Brothers v. Schein, 416 U.S. 386 (1974).

Lockett v. Ohio, 438 U.S. 586 (1978).

Malley v. Briggs, 475 U.S. 335 (1986).

Marek v. Chesny, 473 U.S. 1 (1985).

Mincey v. Arizona, 437 U.S. 385 (1978).

Minnick v. California Department of Corrections, 452 U.S. 105 (1981).

Montana v. United States, 440 U.S. 147 (1979).

Moore v. Illinois, 434 U.S. 220 (1977).

Motor Vehicle Manufacturers Association v. State Farm Mutual Automobile Insurance Co., 463 U.S. 29 (1983).

Mullaney v. Wilbur, 421 U.S. 684 (1975).

National Bank of North America v. Associates of Obstetrics and Female Surgery, 425 U.S. 460 (1976).

New Mexico v. Ralph Rodney Earnest, 477 U.S. 648 (1986).

New York v. Belton, 453 U.S. 454 (1981).

Northern Pipeline Construction Co. v. Marathon Pipe Line Co., 458 U.S. 50 (1982).

Ohralik v. Ohio State Bar Assn., 436 U.S. 447 (1978).

Oneida Indian Nation of New York v. County of Oneida, New York, 414 U.S. 661 (1974).

P. E. Bazemore v. William C. Friday, 106 S.Ct. 3000 (1986).

Papasan v. Allain, 106 S.Ct. 2932 (1986).

Reiter v. Sonotone Corp., 442 U.S. 330 (1979).

Rosales-Lopez v. United States, 451 U.S. 182 (1981).

Rose v. Mitchell, 443 U.S. 545 (1979).

San Diego Gas and Electric Co. v. City of San Diego, 450 U.S. 621 (1981).

Sandstrom v. Montana, 442 U.S. 510 (1979).

Schatzle v. Kirkpatrick, 456 U.S. 966 (1982).

Slodov v. United States, 436 U.S. 238 (1978).

Smith v. Daily Mail Publishing Co., 443 U.S. 97 (1979).

Smith v. Digmon, 434 U.S. 332 (1978).

Steffel v. Thompson, 415 U.S. 452 (1974).

Thornburg v. Gingles, 106 S.Ct. 2752 (1986).

United States v. Bornstein, 423 U.S. 303 (1976).

United States v. Brignoni-Ponce, 422 U.S. 873 (1975).

United States v. Little Lake Misere, 412 U.S. 580 (1973).

United States v. Ortiz, 422 U.S. 891 (1975).

United States v. United States Gypsum Co., 438 U.S. 422 (1978).

Wainwright v. Greenfield, 474 U.S. 284 (1986).

Washington v. Confederated Tribes of the Colville Indian Reservation, 447 U.S. 134 (1980).

Weaver v. Graham, 450 U.S. 24 (1981).

Weinberger v. Wiesenfeld, 420 U.S. 636 (1975).

Wengler v. Druggists Mutual Insurance Co., 446 U.S. 142 (1980).

Wise v. Lipscomb, 437 U.S. 535 (1978).

Witters v. Washington Department of Services for the Blind, 474 U.S. 481 (1986).

Woodard v. Hutchins, 464 U.S. 377 (1984).

Zant v. Stephens, 462 U.S. 862 (1983).

APPENDIX C

Justice Rehnquist's Dissenting Opinions, 1972–1986

Adams v. Texas, 448 U.S. 38 (1980).
Aguilar v. Felton, 473 U.S. 402 (1985).
Ake v. Oklahoma, 470 U.S. 68 (1985).
Allenberg Cotton Co. v. Pittman, 419 U.S. 20 (1974).
Almota Farmers Elevator and Warehouse Co. v. United States, 409 U.S. 470 (1973).
American Bank & Trust Co. v. Dallas County, 463 U.S. 855 (1983).
American Textile Manufacturers Institute v. Donovan, 452 U.S. 490 (1981).
Anderson v. Celebrezze, 460 U.S. 780 (1983).
Anderson v. Liberty Lobby, 477 U.S. 242 (1986).
Antoine v. Washington, 420 U.S. 194 (1975).
Arizona v. Rumsey, 467 U.S. 203 (1984).
Armco Inc. v. Hardesty, 467 U.S. 638 (1984).
Attorney General of New York v. Soto-Lopez, 476 U.S. 898 (1986).
Baker v. Gold Seal Liquors, 417 U.S. 467 (1974).
Bates v. State Bar of Arizona, 433 U.S. 350 (1977).
Beck v. Alabama, 447 U.S. 625 (1980).
Bender v. Williamsport Area School District, 475 U.S. 534 (1986).
Bernal v. Fainter, 467 U.S. 216 (1984).
Berry v. Doles, 438 U.S. 190 (1978).
Bigelow v. Virginia, 421 U.S. 809 (1975).
Blackledge v. Perry, 417 U.S. 21 (1974).
Blue Shield of Virginia v. McCready, 457 U.S. 465 (1982).
Boag v. MacDougall, 454 U.S. 364 (1982).
Board of Education, Island Trees Union Free School District v. Pico, 457 U.S. 853 (1982).
Bob Jones University v. United States, 461 U.S. 574 (1983).
Boeing Co. v. Van Gemert, 444 U.S. 472 (1980).
Bose Corp. v. Consumers Union of United States, 466 U.S. 485 (1984).
Bounds v. Smith, 430 U.S. 817 (1977).
Bowen v. United States Postal Service, 459 U.S. 212 (1983).
Braden v. 30th Judicial Circuit Court of Kentucky, 410 U.S. 484 (1973).
Brandon v. Holt, 469 U.S. 464 (1985).
Brooks v. Tennessee, 406 U.S. 605 (1972).
Brown v. Louisiana, 447 U.S. 323 (1980).

Buckley v. Valeo, 424 U.S. 1 (1976).

Butz v. Economou, 438 U.S. 478 (1978).

Caldwell v. Mississippi, 472 U.S. 320 (1985).

Califano v. Goldfarb, 430 U.S. 199 (1977).

Cantor v. Detroit Edison Co., 428 U.S. 579 (1976).

Carey v. Brown, 447 U.S. 455 (1980).

Carey v. Population Services International, 431 U.S. 678 (1977).

Carlson v. Green, 446 U.S. 14 (1980).

Carter v. Kentucky, 450 U.S. 288 (1981).

Central States, Southeast & Southwest Areas Pension Fund v. Central Transport, 472 U.S. 559 (1985).

Central Hudson Gas and Electric Corporation v. Public Service Commission of New York, 447 U.S. 557 (1980).

Chambers v. Mississippi, 410 U.S. 284 (1973).

Chappelle v. Greater Baton Rouge Airport District, 431 U.S. 159 (1977).

Chardon v. Fumero Soto, 462 U.S. 650 (1983).

City of Burbank v. Lockheed Air Terminal, 411 U.S. 624 (1973).

City of Philadelphia v. New Jersey, 437 U.S. 617 (1978).

City of Riverside v. Rivera, 477 U.S. 561 (1986).

City of Rome v. United States, 446 U.S. 156 (1980).

Clayton v. International Union, United Automobile, Aerospace, & Agricultural Implement Workers of America, 451 U.S. 679 (1981).

Cleavinger v. Saxner, 474 U.S. 193 (1985).

Cleveland Board of Education v. Lafleur, 414 U.S. 632 (1974).

Cleveland Board of Education v. Loudermill, 470 U.S. 532 (1985).

Codispoti v. Pennsylvania, 418 U.S. 506 (1974).

Columbus Board of Education v. Penick, 443 U.S. 449 (1979).

Committee for Public Education & Religious Liberty v. Nyquist, 413 U.S. 756 (1973).

Community Communications Co. v. City of Boulder, Colorado, 455 U.S. 40 (1982).

Concerned Citizens of Southern Ohio, Inc. v. Pine Creek Conservancy District, 429 U.S. 651 (1977).

Connecticut v. Mohegan Tribe, 452 U.S. 968 (1981).

Connor v. Coleman, 425 U.S. 675 (1976).

Cool v. United States, 409 U.S. 100 (1972).

County of Washington, Oregon v. Gunther, 452 U.S. 161 (1981).

Cox Broadcasting Corp. v. Cohn, 420 U.S. 469 (1975).

Craig v. Boren, 429 U.S. 190 (1976).

Cruz v. Beto, 405 U.S. 319 (1972).

Cuyler v. Adams, 449 U.S. 433 (1981).

Davis v. Georgia, 429 U.S. 122 (1976).

Davis v. United States, 417 U.S. 333 (1974).

Dayton Board of Education v. Brinkman, 443 U.S. 526 (1979).

Delaware State Board of Education v. Evans, 446 U.S. 923 (1980).

Delaware v. Prouse, 440 U.S. 648 (1979).

Delta Air Lines v. August, 450 U.S. 346 (1981).

DeMarco v. United States, 415 U.S. 449 (1974).

Department of the Air Force v. Rose, 425 U.S. 352 (1976).

Dickerson v. New Banner Institute, 460 U.S. 103 (1983).

Diedrich v. Commissioner of Internal Revenue, 457 U.S. 191 (1982).

Doe v. Bolton, 410 U.S. 179 (1973).

Doe v. Mcmillan, 412 U.S. 306 (1973).

Douglas v. Seacoast Products, Inc., 431 U.S. 265 (1977).

Dunaway v. New York, 442 U.S. 200 (1979).

Dunlop v. Bachowski, 421 U.S. 560 (1975).

Duren v. Missouri, 439 U.S. 357 (1979).

Eastex v. National Labor Relations Board, 437 U.S. 556 (1978).

Eaton v. City of Tulsa, 415 U.S. 697 (1974).

Edgar v. Mite Corp., 457 U.S. 624 (1982).

Elkins v. Moreno, 435 U.S. 647 (1978).

Evitts v. Lucey, 469 U.S. 387 (1985).

Examining Board of Engineers, Architects and Surveyors v. Flores De Otero, 426 U.S. 572 (1976).

Federal Communications Commission v. League of Women Voters of California, 468 U.S. 364 (1984).

Fidelity Federal Savings & Loan Association v. De La Cuesta, 458 U.S. 141 (1982).

Finch v. United States, 433 U.S. 676 (1977).

First National Bank of Boston v. Bellotti, 435 U.S. 765 (1978).

Flower v. United States, 407 U.S. 197 (1972).

Ford v. Wainwright, 477 U.S. 399 (1986).

Francis v. Franklin, 471 U.S. 307 (1985).

Franks v. Delaware, 438 U.S. 154 (1978).

Fry v. United States, 421 U.S. 542 (1975).

Furman v. Georgia, 408 U.S. 238 (1972).

Garcia v. San Antonio Metropolitan Transit Authority, 469 U.S. 528 (1985).

Gardner v. Florida, 430 U.S. 349 (1977).

Gelbard v. United States, 408 U.S. 41 (1972).

General Atomic Co. v. Felter, 434 U.S. 12 (1977).

Gladstone Realtors v. Village of Bellwood, 441 U.S. 91 (1979).

Golden State Transit Corp. v. City of Los Angeles, 475 U.S. 608 (1986).

Green v. Georgia, 442 U.S. 95 (1979).

Hagans v. Lavine, 415 U.S. 528 (1974).

Hampton v. Mow Sun Wong, 426 U.S. 88 (1976).

Harrison v. PPG Industries, 446 U.S. 578 (1980).

Hathorn v. Lovorn, 457 U.S. 255 (1982).

Henderson v. Morgan, 426 U.S. 637 (1976).

Hensley v. Municipal Court, 411 U.S. 345 (1973).

Herring v. New York, 422 U.S. 853 (1975).

Hess v. Indiana, 414 U.S. 105 (1973).

Hicks v. Oklahoma, 447 U.S. 343 (1980).

Hill v. Stone, 421 U.S. 289 (1975).

Hines v. Anchor Motor Freight, 424 U.S. 554 (1976).

Hughes v. Oklahoma, 441 U.S. 322 (1979).

Hughes v. Rowe, 449 U.S. 5 (1980).

Hutto v. Finney, 437 U.S. 678 (1978).

Hynes v. Mayor and Council of Borough of Oradell, 425 U.S. 610 (1976).

Immigration and Naturalization Service v. Chadha, 462 U.S. 919 (1983).

In Re Primus, 436 U.S. 412 (1978).

Internationnal Union, United Automobile, Aerospace, and Agricultural Implement Workers of America v. Brock, 477 U.S. 274 (1986).

Jimenez v. Weinberger, 417 U.S. 628 (1974).

Johnson v. Board of Education of the City of Chicago, 457 U.S. 52 (1982).

Jones v. Rath Packing Co., 430 U.S. 519 (1977).

Kassel v. Consolidated Freightways Corporation of Delaware, 450 U.S. 662 (1981).

Keyes v. School District No. 1, Denver, Colorado, 413 U.S. 189 (1973).

Kusper v. Pontikes, 414 U.S. 51 (1973).

Larkin v. Grendel's Den, 459 U.S. 116 (1982).

Larson v. Valente, 456 U.S. 228 (1982).

Lawrence County v. Lead-Deadwood School District, 469 U.S. 256 (1985).

Local 28 of the Sheet Metal Workers' International Association v. Equal Employment Opportunity Commission, 106 S.Ct. 3019 (1986).

Local Number 93, International Association of Firefighters v. City of Cleveland, 106 S.Ct. 3063 (1986).

Local 926, International Union of Operating Engineers, AFL-CIO v. Jones, 460 U.S. 669 (1983).

Lockett v. Ohio, 438 U.S. 586 (1978).

Lockheed Aircraft Corp. v. United States, 460 U.S. 190 (1983).

Loper v. Beto, 405 U.S. 473 (1972).

McCarty v. McCarty, 453 U.S. 210 (1981).

Macdonald v. County of Yolo, 477 U.S. 340 (1986).

Malley v. Briggs, 475 U.S. 335 (1986).

Mariscal v. United States, 449 U.S. 405 (1981).

Maryland v. Louisiana, 451 U.S. 725 (1981).

Massachusetts v. United States, 435 U.S. 444 (1978).

Meek v. Pittenger, 421 U.S. 349 (1975).

Memorial Hospital v. Maricopa County, 415 U.S. 250 (1974).

Metromedia v. City of San Diego, 453 U.S. 490 (1981).

Michigan v. Clifford, 464 U.S. 287 (1984).

Michigan v. Jackson, 475 U.S. 625 (1986).

Michigan v. Tyler, 436 U.S. 499 (1978).

Midlantic National Bank v. New Jersey Department of Environmental Protection, 474 U.S. 494 (1986).

Miller v. Fenton, 474 U.S. 104 (1985).

Mincey v. Arizona, 437 U.S. 385 (1978).

Monell v. New York City Department of Social Services, 436 U.S. 658 (1978).

Moses H. Cone Memorial Hospital v. Mercury Construction Corp., 460 U.S. 1 (1983).

Motor Vehicle Manufacturers Association of the United States v. State Farm Mutual Automobile Insurance Co., 463 U.S. 29 (1983).

National Labor Relations Board v. Burns International Security Services, 406 U.S. 272 (1972).

National Labor Relations Board v. International Longshoremen's Assn., 473 U.S. 61 (1985).

National Socialist Party of America v. Village of Skokie, 432 U.S. 43 (1977).

Nevada v. Hall, 440 U.S. 410 (1979).

New Jersey Welfare Rights Organization v. Cahill, 411 U.S. 619 (1973).

Newport News Shipbuilding & Dry Dock Co. v. Equal Employment Opportunity Commission, 462 U.S. 669 (1983).

Nixon v. Administrator of General Services, 433 U.S. 425 (1977).

Nyquist v. Mauclet, 432 U.S. 1 (1977).

Occidental Life Insurance Company of California v. Equal Employment Opportunity Commission, 432 U.S. 355 (1977).

Orr v. Orr, 440 U.S. 268 (1979).

Pacific Gas and Electric Co. v. Public Utilities Commission of California, 475 U.S. 1 (1986).

Papasan v. Allain, 106 S.Ct. 2932 (1986).

Papish v. Board of Curators of the University of Missouri, 410 U.S. 667 (1973).

Parklane Hosiery Co. v. Shore, 439 U.S. 322 (1979).

Payton v. New York, 445 U.S. 573 (1980).

Penn Central Transportation Co. v. New York City, 438 U.S. 104 (1978).

Philadelphia Newspapers v. Jerome, 434 U.S. 241 (1978).

Ramah Navajo School Board v. Bureau of Revenue of New Mexico, 458 U.S. 832 (1982).

Richmond Newspapers v. Virginia, 448 U.S. 555 (1980).

Rinaldi v. United States, 434 U.S. 22 (1977).

Robbins v. California, 453 U.S. 420 (1981).

Roberts v. Louisiana, 431 U.S. 633 (1977).

Roe v. Wade, 410 U.S. 113 (1973).

Santosky v. Kramer, 455 U.S. 745 (1982).

School District of the City of Grand Rapids v. Ball, 473 U.S. 373 (1985).

Secretary of State of Maryland v. Joseph H. Munson Co., 467 U.S. 947 (1984).

Serbian Eastern Orthodox Diocese for the United States of America and Canada v. Milivojevich, 426 U.S. 696 (1976).

Shea v. Louisiana, 470 U.S. 51 (1985).

Simpson v. United States, 435 U.S. 6 (1978).

Smith v. Goguen, 415 U.S. 566 (1974).

Smith v. Illinois, 469 U.S. 91 (1984).

Smith v. Wade, 461 U.S. 30 (1983).

South-Central Timber Development, Inc. v. Wunnicke, 467 U.S. 82 (1984).

Southeastern Promotions, Ltd. v. Conrad, 420 U.S. 546 (1975).

Southern Overlying Carrier Chapter of the California Dump Truck Owners Association v. Public Utilities Commission of California, 434 U.S. 9 (1977).

Spence v. Washington, 418 U.S. 405 (1974).

Sporhase v. Nebraska, 458 U.S. 941 (1982).

Stanton v. Stanton, 421 U.S. 7 (1975).

Steagald v. United States, 451 U.S. 204 (1981).

Stone v. Graham, 449 U.S. 39 (1981).

Strait v. Laird, 406 U.S. 341 (1972).

Sugarman v. Dougall, 413 U.S. 634 (1973).

Supreme Court of New Hampshire v. Piper, 470 U.S. 274 (1985).

Taylor v. Louisiana, 419 U.S. 522 (1975).

Taylor v. McKeithen, 407 U.S. 191 (1972).

Tennessee Valley Authority v. Hill, 437 U.S. 153 (1978).

Thermtron Products v. Hermansdorfer, 423 U.S. 336 (1976).

Thigpen v. Roberts, 468 U.S. 27 (1984).

Thomas v. Review Board of the Indiana Employment Security Division, 450 U.S. 707 (1981).

Thomas v. Washington Gas Light Co., 448 U.S. 261 (1980).

Three Affiliated Tribes of the Fort Berthold Reservation v. Wold Engineering, 467 U.S. 138 (1984).

Three Affiliated Tribes of the Fort Berthold Reservation v. Wold Engineering, 476 U.S. 877 (1986).

Toll v. Moreno, 458 U.S. 1 (1982).

Torres-Valencia v. United States, 464 U.S. 44 (1983).

Transcontinental Gas Pipe Line Corp. v. State Oil and Gas Board of Mississippi, 474 U.S. 409 (1986).

Trimble v. Gordon, 430 U.S. 762 (1977).

Turner v. Murray, 476 U.S. 28 (1986).

Union Labor Life Insurance Co. v. Pireno, 458 U.S. 119 (1982).

United States Department of Agriculture v. Moreno, 413 U.S. 528 (1973).

United States Department of Agriculture v. Murry, 413 U.S. 508 (1973).

United States v. Bornstein, 423 U.S. 303 (1976).

United States v. Clark, 445 U.S. 23 (1980).

United States v. Falstaff Brewing Corp., 410 U.S. 526 (1973).

United States v. Gillock, 445 U.S. 360 (1980).

United States v. Glaxo Group Ltd., 410 U.S. 52 (1973).

United States v. Henry, 447 U.S. 264 (1980).

United States v. Mauro, 436 U.S. 340 (1978).

United States v. Sioux Nation of Indians, 448 U.S. 371 (1980).

United States v. Sotelo, 436 U.S. 268 (1978).

United States v. United States Gypsum Co., 438 U.S. 422 (1978).

United States v. Yermian, 468 U.S. 63 (1984).

United Steelworkers of America v. Weber, 443 U.S. 193 (1979).

Vachon v. New Hampshire, 414 U.S. 478 (1974).

Van Lare v. Hurley, 421 U.S. 338 (1975).

Village of Schaumburg v. Citizens for a Better Environment, 444 U.S. 620 (1980).

Virginia State Board of Pharmacy v. Virginia Citizens Consumer Council, 425 U.S. 748 (1976).

Vlandis v. Kline, 412 U.S. 441 (1973).

Wallace v. Jaffree, 472 U.S. 38 (1985).

Washington Metropolitan Area Transit Authority v. Johnson, 467 U.S. 925 (1984).

Washington v. Confederated Tribes of the Colville Indian Reservation, 447 U.S. 134 (1980).

Weber v. Aetna Casualty & Surety Co., 406 U.S. 164 (1972).

Whalen v. United States, 445 U.S. 684 (1980).

Woodson v. North Carolina, 428 U.S. 280 (1976).

Wooley v. Maynard, 430 U.S. 705 (1977).

Ybarra v. Illinois, 444 U.S. 85 (1979).

Zablocki v. Redhail, 434 U.S. 374 (1978).

Zobel v. Williams, 457 U.S. 55 (1982).

References

Abraham, Henry J. 1980. *The Judicial Process: An Introductory Analysis of the Courts of the United States, England, and France.* 4th ed. New York: Oxford University Press.

——. 1985. *Justices and Presidents: A Political History of Appointments to the Supreme Court.* 2d ed. New York: Oxford University Press.

Ackerman, Bruce A. 1977. *Private Property and the Constitution.* New Haven: Yale University Press.

Arledge, Paula C. 1986. "Justice Stevens and Freedom of Expression, 1975–1985." Paper presented at the 1986 meeting of the Midwest Political Science Association, Chicago.

Austin, John. 1954. *The Province of Jurisprudence Determined.* London: Weidenfeld and Nicolson.

Baker, Leonard 1974. *John Marshall: A Life in Law.* New York: Macmillan.

Baker, Stewart A. 1977. "Federalism and the Eleventh Amendment." *University of Colorado Law Review* 48:139–88.

Barber, Sotirios A. 1976. "*National League of Cities v Usery*: New Meaning for the Tenth Amendment?" *Supreme Court Review* 1976:161–82.

——. 1984. *On What the Constitution Means.* Baltimore: Johns Hopkins University Press.

Berger, Raoul. 1977. *Government by Judiciary.* Cambridge: Harvard University Press.

Beveridge, Albert J. 1916–1919. *The Life of John Marshall.* 2 vols. Boston: Houghton-Mifflin.

Black, Charles L., Jr. 1965. *Structure and Relationship in Constitutional Law.* Baton Rouge: Louisiana State University Press.

——. 1970. "A Note on Senatorial Consideration of Supreme Court Nominees." *Yale Law Journal* 79:657–64.

Bork, Robert H. 1971. "Neutral Principles and Some First Amendment Problems." *Indiana Law Journal* 47:1–35.

Brennan, William J., Jr. 1977. "State Constitutions and the Protection of Individual Rights." *Harvard Law Review* 90:489–504.

Brest, Paul. 1980. "The Misconceived Quest for the Original Understanding." *Boston University Law Review* 60:204–38.

Carter, Lief H. 1985. *Contemporary Constitutional Lawmaking: The*

Supreme Court and the Art of Politics. New York: Pergamon Press.

Cohen, William. 1975. "Congressional Power to Interpret Due Process and Equal Protection." *Stanford Law Review* 27:603–19.

Congressional Record. 1971. 92d Cong., 1st sess. December 6–10.

———. 1986. 99th Cong., 2d sess. September 11–17, S 12378–779.

Cover, Robert M., and T. Alexander Aleinikoff. 1977. "Dialectical Federalism: Habeas Corpus and the Court." *Yale Law Journal* 86:1019–1102.

Cox, Archibald. 1978. "Federalism and Individual Rights under the Burger Court." *Northwestern University Law Review* 73:1–24.

———. 1980. "Foreword: Freedom of Expression in the Burger Court." *Harvard Law Review* 94:1–73.

Coyle, Marcia. 1987. "Court's 'Center' Has an Unlikely New Occupant." *National Law Journal*, July 13, 1987, 1.

Danelski, David J. 1960. "The Influence of the Chief Justice in the Decisional Process." In *Courts, Judges, and Politics*. 2d ed. Edited by Walter F. Murphy and C. Herman Pritchett. New York: Random House, 1974.

Denvir, John. 1983. "Justice Rehnquist and Constitutional Interpretation." *Hastings Law Journal* 34:1011–53.

"Developments in the Law: Section 1983 and Federalism." 1977. *Harvard Law Review* 90:1133–1361.

Dobie, Otis P. 1957. "Recent Judicial Biographies: A Composite View." *Vanderbilt Law Review* 10:403–13.

Dorsen, Norman, and Joel Gora. 1982. "Free Speech, Property, and the Burger Court: Old Values, New Balances." *Supreme Court Review* 7:195–241.

Dunham, Allison. 1962. "Griggs v Allegheny County In Perspective: Thirty Years of Supreme Court Expropriation Law." *Supreme Court Review*, 63–106.

Dunham, Allison, and Philip B. Kurland, eds. 1974. *Mr. Justice*. Chicago: University of Chicago Press.

Dworkin, Ronald. 1977. *Taking Rights Seriously*. Cambridge: Harvard University Press.

———. 1985. *A Matter of Principle*. Cambridge: Harvard University Press.

———. 1986. *Law's Empire*. Cambridge: Harvard University Press, Belknap Press.

Ely, John Hart. 1980. *Democracy and Distrust: A Theory of Judicial Review*. Cambridge: Harvard University Press.

Emerson, Thomas I. 1980. "First Amendment Doctrine and the Burger Court." *California Law Review* 68:422–81.

Faulkner, Robert K. 1968. *The Jurisprudence of John Marshall*. Princeton: Princeton University Press.

229

Fiss, Owen M. 1977. "Dombrowski." *Yale Law Journal* 86:1103–64.

Fiss, Owen M., and Charles Krauthammer. 1982. "The Rehnquist Court." *New Republic*, March 10, 14–23.

Fletcher, William A. 1983. "A Historical Interpretation of the Eleventh Amendment: A Narrow Construction of an Affirmative Grant of Jurisdiction Rather Than a Prohibition against Jurisdiction." *Stanford Law Review* 35:1033–1131.

Friedman, Leon, and Fred L. Israel, comps. 1969. *The Justices of the United States Supreme Court, 1789–1968: Their Lives and Major Opinions.* 4 vols. New York: Chelsea House.

Friedman, Leon, comp. 1979. *The Justices of the United States Supreme Court: Their Lives and Major Opinions.* Vol. 5, *The Burger Court, 1969–1978.* New York: Chelsea House.

Goldman, Sheldon. 1985. "Reorganizing the Judiciary: The First Term Appointments." *Judicature* 68: 313–29.

Graham, Fred P. 1971a. "Rights Aids Call Rehnquist Racist." *New York Times*, November 10.

———. 1971b. "Rehnquist Says '52 Memo Outlined Jackson's Views." *New York Times*, December 9.

Grey, Thomas C. 1975. "Do We Have an Unwritten Constitution?" *Stanford Law Review* 27:703–18.

Gunther, Gerald. 1985. *Constitutional Law.* 11th ed. Mineola, N.Y.: Foundation Press.

Hale, Robert L. 1944a. "The Supreme Court and the Contract Clause." *Harvard Law Review* 57:512–57.

———. 1944b. "The Supreme Court and the Contract Clause: II." *Harvard Law Review* 57:621–74.

———. 1944c. "The Supreme Court and the Contract Clause: III." *Harvard Law Review* 57:852–92.

Harris, William F., III. 1982. "Bonding Word and Polity: The Logic of American Constitutionalism." *American Political Science Review* 76:34–45.

Hart, H.L.A. 1961. *The Concept of Law.* London: Oxford University Press.

Heck, Edward V., and Albert C. Ringelstein. 1985. "The Burger Court and 'The Central Meaning of the First Amendment.' " Paper presented at the annual meeting of the American Political Science Association, New Orleans, August.

Heck, Edward V. 1986. "Justice Brennan and Freedom of Expression Doctrine in the Burger Court." Paper presented at the 1986 meeting of the Midwest Political Science Association, Chicago.

Holmes, Oliver Wendell, Jr. 1897. "The Path of the Law." *Harvard Law Review* 10:457. Reprinted in George C. Christie, *Jurisprudence: Text and Readings on the Philosophy of Law*, 648–63. St Paul, Minn.: West Publishing Co., 1973.

REFERENCES

Howard, A. E. Dick. 1986. "A Key Fighter in Major Battles." *American Bar Association Journal*, June 15, 47–49.

Howe, Mark DeWolfe. 1957–1963. *Justice Oliver Wendell Holmes*. 2 vols. Cambridge: Harvard University Press.

Jenkins, John A. 1985. "The Partisan: A Talk with Justice Rehnquist." *New York Times Magazine*, March 3.

"Justice Rehnquist's Theory of Property." 1984. *Yale Law Journal* 93:541–60.

Justice, William W. 1980. "A Relativistic Constitution." *University of Colorado Law Review* 52:19–32.

Kleven, Thomas. 1982. "The Constitutional Philosophy of Justice William H. Rehnquist." *Vermont Law Review* 8:211–47.

Kluger, Richard. 1975. *Simple Justice: The History of Brown v Board of Education and Black America's Struggle for Equality*. New York: Vintage Books.

Kobylka, Joseph F. 1986. "Justice Blackmun and Expression Issues: Intracourt Dynamics and a Flexible Role Conception." Paper presented at the 1986 meeting of the Midwest Political Science Association, Chicago.

Konefsky, Samuel J. 1956. *The Legacy of Holmes and Brandeis: A Study in the Influence of Ideas*. New York: Macmillan.

Lardner, George Jr., and Al Kamen. 1986. "Civil Rights, Women's Groups to Fight Rehnquist Confirmation." *Washington Post*, July 29.

Leeds, Jeffrey T. 1986. "A Life on the Court." *New York Times Magazine*, October 5.

Levinson, Sanford. 1979. "The Constitution in American Civil Religion." *Supreme Court Review* 1979:123–51.

———. 1982. "Law as Literature." *Texas Law Review* 60:373–403.

Levy, Leonard W. 1974. *Against the Law: The Nixon Court and Criminal Justice*. New York: Harper and Row.

Lewis, Anthony. 1986. "The Court: Rehnquist." *New York Times*, June 20.

Lind, Robert C., Jr. 1980. "Justice Rehnquist: First Amendment Speech in the Labor Context." *Hastings Constitutional Law Quarterly* 8:93–123.

Luneburg, William V. 1982. "Justice Rehnquist, Statutory Interpretation, the Policies of Clear Statement, and Federal Justisdiction." *Indiana Law Journal* 58:211–47.

McCloskey, Robert G. 1960. *The American Supreme Court*. Chicago: University of Chicago Press.

Mason, Alpheus T. 1956. *Brandeis: A Free Man's Life*. New York: Viking Press.

Massey, Stephen J. 1984. "Justice Rehnquist's Theory of Property." *Yale Law Journal* 93:541–60.

Meiklejohn, Alexander. 1965. *Free Speech and Its Relation to Self-Government*. Collected with additional Meiklejohn papers in *Political Freedom: The Constitutional Powers of the People*. New York: Oxford University Press.

Mendelson, Wallace 1961. *Justices Black and Frankfurter: Conflict in the Court*. Chicago: University of Chicago Press.

Michelman, Frank F. 1977. "States' Rights and States' Roles: Permutations of 'Sovereignty' in *National League of Cities v Usery*." *Yale Law Journal* 86:1165–95.

Michelman, Frank I. 1967. "Property, Utility, and Fairness: Comments on the Ethical Foundations of 'Just Compensation' Law." *Harvard Law Review* 80:1165–1258.

Monaghan, Henry Paul. 1977. "Of 'Liberty' and 'Property.' " *Cornell Law Review* 62:405–37.

———. 1981. "Our Perfect Constitution." *New York University Law Review* 56:353–96.

Murphy, Walter F., and Joseph Tanenhaus. 1972. *The Study of Public Law*. New York: Random House.

Murphy, Walter F. 1978. "Constitutional Interpretation: The Art of the Historian, Magician, or Statesman?" *Yale Law Journal* 87:1752–71.

———. 1980. "An Ordering of Constitutional Values." *Southern California Law Review* 53:703–60.

Murphy, Walter F., James E. Fleming, and William F. Harris II. 1986. *American Constitutional Interpretation*. Mineola, N.Y.: Foundation Press.

Neuborne, Bert. 1977. "The Myth of Parity." *Harvard Law Review* 90:1105–31.

Newmeyer, R. Kent. 1968. *The Supreme Court under Marshall and Taney*. New York: Thomas Y. Crowell.

O'Brien, David M. 1986. *Storm Center: The Supreme Court in American Politics*. New York: W. W. Norton.

Peltason, J. W. 1964. "Supreme Court Biography and the Study of Public Law." In Gottfried Dietze, ed., *Essays on the American Constitution*, 215–27. Englewood Cliffs, N.J.: Prentice-Hall.

Perry, Michael. J. 1985. "The Authority of Text, Tradition, and Reason: A Theory of Constitutional 'Interpretation.' " *Southern California Law Review* 58:551–602.

Powell, Jeff. 1982. "The Compleat Jeffersonian: Justice Rehnquist and Federalism." *Yale Law Journal* 91:1317–70.

Powell, Lewis. 1976. "What the Justices are Saying . . ." *American Bar Association Journal* 62:1454.

Pritchett, C. Herman. 1948. *The Roosevelt Court: A Study in Judicial Politics and Values, 1937–1947*. New York: Macmillan.

REFERENCES

"A Process Oriented Approach to the Contract Clause." 1980. *Yale Law Journal* 89:1623–51.

"Reagan's Mr. Right." 1986. *Time*, June 30, 1986.

"Rediscovering the Contract Clause." 1984. *Harvard Law Review* 97:1414–31.

Redish, Martin H. 1978. "The Doctrine of *Younger v. Harris*: Deference in Search of a Rationale." *Cornell Law Review* 63:463–88.

———. 1980. *Federal Jurisdiction: Tensions in the Allocation of Judicial Power*. Indianapolis, Ind.: Michie Company.

"The Rehnquist Court Still Seems an Appointment Away." 1986. *New York Times*, September 21.

Rehnquist, William H. 1958. "The Bar Admission Cases: A Strange Judicial Aberration." *American Bar Association Journal* 44:229.

———. 1973. "The Supreme Court Past and Present." *American Bar Association Journal* 59:361–64.

———. 1974. "Whither the Courts." *American Bar Association Journal* 60:787–90.

———. 1976a. "The Notion of a Living Constitution." *Texas Law Review* 54:693–706.

———. 1976b. "The Cult of the Robe." *Judges Journal* 15:74–77.

———. 1978. "The Adversary Society: Keynote Address of the Third Annual Baron de Hirsch Meyer Lecture Series." *University of Miami Law Review* 33:19.

———. 1980. "Government by Cliché: Keynote Address of the Earl F. Nelson Lecture Series." *Missouri Law Review* 45:379–93.

———. 1985. "Presidential Appointments to the Supreme Court." *Constitutional Commentary* 2:319–30.

———. 1987a. "Remarks by the Chief Justice at the Conference on the Judicial Interpretation of the Constitution." Washington, D.C., June 12.

———. 1987b. *The Supreme Court: How It Was, How It Is*. New York: William Morrow.

Reich, Charles. 1964. "The New Property." *Yale Law Journal* 73:733–87.

———. 1965. "Individual Rights and Social Welfare: The Emerging Legal Issues." *Yale Law Journal* 74:1245–57.

"Revival of the Contract Clause: *Allied Structural Steel Co. v Spannaus* and *United States Trust Co. v New Jersey*." 1979. *Virginia Law Review* 65:377–402.

Riggs, Robert E., and Thomas D. Proffit. 1983. "The Judicial Philosophy of Justice Rehnquist." *Akron Law Review* 16:555–604.

Roberts, Steven V. 1986. "Approval Called Likely for High Court Choices." *New York Times*, June 19.

Roche, John P. 1957. "The Utopian Pilgrimage of Mr. Justice Murphy." *Vanderbilt Law Review* 10: 369–94.

Rydell, John R. 1975. "Mr. Justice Rehnquist and Judicial Self-Restraint." *Hastings Law Journal* 26:875–915.

Sax, Joseph L. 1964. "Takings and the Police Power." *Yale Law Journal* 74:36–75.

———. 1971. "Takings, Private Property, and Public Rights." *Yale Law Journal* 81:149–86.

Schmidt, Benno C., Jr. 1986. "The Rehnquist Court: A Watershed." *New York Times*, June 22.

Schubert, Glendon. 1965. *The Judicial Mind*. Evanston, Ill.: Northwestern University Press.

Shapiro, David L. 1976. "Mr. Justice Rehnquist: A Preliminary View." *Harvard Law Review* 90:293–357.

———. 1984. "Wrong Turns: The Eleventh Amendment and the *Pennhurst* Case." *Harvard Law Review* 98:61–85.

Silverstein, Mark. 1984. *Constitutional Faiths: Felix Frankfurter, Hugo Black, and the Process of Judicial Decision Making*. Ithaca: Cornell University Press.

Simon, James F. 1973. *In His Own Image: The Supreme Court in Richard Nixon's America*. New York: David McKay.

———. 1980. *Independent Journey: The Life of William O. Douglas*. New York: Penguin Books.

Soifer, Aviam, and H. C. Macgill. 1977. "The *Younger* Doctrine: Reconstructing Reconstruction." *Texas Law Review* 55:1141–1215.

Soifer, Aviam. 1980. "Rehnquist: Trying to Capture an Imaginary, Idyllic Past." *National Law Journal*, February 18.

"Statutory Entitlement and the Concept of Property." 1977. *Yale Law Journal* 86:695–714.

Steamer, Robert J. 1986. *Chief Justice: Leadership and the Supreme Court*. Columbia: University of South Carolina Press.

Stephenson, Grier, Jr. 1981. *The Supreme Court and the American Republic: An Annotated Bibliography*. New York: Garland.

Stevens, John Paul. 1985. "Deciding What to Decide: The Docket and the Rule of Four." Ch. 8 in *Views From the Bench*. Edited by Mark W. Cannon and David M. O'Brien. N.J.: Chatham House.

Stone, Geoffrey R. 1983. "Content Regulation and the First Amendment." *William and Mary Law Review* 25:189–231.

"*Sumner v Mata*: Muddying the Waters of Federal Habeas Court Deference to State Court Findings." 1983. *Wisconsin Law Review* 1983:751–73.

"Supreme Court: Memo From Rehnquist." 1971. *Newsweek*, December 13.

"Supreme Court, 1971 Term, The." 1972. *Harvard Law Review* 86:1–306.

Swisher, Carl B. 1935. *Roger B. Taney*. New York: Macmillan.

Taylor, Stuart Jr. 1985a. "Brennan Opposes Legal View Urged by Administration." *New York Times*, October 13.

———. 1985b. "Justice Stevens, in Rare Criticism, Disputes Meese on
Constitution." *New York Times.* October 26.

———. 1986. "Opposition to Nomination of Rehnquist Hardens as New
Charges Emerge." *New York Times.* July 27.

Terrell, Timothy P. 1982. "Property, Due Process, and the Distinction
between Definition and Theory in Legal Analysis." *Georgetown
Law Journal* 70:861–941.

"Transcript of the President's Announcement on Two Nominees for Supreme Court." 1971. *New York Times*, October 22.

Tribe, Laurence H. 1978. *American Constitutional Law.* Mineola, New
York: Foundation Press.

———. 1985a. *Constitutional Choices.* Cambridge: Harvard University
Press. Ch. 12.

———. 1985b. *God Save This Honorable Court: How the Choice of Supreme Court Justices Shapes Our History.* New York: Random
House.

Tushnet, Mark. 1975. "The Newer Property: Suggestion for the Revival
of Substantive Due Process." *Supreme Court Review* 1975:261–
88.

U.S. Congress. Senate. 1971a. Committee on the Judiciary. *Nominations
of William H. Rehnquist and Lewis F. Powell, Jr.: Hearings before
the Committee on the Judiciary.* 92d Cong., 1st sess. November
3, 4, 8, 9, 10.

———. 1971b. *Nomination of William H. Rehnquist.* 92d Cong., 1st
sess. Senatorial Executive Report no. 92–16, November 30.

———. 1986a. Committee on the Judiciary. *Nomination of William
Hubbs Rehnquist to be Chief Justice of the United States: Hear-
ings before the Committee on the Judiciary.* 99th Cong., 2d sess.
July 29, 30, 31, and August 1.

———. 1986b. *Nomination of William H. Rehnquist to be Chief Justice
of the United States.* 99th Cong., 2d sess. Senatorial Executive
Report no. 99–18, September 8.

Van Alstyne, William W. 1968. "The Demise of the Right-Privilege Distinction in Constitutional Law." *Harvard Law Review* 81:1439–
64.

———. 1977. "Cracks in 'the New Property': Adjudicative Due Process
in the Administrative State." *Cornell Law Review* 62:445–93.

———. 1980. "The Recrudescence of Property Rights as the Foremost
Principle of Civil Liberties." *Law and Contemporary Problems*
43:66–82.

Weaver, Warren. 1974. "Mr. Justice Rehnquist Dissenting." *New York
Times Magazine*, October 13.

Wechsler, Herbert. 1954. "The Political Safeguards of Federalism: The

Role of the States in the Composition and Selection of the National Governments." *Columbia Law Review* 54:543–60.

Weinberg, Louise. 1977. "The New Judicial Federalism." *Stanford Law Review* 29:1191–1244.

Wells, Michael. 1981. "The Role of Comity in the Law of Federal Courts." *North Carolina Law Review* 60:59–86.

White, G. Edward. 1971. "The Rise and Fall of Justice Holmes." *University of Chicago Law Review* 39:51–77.

—— 1976. *The American Judicial Tradition.* New York: Oxford University Press.

—— 1982. *Earl Warren: A Public Life.* New York: Oxford University Press.

Whitman, Christina. 1980. "Constitutional Torts." *Michigan Law Review* 79:1–71.

Wright, Charles Alan. 1983. *The Law of Federal Courts.* 4th ed. St. Paul, Minn.: West Publishing Co., 268–346.

Yarbrough, Tinsley E. 1971. "Mr. Justice Black and Legal Positivism." *Virginia Law Review* 57:375–407.

Index

Abelman v. Booth (62 U.S. 506 [1859]), 153

Abood v. Detroit (431 U.S. 347 [1976]), 90

abortion, 12, 27, 50, 77, 82, 191

Abrams v. United States (250 U.S. 616 [1919]), 67

affirmative action, 20, 60–62, 64, 191, 207

AFL-CIO, 13

Agins v. City of Tiburon (447 U.S. 255 [1980], 117–118

Allen v. McCurry (449 U.S. 90 [1980]), 181

Allied Structural Steel Co. v. Spannaus (438 U.S. 234 [1978]), 127–128, 129

Almota Farmers Elevator and Warehouse Co. v. United States (409 U.S. 470 [1973]), 122

American Bar Association Standing Committee on Federal Judiciary, 5, 8, 193–194

American Civil Liberties Union, 13, 194

American Textile Manufacturers Institute v. Donovan (452 U.S. 490 [1981]), 26

Americans for Democratic Action, 13

Anderson v. Celebrezze (460 U.S. 780 [1983]), 88

Andrus v. Allard (444 U.S. 51 [1979]), 116

Anti-Injunction Act, 176, 177

Arizona Public Service Co. v. Snead (441 U.S. 141 [1979]), 137

Armco Inc. v. Hardesty (467 U.S. 638 [1984]), 139

Armstrong v. United States (364 U.S. 40), 121

Arnett v. Kennedy (416 U.S. 134 [1974]), 102–104, 105, 106, 108

Atascadero State Hospital v. Scanlon (473 U.S. 234 [1985]), 158–159

Atlantic Coastline R.R. v. Brotherhood of Locomotive Engineers (398 U.S. 281 [1970]), 176

Austin, John, 21

Baker v. McCollan (443 U.S. 137 [1979]), 163

Bankruptcy Reform Act of 1978, 119–120

Barron v. Baltimore (7 Pet. 243 [1833]), 43–44

Barsky v. Board of Regents (347 U.S. 442 [1954]), 99

Bates v. State Bar of Arizona (433 U.S. 350 [1977]), 79

Batson v. Kentucky (106 S.Ct. 1712 [1986]), 58

Bayh, Birch, 10, 12, 13

Beauharnais v. Illinois (343 U.S. 250 [1952]), 71

Begelow v. Virginia (421 U.S. 809 [1975]), 73

Bell v. Burson (402 U.S. 535 [1971]), 100

Bell v. Wolfish (441 U.S. 520 [1979]), 91

Bentson, Wayne, 197

Bickel, Alexander, 16

Biden, Joseph R., 191, 193, 196, 197, 198, 200

Bigelow v. Virginia (421 U.S. 809 [1975]), 77, 81

Bill of Rights, 12, 13, 23, 24, 29, 34, 35, 43, 44, 45, 143, 153, 191, 192, 204, 205; incorporation of, 24, 29, 43–44, 64, 71, 196, 203, 206